Communication for a
Global Society

National Business Education Association Yearbook, No. 43

2005

Editor
James Calvert Scott
Utah State University
Logan, Utah

Assistant Editors

Carol Blaszczynski
California State University, Los Angeles
Los Angeles, California

Diana J. Green
Weber State University
Ogden, Utah

Published by

NBEA

National Business Education Association
1914 Association Drive
Reston, VA 20191-1596
(703) 860-8300 • Fax: (703) 620-4483
www.nbea.org

Communication for a Global Society

Copyright © 2005 by the National Business Education Association

National Business Education Association
1914 Association Drive
Reston, VA 20191-1596

ISBN 0-933964-62-5

TABLE OF CONTENTS

PREFACE

You and I live in a different world from that of our grandparents and parents. For our grandparents, the world primarily revolved around life in their immediate community. For our parents, the world centered on community and on life in the larger entity of their state of residence and, with the exception of wartime, only occasionally on national events. For you and me, the world has expanded, adding a national and international dimension to everyday life. We are members of a global society—a world made possible by communication in its many forms.

Given the varied faces and forms of communication and given its growing importance in the effective functioning of an increasingly interdependent world, it is fitting that National Business Education Association devotes its 2005 yearbook to the topic of communication for a global society. Communication, the lifeblood of all business-related activities, plays a pivotal role in a global society composed of diverse individuals dispersed around the world. Effective business communication allows people from different cultural backgrounds to achieve something approaching oneness of meaning, which makes possible the transaction of business on an international scale. In our interdependent world, everyone relies on communication. This yearbook acknowledges the importance of effective communication within a global society.

Communication for a Global Society is designed to inform and to inspire business educators as it explores the many dimensions of communication in a global context. Part I reviews the foundations upon which global business communication is built. Part II focuses on preparing people for cross-cultural communication and its aftermath. Part III addresses wide-ranging matters that bear on effective communication around the world. Regardless of what you already know about communication in a global society, this yearbook offers something of value to you as a business educator—be it breadth or depth of topic coverage or related instructional information that is useful in a wide variety of settings.

Communication for a Global Society is reflective of its era: it is truly the product of a global society. Not only does it contain insights from authors who have spent significant amounts of time in other countries exploring aspects of local communication systems, but also it was developed and brought to fruition while I was on a yearlong sabbatical leave attached to the Bristol Business School in Bristol, United Kingdom. As a result, it was global communication taking place between the authors, my coeditors, and me that produced the yearbook that you hold in your hands today. Without the marvels of advanced global communication technology, this yearbook could not have been created.

Communication for a Global Society is not the product of one person; instead, it is an ensemble effort of many dedicated professionals who, in spite of challenges, had the will to make it happen. As editor I am grateful to the authors of the various chapters, who willingly accepted the task of sharing important communication-related information to meet the diverse needs of business educators. Their names and affiliations appear at the beginnings of their respective chapters. I also express appreciation to the many persons who constructively reviewed yearbook chapters to ensure high quality and meaningful content. Their names appear on the following page. Thanks are also due to the members of the NBEA Publications Committee, especially its chairperson, Kenneth L. Gorman, and to the NBEA headquarters staff, especially Susan O'Brien, for their direction, guidance, and assistance. Their faith in me as editor of my second NBEA yearbook has been unflinching.

Finally, I am deeply indebted to and consequently extend special thanks to my two highly competent associate editors who faithfully labored stateside while I labored abroad on this yearbook. Without the strong commitment and unwavering professional support of Carol Blaszczynski and Diana J. Green, this yearbook would not have become a reality.

James Calvert Scott, Editor
Utah State University
Logan, Utah
and
University of the West of England, Bristol
Bristol, United Kingdom

ACKNOWLEDGMENTS

The following business educators devoted their time, effort, and expertise to reviewing the *2005 NBEA Yearbook, Communication for a Global Society*:

Marcia A. Anderson	Beryl C. McEwen
Shirley J. Barton	Peter F. Meggison
Betty J. Brown	Sharon Lund O'Neil
Lillian H. Chaney	Larry G. Pagel
John E. Clow	Heidi R. Perreault
Tena B. Crews	Jean A. Pratt
Donna R. Everett	Ann M. Remp
Kenneth L. Gorman	Kathleen Richards
Lisa E. Gueldenzoph	Allyson Saunders
Mary Ellen Guffey	Jean Anna Sellers
Janice C. Harder	Bonnie J. Sibert
Susan Jaderstrom	Dana H. Swensen
Carol A. Johnson	Alden A. Talbot
Carol Larson Jones	Colleen Vawdrey
Marguerite P. Joyce	William J. Wilhelm
Marianna P Larsen	Janet K. Winter
Melinda M. McCannon	

Yesterday, Today, and Tomorrow: Communicating in a Global Society

Diana J. Green
Weber State University
Ogden, Utah

Communication is a founding block of society and a part of virtually every facet of human existence. Guffey (1994) stated that communication is "the mortar that holds together organizations—and the entire knowledge society...Without communication, information could not be processed or exchanged" (p. 7). Now, more than ever before, communication plays an integral role in a global society. Communication provides the means for governments, organizations, and individual citizens to communicate for virtually every purpose imaginable. As humans have progressed through the decades of time, so have the ways in which humans communicate. This chapter discusses (a) the milestones of communication from prehistoric to contemporary times; (b) the influence of communication on business, government, and education; and (c) the major topics that follow in this yearbook.

MILESTONES OF COMMUNICATION

Milestones of communication show how people have exchanged information through the ages by marking significant points in the development of communication technologies and systems. People are driven to find new and better ways to communicate using methods and inventions, each setting goals to surpass the previous method or invention. Milestones reflect culture, time, and people. They guide people through time, from prehistoric ages with individuals living in closed communities and never communicating with outsiders, to today, a time when virtually everyone has the potential to communicate with individuals all over the world.

Milestones of communication include early drawing and writing, the printing press, signaling, telegraph, underwater telegraph cable, telephone, radio, television, satellites, computers, the Internet, and telecommunications.

Drawing and Writing

Milestones of communication begin with prehistoric people drawing pictures of animals on cave walls (Gordon, 1989). This included such groups as the Cro-Magnon people, Paleolithic hunters, and Neolithic herdsmen and farmers. Their drawings addressed such subjects as animals and fertility. Inferences of the artwork also included magic qualities. "The art of nonliterate peoples served the functions of all artistic communication: to relate individual imagination and vision to the common consciousness of a culture" (Gerbner, 1999, p. 424).

As times advanced, rulers and priests acquired property that needed to be identified. These individuals used brands and markings to show ownership. Other events such as the recording of seasons and calendars and the using of precious metals stamped with the mark of trading value (i.e., money) were some of the first forms of sign or picture writing (Gerbner, 1999). These examples of pictograms denoted items but could not make statements equivalent to the spoken word. Individuals turned to creating symbols that could represent human speech. People of Sumer, who inhabited Mesopotamia about 3000 B.C., first bridged the gap between sign or picture writing and sound writing by inventing a wedge-shaped stylus that was used to stamp their signs on soft clay. Through this and other cultural developments, as well as contacts with trading partners who spoke different languages, came further simplification and syllabification of script, the association of signs with the sounds and meanings of a number of languages, and the eventual transition to phonetic writing and the development of the alphabet (Gerbner, 1999).

> Writing ranked second only to speech among the most important early inventions in communication. Writing enabled people to exchange messages over long distances without depending on a messenger's memory. Information also could be kept for later use. With the invention of writing, prehistoric times ended and the period of written history began. (Gordon, 1989, p. 882)

Printing Press

The invention of the printing press moved the means of communication forward. Most credit for the printing press is given to Johann Gutenberg in Germany in 1452, although the same type process that he used had been used in Asia since the 1000s. Gutenberg applied movable type, paper, and ink to the hand press. Other individuals set up similar presses in France and England, making the written word more readily available to the populace. Most of the written documents focused on the Bible and other religious books. The printing press was advanced with the invention in 1751 of the steam engine, and copies were printed by the thousands. More and more people were becoming literate. After printed copies of the Bible were available, printed copies of literature and other writing became more readily accessible to the populace. People could be taught using such written sources. Businesses could use written documents for business contracts and other dealings. Having copies facilitated the expansion of communication to many more individuals located in other localities, cities, and countries, thus moving toward a more global society.

Signaling

Another communication method that has had an impact on mankind is that of signaling. Communication once depended on the ability of humans to travel from one place to another, carrying their messages with them. Factors influencing successful communication were the length of time individuals needed to travel and the reality of being able to reach their destinations. Individuals looked for ways to communicate without the travel and the uncertainties. One type of communication that did not require travel over distance was signaling. The Chappe brothers of France in the 1790s set up a signaling system between a private house in Parcé and a castle in Brûlon approximately 10 miles (16 km) away using two pendulum clocks. Later the Chappe brothers developed "a semaphore system which appeared to mimic a person with wide-outstretched arms, holding a signal flag in each hand. They were able to signal hundreds of symbols" (Jones, 1999, para. 6). They were able to communicate with each other without having to travel, without the factor of travel time, and without the possibility of not reaching their destinations.

Telegraph

Signaling worked well in daylight and good weather. But other inventors looked for ways to communicate day or night in good weather or bad weather. The telegraph was one of those ways and a major milestone in long-distance communication. Samuel Morse utilized the idea of sending electrical impulses using a code of dots and dashes across a telegraph wire. On May 24, 1844, he sent the message "What hath God wrought?" from the old Supreme Court chamber in the United States Capitol to his partner in Baltimore (About.com, 2003). Newspapers began to use the Morse telegraph immediately. Stockbrokers also used the telegraph to move information rapidly. The Magnetic Telegraph Company saw the opportunity to build a communication system linking the main commercial routes of the United States. This further led to the railroad's building of telegraph lines along railroad rights of way. A national communication infrastructure was now closer to reality. By the 1860s most cities in the United States were connected through the telegraph. The telegraph influenced the way business was transacted. New partnerships were formed between businesses such as the railroad and telegraph companies. Companies expanded their numbers of offices and their locations away from headquarters. Corporations spread information about goods and services to their customers more quickly. Newspaper agencies were able to more quickly send information to their offices throughout the country and to have the information appear in their newspaper headlines soon after the occurrence of the actual events. The telegraph greatly influenced the means of sending and receiving messages for the military during the Civil War. Educational opportunities opened in which students learned more quickly about what was happening in their own cities and towns as well as in other locations throughout the United States. Information could be spread more quickly and to more individuals, which influenced all aspects of life including culture, education, business, and government (Marvin, 1989). This was also happening in cities in Europe (Schietinger & Brüggemann, 2001). The next goal was to connect the people of different continents.

Underwater Telegraph Cable

Cyrus Field, a 35-year old retired newspaper merchant, was interested in the idea of linking continents with a transatlantic telegraph cable. He founded the New York Newfoundland and London Telegraph Company in the U.S. and the Atlantic Telegraph Company in London. After several unsuccessful tries between 1855 and 1866, Field was finally successful in laying the first functional underwater telegraph line, and messages were sent between the two continents (Schietinger & Brüggemann, 2001). With this development in long-distance communication, individuals could now send and receive messages from greater distances more quickly and more reliably. These messages included business contracts, government decisions, and personal information.

Telephone

Alexander Graham Bell took Morse's idea of sending electrical codes across wires and extended it to sending sounds across wires. In 1876 Bell patented the telephone. Bell's patent included a means of sending "vocal or other sounds" (Rowe, 2002, p. 38) through electrical transmission. His invention was often referred to as a talking telegraph that now competed with the telegraph companies. Shortly following this event, the Bell Telephone Company was created; and by the fall of 1877, the company had approximately 600 telephone subscribers. With the original setup of the wiring, each subscriber had to have a pair of wires from his or her telephone to another subscriber's telephone in order to communicate. Since it was impossible to have 600 wires going to each subscriber's location, the Bell Telephone Company invented a telephone exchange with an operator who handled the switching of wires for different callers. Using a series of plugs and jacks, the operator connected calls made between subscribers, thus eliminating the need for many wires at each subscriber's location (Rowe, 2002).

In 1878 Western Union Telegraph Company set up its own telephone company, taking advantage of its own network of telegraph wires (Rowe, 2002). The Bell Telephone Company sued Western Union Telegraph Company for patent infringement. The two companies settled out of court, with the Western Union Telegraph Company selling its network to The Bell Company. In 1885 American Telephone & Telegraph Company was formed. It built a network of telephone lines that provided telephone service throughout the country (Rowe, 2002). All of the advantages attributed to the use of the telegraph were now available using the telephone. Governments, businesses, newspapers, and individuals were able to share information using vocal means.

Radio

With the ability to transmit voice from one telephone user to another, the idea of transmitting voice from one individual to many individuals simultaneously was the next focus of attention. The Italian inventor Guglielmo Marconi in 1895 combined two theories: one, developed by the British physicist James Clerk Maxwell, held that electromagnetic waves traveled through space at the speed of light; the other, demonstrated by German physicist Heinrich Hertz's experiments, proved the existence of these waves. The resultant invention was called the wireless telegraph. Later, it was called the radio. Before the invention of the radio, communication by wire was essentially between two individuals. Radio provided the new concept of broadcasting, which is sending out signals to many individuals simultaneously (Rowe, 2002).

In 1922 station WEAF in New York accepted a fee from the Queensboro Corporation of New York to advertise real estate on the air (Gordon, 1989). This was the first radio commercial. Subsequently, other businesses began paying for advertisements of their products and services on the radio. "The growth of radio stations went from 2 in 1920 to 471 in five years, 2,000 in 30 years, and 5,800 in 60 years" (Gerbner, 1999, p. 426). The radio made it possible to share communication from one source to thousands of individuals all at the same time. The ability to communicate with the masses was now a reality. According to Rowe (2002), people today are "bombarded by broadcasts designed to entertain, sell, and provide information" (p. 3) through the radio.

Television

Recognizing that the human voice could be sent over radio waves, inventors worked until they were able to send pictures using radio waves. This was accomplished by John Logie Baird, a Scottish engineer, in 1926 and by Vladimir K. Zworykin, a Russian-born American physicist, in 1929. The British Broadcasting Corporation (BBC) transmitted the world's first open-circuit TV broadcasts. In 1929 Vladimir K. Zworykin demonstrated the first practical all-electronic TV system (Gordon, 1989). The Radio Corporation of America (RCA Corporation) began regular telecasts in 1939. By the early 1950s, television stations were broadcasting throughout the United States (Gordon, 1989). The use of the television provided the means to see and hear advertisements while viewing the related products or services. Entertainment incorporated the dimensions of seeing as well as hearing. News broadcasters could show news stories in addition to reporting about them. Thus, the television is another invention that has influenced the way communication is delivered.

Satellites

Satellite technology began in the 1940s and gained real prominence in the 1960s, after the Russians launched Sputnik I in 1957. John R. Pierce of AT&T's Bell Telephone Laboratories in 1955 shared his vision that a satellite would be worth a billion dollars based on the first transatlantic telephone cable (TAT-1), which cost $30-$50 million and could carry 36 simultaneous telephone calls. Pierce estimated that a satellite would be able to carry 1,000 simultaneous telephone calls and cost a billion dollars. He wondered if it was worth it (Whalen, 2003). Others have caught his vision and continually developed and improved the satellite system to where it has become a multibillion dollar business.

According to Regis Leonard (n.d.) for NASA Lewis Research Center, "The nature of future satellite communication systems will depend on the demands of the marketplace (direct home distribution of entertainment, data transfers between businesses, telephone traffic, cellular telephone traffic, etc.)" (para. 1). Satellites are used in numerous ways. Scientists use them to study the earth's surface. Weather experts use satellites to improve communication of global weather forecasting, particularly in events such as hurricanes and floods, where evacuation notices can prevent disaster and loss of human life, and where satellites have provided a means for search and rescue groups to locate stranded victims. Satellites are used to relay telephone calls to virtually any location around the globe or to relay television signals that share events occurring at that same point in time with viewers in distant locations (NASA, 2004). Satellites have been absolutely critical in the past forty years to commerce, communication, and national security and will continue to determine America's success in military and commercial dominance ("The future of satellites," 2003). The use of satellites will continue to expand as individuals incorporate them into all aspects of life. As NASA puts it, "For satellites and the future, the sky is the limit" (NASA, 2004, para. 43).

Computers

Computers have evolved through many stages, starting with the first generation of computers that included the freely programmable computer by Zuse in 1936, to the ABC Computer by Atanasoff and Berry in 1942, to the ENIAC 1 Computer in 1946, to the fifth generation of computers that now have been designed to have artificial intelligence, spoken-word instructions, parallel processing, and superconductor technology (LaMorte & Lilly, 1995). "Nothing epitomizes modern life better than a computer" (LaMorte & Lilly, 1995, para. 1). Computers are used to calculate grocery bills at supermarkets, transmit and receive millions of telephone calls, issue money at automatic teller machines, conduct banking transitions from anywhere in the world, and assist doctors in making diagnoses (LaMoret & Lilly, 1995). "Computers have infiltrated every aspect of our society" (LaMoret & Lilly, 1995, para. 1). "Computers are the future and are definitely a way of life. . . . Their uses are phenomenally boundless" (Antolick, 2004, para. 11).

Internet

The launching of Sputnik in 1957 by Russia spurred then United States President Dwight D. Eisenhower to issue an order to the Department of Defense to create the Advanced Research Project Agency (ARPA). It created a network of computers that could communicate without disruption from a nuclear attack. The four-node network connected the University of California, Los Angeles; Stanford Research Institute (SRI); University of California, Santa Barbara (UCSB); and the University of Utah, Salt Lake City. The network was called ARPANET and was used for research purposes in addition to defense purposes. Recognizing the potential of ARPANET, the connections spread from the universities and research institutes to other government agencies. The network was opened to private corporations and then to everyday users. It has become the Internet (Rowe, 2002). "The Internet today is a massive network of networks, a networking infrastructure. It connects millions of computers together globally, forming a network in which any computer can communicate with any other computer as long as they are both connected to the Internet" (Webopedia.com, 2002, para. 2).

With millions of users connected to the Internet, the Internet can be used for a variety of purposes such as communication, dissemination of information, research and education, marketing and public relations, and public growth and entertainment (UALC Information for Life Taskforce, 2001).

Telecommunication

Telecommunication is the buzzword used for discussing communication over distance—across oceans, over mountains, or around the globe. As telecommunication technology has changed, emphasis has been placed on efficiency, magnitude, availability, and speed. The evolution of cabling from coaxial to twisted pair to fiber optic has advanced telecommunication in the areas of increased signal transfer speeds, numbers of signals handled simultaneously, and better security. Wireless communication abets telecommunication in the process of routing information through the free-space environment rather than by wire (Ciampa, 2002). Wireless technology involves the use of a variety of devices that include laptop computers, personal digital assistants (PDAs), pagers, and cellular phones. Through wireless technology, users can be connected to networks in such places as home, school, work, hotels, and airplanes. With global positioning systems (GPS) and satellites, individuals can also be connected to networks in the mountains, on the deserts, and on the seas. The use of wireless technology has grown and will continue to grow.

Due to its versatility and availability, more and more individuals are using wireless technology. According to Brian Cruikshank, senior vice president of Ipsos-Insight's Technology and Communications Practice, "Wireless Internet trial and usage in leading-edge and advancing markets is rapidly expanding with double, and in many countries, triple-digit growth" (Ipsos News Center, 2004, para. 3). In the same report, Ipsos News Center cited the following facts on the growth of wireless systems:

- *The Face of the Web 2003* study involving respondents from 13 key global markets found an increase in wireless Internet usage of 145% (para. 1).

- The growth of wireless communication is being influenced by wireless digital devices such as laptops, PDAs, and mobile phones. Close to 130 million households in the markets studied own a laptop . . . [and] 8% of the household mobile phones have PDA functionality" (para. 4).

- As users grow accustomed to integrating the online medium into their everyday lives, they are also increasingly demanding access to it from any place, at any time (para. 2).

Thus, the milestones of early drawings and writings, the printing press, signaling, telegraph, underwater telegraph cable, telephone, radio, television, computers, Internet, satellites, and telecommunications have provided increasingly sophisticated ways and means by which communication has advanced, ultimately linking people, companies, and governments around the globe. The limitations of space and distance are no longer the

7

issues that they were hundreds of years ago, or even ten years ago. Because of these communication milestones, the people of the world have become a global society. The present use of computers in combination with satellites, the Internet, and telecommunications has had a direct impact on the way business, government, and education disseminate information.

INFLUENCES OF COMMUNICATION ON BUSINESS, GOVERNMENT, AND EDUCATION

Businesses are taking advantage of the advancements in communication in the ways they disseminate information about products and services to their customers and in how they conduct business within their organizations. Governments are utilizing these same advancements to further the infrastructures in their countries. Educational institutions are using computers and the Internet to further educational opportunities. Former Vice President Al Gore indicated that the global information infrastructure (GII), which is a massive network of communication networks, would change the ways that citizens everywhere will live, learn, work, and communicate (Gore, 1998).

According to Garcia (1998), "Communication and information technologies are the foundation of the new global information-based economy" (para. 1). More and more countries are installing new technologies, making it possible for governments and businesses to enhance their services and to improve their efficiency and competitiveness. They are offering their customers better goods and services at lower prices. The influences of communication on business and education are discussed in the following sections: Internet service providers; e-business; national, international, and multinational firms; governments; and distance learning education.

Internet Service Providers

Internet service providers (ISPs) are companies that provide Internet and World Wide Web access through dial up or cable connections. ISPs offer their services to businesses, individuals, and organizations. Additional services that ISPs offer include Web hosting, domain name services, and proprietary online services (North Dakota State University Extension Service, 2004). Internet service providers offer services that include simple dial-up connections to e-business programming and secure data transports. Web hosting and e-mail services are also a part of the services offered by ISPs (St-louis.net, 2004). Internet service providers are a few of the key businesses that are making it possible for other businesses and organizations to enhance their offerings to customers around the globe. Those computer-based information service providers include three types of companies: "Internet access providers, which provide the general public with links to the global Internet; commercial online services like America Online, MSN, and Prodigy, which offer the general public both simple Internet access and also their own proprietary networks and content; and sophisticated business services like Electronic Data Systems, Dow Jones, and Dun and Bradstreet, which provide highly specialized and expensive proprietary systems and information to corporate and institutional clients" (Windhausen, 1998, para. 20).

E-Business

Technology influences the way in which businesses operate and engage in business. E-business is the conducting of business on the Internet. It refers to buying and selling online as well as servicing customers and collaborating with business partners (mariosalexandrou.com, 2004). Through the use of computers and the Internet, individuals can now shop for goods or services globally from the comfort of their own homes. Companies utilize the Internet to reach more customers. Some of the E-companies found on the Fortune E-50 list include Amazon.com, Ameritrade Holding, AOL Time Warner, Charles Schwab, CNet, DoubleClick, E*Trade Group, eBay, FreeMarkets, Knight/Trimark Group, RealNetworks, USA Networks, Yahoo, Adobe Systems, EarthLink, Microsoft, Macromedia Network Associates, Oracle, United Parcel Service, Cisco, Corning, Intel, International Business Machines (IBM), Texas Instruments, AT&T, MCI WorldCom, and Qwest (AskJeeves.com, 2004). IBM was one of the first companies to use the term "eBusiness." In order to stay competitive, companies are rethinking their businesses in terms of the Internet and it capabilities (mariosalexandrou.com, 2004). "Exploiting the convenience, availability, and global reach of the Internet, many companies, both large and small, have already discovered how to use the Internet successfully" (mariosalexandrou.com, 2004, para. 2).

National, International, and Multinational Firms

National companies focus their business dealings within their own countries. International and multinational companies have extended business dealings outside of their home countries. Each of these types of firms utilizes technology in similar ways to further their communication abilities. National, international, and multinational companies use computer networks and intranets (networks within companies) for information sharing and processing with their employees as well as their customers. They communicate with their employees and clients using the now more popular method of communication—e-mail. In an American Management Association survey, 36% of the executives preferred using e-mail rather than the telephone. Some even preferred e-mail to face-to-face meetings. Companies are utilizing pagers and cellular telephones to communicate between employees and with clients. These companies have company Web sites to advertise their services or products. Their clients use their Web sites to place orders and make purchases, and prospective clients use their Web sites to make inquiries. Where cost and location limited national companies prior to the technology age, these limitations are now being overcome by using technology, making it possible for national companies to be international and multinational. Networks that are connected to the Internet make it possible to connect to company locations throughout the world. By utilizing technology to access customers all over the world, businesses can operate on a larger scale. They can become more competitive with a broader base of customers. Small- and medium-sized firms can partner with multinational firms to enter areas of business that were not a reality prior to electronic technology (Garcia, 1998). "With the help of networking, small businesses can use technology to help level the playing field, and enable them to do everything from communicating with remote employees to managing international clients" (Muehleman, 2000, para. 4).

A number of challenges have emerged as a result of companies' becoming international or multinational. One of these challenges is dealing with differences in culture. Varner and Beamer (2005) suggest an intercultural business communication strategy involves three parts—business strategy, intercultural strategy, and intercultural business communication strategy. They believe that fusing these three strategies together in a firm's environment will assist with successful business communication. Another suggestion for dealing with diversity within an organization is creating self-awareness of one's own culture, mapping differences among cultures, bridging gaps and identifying synergies, developing strategies to integrate differences, and assessing results of the team-building process (Varner & Beamer, 2005).

A second challenge deals with language. Varner and Beamer (2005) suggest that if businesses in the U.S. want to expand into international markets, their employees need to learn the languages used in the potential markets. Individuals from countries that do not have English as the first language may desire to learn English since English is the lingua franca of international business (Varner & Beamer, 2005).

Government

In past years the big industrialized countries were the major forces in the international markets. Now smaller countries are becoming involved because of the advancements of telecommunications. "If developing countries deploy advanced communication technologies in tandem with developed countries, they can also compete in the expanding global services market on a more equal basis" (Garcia, 1998, para. 12).

Governments are involved in building strong communication infrastructures. The Federal Telecommunications System 2000 (FTS2000) program for the United States has been involved in assessing the current and emerging telecommunications technologies and the federal agency requirements over the next 15 years (Fisher, 1999) to ensure that appropriate technology choices are made. Governments are interested in keeping current and effective. They also want to protect the interests of their nations, and yet open their borders to other nations for needed goods and services. With the expansion of business across national borders, governments are faced with additional issues of regulation, particularly regarding international and multinational businesses. "Each country establishes its own laws and rules for competition, taxation, employment, and product quality" (Beamer & Varner, 2001, p. 282). Government officials have to decide how strict the regulations should be without discouraging international exchanges and still protect the interests of the individual nations. The U.S. government is utilizing the Harris Corporation to provide communication with "precise, highly-reliable, high-speed communications for improved productivity and information processing" (Government Communications Systems Division, 2004, para. 2).

Distance Learning Education

Telecommunication technology has also created a milestone in learning. Many colleges and universities are offering courses online that were traditionally offered in a classroom setting with a teacher and students in one physical location. Today courses are offered in a setting where the teacher is in one location and students are at locations throughout the world, connected by computers, satellites, and the Internet. The Western Governors University was founded by governors of 19 Western states in 2000 to offer competency-based online degrees. It is the only accredited university in the U.S. of its kind (WGU.edu, 2004). It is growing by approximately 10%, or 200 students each month, with about 1,800 students from all 50 states, Guam, Puerto Rico, and eight different countries (Speckman, 2004). WorldWideLearn.com teams with a variety of colleges and universities to offer over 249 categories of online courses. Individuals interested in obtaining an associates, bachelors, or masters degree using online courses can do so using the World Wide Web (WorldWideLearn.com, 2004). The International Distance Learning Course Finder has a compilation of over 55,000 distance learning courses and programs from 130 countries offered by a multitude of universities, colleges, and businesses (The International Distance Learning Course Finder, 2003).

Thus, businesses are taking advantage of the advancements of communication in the ways they disseminate information about products and services to their customers and in how they conduct business within their organizations. Governments are utilizing these same advancements to further the infrastructures of their countries. Educational institutions are using computers and the Internet to further educational opportunities.

MAJOR TOPICS OF THIS YEARBOOK

Part I of *Communication for a Global Society* reflects on how communication has changed over time and on the foundations upon which business communication is built. It explores listening, the most common communication activity, and its complementary process, speaking, before moving on to another set of complementary communication processes, reading and writing. Part I also addresses the increasingly important aspects of communicating through numeracy and computations and through visualizations to reach diverse audiences.

Part II of *Communication for a Global Society* discusses preparing specifically for global communication. Effective intercultural communication, the process through which cultural differences are bridged and diverse people are united to achieve a common goal, is critical for life in a global society. People interacting with others who are culturally different from them also need to understand culture shock, the cycle of adjustment experienced as they encounter a different culture, and reverse culture shock, the cycle of readjustment experienced when they return to their native culture after having encountered another culture.

Part III of *Communication for a Global Society* discusses divergent matters relating to communication in an interdependent world. For example, a chapter focuses on the English language and its role as a global communication medium. Another explores the silent but important role of nonverbal communication across cultures. The relative directness of intercultural communication, known as contexting, is the topic of another chapter. Still another chapter addresses Western and Eastern perspectives about "face," a person's moral and social status within a group, as exemplified by the American and the

Chinese business subcultures. The chapter on group dynamics offers guidance about how to work effectively with others in a multicultural setting. One of the chapters in Part III develops the topic of negotiating with business partners from around the world. Yet another chapter explores the enigma of time and its effects on intercultural communication. The final chapter takes a critical look at computer-mediated communication in cross-cultural communication settings, exposing both promises and pitfalls.

Thus, the three parts of *Communication for a Global Society* together focus attention on relevant aspects of communication in an interdependent world.

SUMMARY

In summary, the milestones made in communication and their influences on governments, businesses, and people have moved the world toward a global society. The human race has progressed through drawing and writing to the Internet and telecommunications. The greatest drive behind all of these changes, inventions, and methods has been the need to communicate with one another. That need to communicate will continue throughout time. Businesses have become international and multinational organizations, many of which have become e-businesses. They are using telecommunication and the Internet to further their business pursuits. Governments are utilizing the latest technology to improve and enhance their communication abilities. Education is also expanding its offerings through telecommunication and is available through distance learning and the Internet. People increasingly share information utilizing new technologies, making this world a global society.

REFERENCES

About.com. (2003). *The history of the telegraph and telegraphy*. Retrieved January 5, 2004, from http://inventors.about.com/library/inventors/bltelegraph.htm

Antolick, L. (2004). *Computer history*. Retrieved May 29, 2004, from http://www.edu.pe.ca/ montaguehigh/grass/comp/HistComp/lydiaal.htm

AskJeeves.com. (2004). *What do e-businesses do?* Retrieved June 2, 2004, from http://web.ask .com

Beamer, L., & Varner, I. (2001). *Intercultural communication in the global workplace* (2nd ed.). New York: The McGraw-Hill Companies, Inc.

Ciampa, M. (2002). *Guide to wireless communication*. Boston: Course Technology.

Fisher, J. L. (1999). *Networking for reinvented government: Federal telecommunications requirements and industry*. Retrieved March 18, 2004, from http//post.fts.2k.gsa.gov/ gsa_docs/FCSWG_9311/sec1.asp

Garcia, D. L. (1998). *Opportunities for developing countries in the global information economy*. Retrieved January 2, 2004, from http://usinfo.state.gov/products/pubs/ archive/telecomm/ garcia.htm

Gerbner, G. (Ed.). (1999). Communication. *The encyclopedia Americana international edition* (Vol. 7, pp. 423-430). Danbury, CT: Grolier Incorporated.

Gordon, G. N. (Ed.). (1989). Communication. *The world book encyclopedia* (Vol. 4, pp. 879-890). Chicago: World Book, Inc.

Gore, A. (1998). *Information age*. Retrieved January 2, 2004, from http://usinfo.state.gov/ products/pubs/archive/telecommm/gore.htm

Government Communications Systems Division. (2004). *Civil*. Retrieved June 6, 2004, from http://www.govcomm.harris.com/solutions/marketindex/market.asp?source =market&market_id=89

Guffey, M. E. (1994). *Business communication: Process and product*. Belmont, CA: Wadsworth, Inc.

The International Distance Learning Course Finder. (2003). *Welcome to the galaxy of distance learning!* Retrieved June 6, 2004, from http://www.dlcoursefinder.com/

Ipsos News Center. (2004, May 11). *Wireless Internet access set to flourish*. Retrieved May 31, 2004, from http://www.ipsoso-na.com/news/presssreleast.cfm?id=2228

Jones, R. V. (1999). *Synchronous telegraph experiments (1790-1791)*. Retrieved January 5, 2004, from http://vvv.it.kth.se/ docs/early_net/ch-2-2.2.html

LaMorte, C., & Lilly, J. (1995). *Computers: History and development*. Retrieved May 29, 2004, from http://dia.eui.upm.es/asignatu/sis_op1/comp_hd/comp_hd.htm.

Leonard, R. (n.d.). *Future communications satellites*. Retrieved May 28, 2004, from http:// ctd .grc.nasa.gov/rleonard/regsliv.html

Mariosalexandrou.com. (2003). *eBusiness definition*. Retrieved June 2, 2004, from http:// www. mariosalexandrou.com/glossary/egusiness.asp

Marvin, C. (Ed.). (1989). Telegraph. *The world book encyclopedia* (Vol. 19, pp. 94-97). Chicago: World Book, Inc.

Muehleman, F. (2000). Networking: Lifeline for small firms' computers. *Austin Business Journal*. Retrieved May 31, 2004, from http://www.bizjournals.com/ austin/stories/2000/ 05/01/smalb4.html?t=printable

National Aeronautics and Space Administration (NASA). (2004). *Satellites*. Retrieved November 4, 2004, from http://pao.gsfc.nasa.gov/gsfc/service/gallery/fact_sheets/ general/satsum.htm

North Dakota State University Extension Service. (2004). *What is an Internet service provider?* Retrieved June 2, 2004, from http://www.ext.nodak.edu/miv/ 15min/isp/ sld009.htm

Rowe, S. H., II. (2002). *Telecommunications for managers* (5th ed.). Upper Saddle River, NJ: Prentice Hall.

Schietinger, J., & Brüggemann, L. (2001). 1866: The transatlantic telegraph. *The history of telecommunications from 1840 to 1870*. Retrieved January 10, 2004, from http://www2 .fht-esslingen.de/telehistory/1840-.html#1866

St. Louis Internet. (2002). *Web hosting rate plans*. Retrieved June 2, 2004, from http:// www.st-louis.net/rateplanprices.htm

Speckman, S. (2004, February 22). Utah's online university growing by 200 a month. *Deseret Morning News*. Retrieved March 18, 2004, from http://deseretnews.com/dn/ view/ 0,1249,590045031,00.html

The future of satellites. (2003, Fall). [Electronic Version]. *The New Atlantis*, *3*, 114-115. Retrieved May 28, 2004, from http://www.thenewatlantis.com/archive/ 3/soa/sats.htm

UALC Information for Life Taskforce. (2001). *Internet navigator*. Retrieved May 28, 2004, from http://medstat.med.utah.edu/navigator/about.htm

Varner, I., & Beamer, L. (2005). *Intercultural communication in the global workplace* (3rd ed.). New York: McGraw-Hill Companies, Inc.

Webopedia.com. (2002). *The difference between the Internet and the World Wide Web.* Retrieved February 7, 2004, from http://www.webopedia.com/DidYouKnow/Internet/ 2002/Web_vs_Internet.asp

WGU.edu. (2004). *Western governors' university.* Retrieved March 18, 2004, from http:// www .wgu.edu/wgu/index.html

Whalen, D. J. (3 April 2003). *Communications satellites: Making the global village possible.* Retrieved February 7, 2004, from http://www.hq.nasa.gov/office/pao/History/ satcomhistory.html

Windhausen, J. (1998). *Business strategies and markets in transition.* Retrieved January 2, 2004, from http://usinfo.state.gov/products/ pubs/archive/telecomm/wind.htm

WorldWideLearn.com. (2004). *Looking for online education?* Retrieved June 6, 2004, from www.worldwidelearn.com

Listening: The Forgotten Skill

Bobbye J. Davis
Southeastern Louisiana University
Hammond, LA

Clarice P. Brantley
Innovative Training Team
Pensacola, FL

Effective listening promotes success in both personal and professional endeavors. As a cornerstone to achievement, the "forgotten skill" of listening furthers interpersonal relationships and increases intercultural understanding. This chapter provides an overview of the significance, processes, levels, purposes, barriers, strategies, and activities associated with listening, including comments related to intercultural sensitivity.

LISTENING SIGNIFICANCE

From the classroom to the workplace, listening affects achievement. Lyman Steil's scientific research finding (as cited in Harris & Moran, 2000) indicated that listening is the most used but least taught communication skill. Recent studies reveal that students spend between 50 and 75% of classroom time listening to teachers, other students, or audio media (Smith, 1992).

According to Wolvin and Coakley (1991), listening correlates positively with job success, general career competence, managerial competency, and enduring relationships. In the workplace approximately 45% of a manager's time is spent listening; some managers state they earn up to 60% of their salaries by listening (Raudsepp, n.d.). Chambers and Asher (1998) reported that listening is the most important skill for business managers. They also described poor listening in business and in life as self-centered and ill-mannered.

Listening is especially important when communicating with persons from another culture. Thomlison (1991) stated that transportation and technology connect different parts of the world, allowing increasing intercultural contact for individuals and businesses. Intercultural communication has thus increased and will continue to expand. All communication, and especially listening, will directly affect successful multinational ventures, as business people listen to current and potential customers from all parts of the world.

These compelling statistics on listening from Harris and Moran, Wolvin and Coakley, Raudsepp, and Thomlison document that mastering listening skills is necessary for achieving personal and professional success. However, limited attention has been given to developing listening skills.

LISTENING PROCESSES

Kline (2003) stated, "Hearing is the reception of sound; listening is the attachment of meaning to the sound" (p. 11). Listening, a cyclical activity, potentially involves five related processes. Three of the processes generally occur in sequence: receiving, attending, and interpreting. The other activities, responding and remembering, may or may not occur (Bovee, Thill, & Schatzman, 2003).

Receiving

Listeners physically hear the message and make note of the information in mental, written, or both formats. Individuals should remember, though, that a difference exists between hearing and listening. While hearing is an important part of the listening process, listeners must actively engage their minds when they actually receive information (Kline, 2003).

Attending

When receivers consciously listen to speakers, they pay attention to the messages. When stimuli, external or internal, intervene and compete for listeners' concentration, the remaining listening processes are delayed or deleted.

Interpreting

Effective listening occurs when listeners receive, interpret, and understand messages as intended by senders. Interpreting is especially important in the listening cycle and crucial when communicating interculturally. Words used and the manner in which they are delivered may have different meaning among listeners and speakers.

Responding

Even though the listening process may end after interpreting the message, a response enhances or strengthens the cycle. Responding lets the sender know that the message was received, attended to, and interpreted. Responses may be verbal (affirming, clarifying, or paraphrasing) or nonverbal (nod of the head, smile, or show of hands).

Remembering

Listeners retain information needed for future reference by taking notes or by making mental outlines. In a classroom setting, providing students with notetaking techniques will increase the likelihood of their retaining and recalling information.

Listening encompasses five processes (receiving, attending, interpreting, responding, and remembering). However, some types of listening may not require two of those processes (responding and remembering). Even though word connotations and delivery methods may vary, the listening processes remain significant within and between all cultures.

LISTENING LEVELS

Listening can be passive or active. Passive listening requires no verbal response, even though the listener may send nonverbal messages such as eye contact, facial expressions, or body movement. However, active listening, a cyclical process, requires feedback (Mentoring Skills, 1998).

Active listening begins with the speaker, travels to the message listener, stimulates feedback to the speaker, and the process repeats. Listeners interpret spoken words based on numerous factors such as age, gender, education, economic status, religious beliefs, specific situations, and cultural backgrounds (Kline, 2003). These factors split the listening levels into three categories: intrapersonal, interpersonal, and intercultural.

Listening Intrapersonally

Intrapersonal listening, often referred to as casual or passive listening, provides personal enjoyment or background while the listener engages in other activities. Students listen to music while studying, people dial radio stations while driving, and homemakers play television while completing household chores; all of these activities are examples of intrapersonal listening. Since listeners are under no pressure to comprehend or recall, intrapersonal listening requires only passive efforts (Galle, Nelson, Luse, & Villere, 1996).

Listening Interpersonally

Listening interpersonally demands active, intensive participation. The listener must exercise extra effort to absorb intended information, since the speaking rate is usually 120 to 150 words per minute, while the listener can process information 500 to 600 words per minute (Collins, 1997; Winzurk, 2000). The difference in speaking rate and listening rate, referred to as *lag time* by Lehman and Dufrene (2002), allows listeners' minds to wander. To lessen the possibility of their minds wandering, listeners must actively involve themselves in the interpersonal listening process.

Listening Interculturally

Increasing diversity within the United States, expanding international markets, and the growing availability of technological communication mandate that listeners become adept at intercultural listening (Beamer & Varner, 2001; Chen & Starosta, 1998). Most

Western cultures place more emphasis on speaking than on listening, whereas non-Western cultures emphasize listening rather than speaking. Intercultural listening presents complex challenges based on such differences as language systems (verbal and nonverbal) and values (Thomlison, 1991).

In verbal systems word usage alone may present special dilemmas. One language may not have equivalent words in another language. For example, Spanish does not have an equivalent word for "yuppie." In Vietnamese a term does not exist for the expression "OK" (K. Nguyen, personal communication, January 22, 2004). An object may be identified with different words even within the same country—a water fountain in Florida is a "bubbler" in Wisconsin (Brantley & Miller, 2002).

Nonverbal systems differ widely among cultures. To enhance intercultural listening, communicators must understand gestures and expressions. In Russia the OK sign may be interpreted as vulgar; in Taiwan blinking the eyes at someone is impolite; and in Japan laughter might not indicate joy or amusement but may be a sign of embarrassment (Chan-Herur, 1994).

Values are standards of cultural patterns prevalent in a particular society. Values differ across cultures and must be considered when listening (Terpstra & David, 1991). Among the value differences are views about time management, directness, and formality. In the United States, speakers and listeners expect strict adherence to appointment and class times while other cultures may place less emphasis on time. Directness and openness are valued in the United States, while indirectness (saving face) appeals to various other cultures. Informal dress and casual conversation often used by U.S. residents may be interpreted as inappropriate or even disrespectful by listeners in other countries (Thomlison, 1991). Understanding cultural differences will improve rather than deter intercultural listening effectiveness.

Interpersonal and intercultural listening necessitate active participation, whereas intrapersonal listening may require only passive efforts. Intercultural listening reflects potential differences in verbal and nonverbal language systems and values, thereby requiring concentrated effort and additional knowledge of various cultures.

LISTENING PURPOSES

To listen effectively, individuals must determine the reasons for listening. The more important the reason or purpose for listening, the more attention listeners give speakers. People listen to interact socially and professionally, receive information, share feelings, solve problems, and understand global implications.

Interacting Socially and Professionally

Listening builds relationships in social and professional settings. Casual conversations with friends require less attention than do professional dialogues with supervisors or coworkers. Casual listeners also may be selective listeners with friends as they choose when to tune in or out of conversations. Casual listening may occur in professional

18

settings when persons introduce workers to each other, plan after-work social gatherings, or discuss vacation activities. Professional conversations are more intense than casual conversations but less intense than formal meetings (Burley-Allen, 1995; Lehman & Dufrene, 2002).

Receiving Information

When receiving information is the purpose for listening, less two-way dialogue occurs. The speaker delivers content, and the listener receives the message. According to Kline (2003), this type of listening requires more concentration than does casual listening. In classroom or business settings, listeners should remain focused on the message, though to do so for long time periods is extremely difficult.

Sharing Feelings

Sharing feelings with empathetic listeners is valued in professional and private settings. Listening empathetically assists teachers, parents, counselors, and managers in nurturing and promoting successful students, children, clients, and employees. Empathetic listeners withhold advice; their goal is to understand speakers' perceptions and emotions without necessarily agreeing with them (Kline, 2003; Smith, 1992).

Solving Problems

Solving problems involves intensive, critical listening. Listeners not only understand the meaning but also evaluate the speaker's message. Critical listening follows a problem-solving process as listeners identify and assess the (1) logic of information (2) strength of evidence (3) validity of conclusions (4) implications of the message for listeners and organizations (5) intentions and motives of speakers, and (6) omission of important, relevant points (Bovee, Thill, & Schatzman, 2003).

Understanding Global Implications

Regardless of the purpose, listening in an intercultural environment requires additional concentration and interaction. Attentive listeners show intercultural speakers that their contributions are valued and respected. Listeners may show support and build rapport with three techniques: confirming, supporting, and building. In confirming, listeners may say, "Let me repeat what you said"; in supporting, "That's a great point"; and in building, "May I add a thought?" (Three Secrets, January 2004). Harris and Moran (2000) and Varner (2000) further recommended that paying attention to the person and the message in intercultural exchanges enables listeners to focus on the purpose.

Listening purposes vary widely, depending on various situations and participants' intents. When the purpose is to interact casually in a social or professional setting, listeners frequently offer fewer responses and commit less information to memory. Listening for receiving information, sharing feelings, and solving problems requires more active participation. Listeners in intercultural environments must devote additional thought and effort to create understanding and rapport among listeners and speakers.

LISTENING BARRIERS

Barriers, interferences with listening, negatively affect the listening process. Good listeners recognize and attempt to overcome potential barriers. Listening barriers may be physical, emotional, and/or psychological.

Distracting Physical Conditions

The listening environment may negatively affect the listening process. External factors may include noises (mechanical or people sounds), poor lighting, uncomfortable temperature, and room arrangement. Winzurk (2000) suggested additional external issues that may involve the speaker's mannerisms, voice, delivery, and appearance. Internal factors may include impaired hearing, hunger, fatigue, or illness (Bly, 2000).

Existing Emotional Reactions

Emotional barriers, often referred to as roadblocks, vary with individuals and are seldom observable. Emotional barriers take place within listeners' minds and bodies. Emotional roadblocks may range from worries or concerns to a poor personal or professional relationship with the speaker (Winzurk, 2000; Johnson 1996).

Existing Mental Perceptions

Individuals' mental perceptions often become one of the greatest barriers to listening. The following habits interfere with listening (Why We Don't, n.d.; The Top Seven Mistakes, n.d.):

- Interrupting—thinking of the next question when the speaker has not asked for input

- Talking too much—monopolizing time with personal questions and comments

- Editorializing—interjecting comments that reflect emotional feelings

- Jumping to conclusions—making decisions about the content before the message is heard and the content evaluated

- Judging—prejudging somebody as incompetent or uninformed

- Filtering—hearing only what the listeners want to hear (selective listening)

- Dreaming—pretending to listen while drifting into internal fantasies

- Placating—agreeing with everything just to be nice or to avoid conflict

According to Johnson (1996), recognizing the environmental, emotional, and barriers exist is the first step in selecting strategies for improved listening.

Three barrier categories (physical, emotional, and psychological) may impede the listening process. Physical barriers include both external and internal factors. Although emotional reactions and psychological perceptions may remain unseen, these barriers create a negative listening state.

LISTENING STRATEGIES

To develop better skills, listeners identify potential barriers and incorporate strategies for improvement into an action plan. The plan contains four elements: preparing for listening, removing distractions, remaining attentive, and considering intercultural components.

Preparing for Listening

According to Kline (2003), mental planning may be divided into three preparation stages: long-term, mid-term, and short-term. Long-term preparation means ongoing practice. Individuals may listen to challenging topics such as debates, news programs, and lectures. They need to maintain a vocabulary building program because an extensive vocabulary improves the likelihood of becoming a better listener.

Mid-term preparation requires background research. For students mid-term listening preparation means reading assigned material and possibly locating additional resources. Other listeners review files, participate in briefings, and locate resources as preparation for listening.

Short-term planning involves focusing on the proposed topic and forgetting personal agendas (Schoombie, 1999). Listeners need to begin listening when the first word is spoken and remain attentive until the speaker ends the discussion.

Removing Distractions

In physical arrangements listeners need to control or eliminate distracting mechanical noises, set the temperature control within a comfortable range, and arrange seating to accommodate visual and verbal interactions between listeners and the speaker. Accommodating personal distractions related to the speaker or the receiver before the communication process will boost successful listening. Although listeners cannot alter a speaker's appearance, mannerisms, and delivery, they must look beyond those distractions to the message (Wilson, n.d.).

Remaining Attentive

Active listening is hard work. Walker (n.d.) and Raudsepp (n.d) recommended that listeners improve awareness and efficiency by observing the following guidelines:

- Suspend other activities

- Focus attention on content

- Maintain eye contact

- Show appropriate facial expressions, posture, and gestures

- Recognize individual feelings and opinions

- Separate main points from supporting material

- Restate the speaker's messages

- Ask clarification questions when needed

- Use lag time wisely

Attentive listening is an individual task; therefore, listeners may develop other techniques for lengthening concentration.

Considering Intercultural Components

Intercultural listening offers challenges seldom admitted or recognized because of the erroneous assumption that all cultures adhere to the same standards, behaviors, and customs (Bovee, Thill, & Schatzman, 2003). To address some of the issues in intercultural listening, Murray (2003) recommended these basic guidelines:

- Show interest and attention

- Learn to paraphrase

- Use appropriate body language

- Avoid interrupting

- Hold questions for appropriate time

- Enjoy every word heard

- Continue dialogue after the presentation

- Grasp others' viewpoints and demonstrate empathy

Active listening guidelines may need adjustment when listeners and speakers come from different countries or even different parts of the same country. For example, listeners and speakers in the U.S. expect direct eye contact, while some cultures (Middle and Far Eastern) maintain limited to no contact (Foster, 2000).

Vocal cues such as word choice, pronunciation, intonation, and accent affect understanding. While U. S. speakers pronounce a series of actions leading to an end as "pro'cess," the British pronunciation is "prô'cess." Venezuelans end each sentence with a lilt, as though statements are questions. Yala people in Nigeria vary the pitch of certain words to change their meaning. Listeners unfamiliar with language sounds may not distinguish or recognize intended meanings (Thomlison, 1991). Within the United States, regional accents are troublesome to international students (Davis & Walker, 2000).

To address known barriers, listeners can develop strategies for improving listening skills. They can prepare for listening, remove as many distractions as possible, and remain focused on the speaker. Incorporating the suggested guidelines for intercultural listening will improve communication both within a culture and among cultures.

LISTENING ACTIVITIES

Individual and group activities can help students to improve listening skills. Before activities or exercises are assigned, participants may complete a pretest of perceived listening effectiveness (Johnson, Pearce, Tuten, & Sinclair, 2003). URLs for online listening evaluation instruments are the following:

- http://www.lahc.cc.ca.us/tutortraining/listtest.html

- http://homepages.ius.edu/KBALDRID/activities/LISTNING.HTM

- http://www.careerjournal.com/sidebars/20021224-raudsepp-quiz.html

After listeners complete evaluation instruments, instructors select activities that are relevant and authentic. Relevant exercises have a stated purpose and are based on participants' interests or job-related tasks. The language in authentic exercises reflects real conversations, including hesitations, rephrasing, and a variety of accents.

Numerous activities are available in print and electronic formats. "The Dolittle Method of Listening" (Batty-Herbert, K., 1999) may be retrieved from the following URL: http://old.weber.edu/comm/IlaListening%20Exercises/dolittle.htm.

Learners' needs, whether in a business or a classroom setting, will determine the selection of appropriate listening activities. Suggested listening activities include the following:

Activity 1. Transmitting Information

Procedure. Select any recent 2-3 paragraph article. Divide the group into teams of 4 people each. Tell them to count off, 1, 2, 3, and 4 so that each person is identified in sequence. Ask those numbered 1 to stay in the room and all others to move outside the room. Then, tell those remaining to listen to a story; listeners should not take notes nor ask questions. After listening to the story, ask the #2s to return to their team. The #1s will repeat the story to the #2s. Then the #3s return to their groups and hear the story from the #2s, while the #1s observe. Continue the sequence until all have participated. Then at random ask some of the number #4s to repeat what they heard.

Discussion questions. (a) How much information was lost in each transmittal? How much embellishment occurred? (b) What errors or differences were observed as the story was told by the group members? (c) What would have increased both the facts and the understanding?

Activity 2. Following Spoken Instructions
Procedure. Students listen carefully to each item and complete all calculations mentally, writing *only* the answers on their paper. Read the items at a normal rate of speed.

(a) Start with 8; double it; add 4; divide by 5; the answer is _____.

(b) Start with 11; subtract 3; add 4; add 3; divide by 3; the answer is _____.

(c) Start with 15; add 10; divide by 5; multiply by 6; add 6; divide by 4; the answer is _____.

(d) From a number that is 4 larger than 13, add 5; divide by 2; subtract 3; the answer is _____.

(e) From a number that is 2 smaller than 9, add 6; add 5; multiply by 2; divide by 4; the answer is _____.

Discussion questions. (a) How many just quit listening after becoming confused or lost with a question? (b) When others are talking, do listeners quit listening? (c) What can be done to encourage better listening when communicating with others?

Activity 3. Willing Self to Listen: Can You?
Procedure. Tape two conversations that include names, dates, times, and addresses. After participants listen to the first conversation, ask 6-8 questions on items included in the message. Most people will correctly answer only half of the questions. Play the second conversation and ask participants to listen intently. Again ask 6-8 questions. Compare the number of correct responses between the first and the second conversations.

Discussion questions. (a) What barriers to effective listening did this exercise illustrate? (b) Were listening quotients better on the second exercise? If so, why?

Activity 4. Listening with Interest
Procedure. Select any 2-3 paragraph article of a nonbusiness nature, preferably one in which most listeners would have little interest. Read the article to the group. Ask the listeners to write what they heard.

Then read a second article from a trade journal or magazine related to most listeners' interest. Again ask listeners to write what they heard. Compare the results.

Discussion questions. (a) Why was recall difficult on the first article? (b) Research shows most listeners immediately forget 50% of what they have heard. Why was recall improved on the second article? (c) What additional listening barriers does this activity illustrate?

For additional testing instruments and activities, instructors may conduct online searches using keywords such as "listening skills quiz," "listening self-evaluation," and "listening activities."

SUMMARY

Effective listening significantly enhances communication in personal and professional endeavors. Listening affects intercultural understanding, business relationships, and learning environments. Knowing the cyclical listening process and listening levels increases the possibilities of improved intrapersonal, interpersonal, and intercultural communication. While all listening can be challenging, listening interculturally demands concentrated effort and attention as listeners attempt to show support and build rapport with those from other cultures.

Listening purposes encompass interacting socially and professionally, receiving information, sharing feelings, solving problems, and understanding global implications. Communication situations and participants' intents may alter listening purposes.

Barriers to listening in all settings include physical conditions, emotional reactions, and psychological perceptions. Strategies for lessening the effect of barriers encompass both mental and mechanical elements. The elements include preparing to listen, removing distractions when possible, and remaining attentive to the speaker. Intercultural listening requires intensified strategic planning.

Activities for improving listening begin with assessing listening skills. Many brief and relevant activities appear in written and electronic formats.

The "forgotten" skill of listening, both within cultures and among cultures, can be developed and/or enhanced by devoting careful attention to listening processes, levels, purposes, barriers, strategies, and activities for improvement.

REFERENCES

Batty-Herbert, K. (1999). *The Dolittle method of listening.* Retrieved August 8, 2003, from http://old.weber.edu/comm/IlaListening%20Exercises/dolittle.htm

Beamer, L., & Varner, I. (2001). *Intercultural communication in the global workplace* (2nd ed.). Burr Ridge, IL: Irwin McGraw-Hill.

Bly, R. W. (2000). *Improving your listening skills.* Retrieved October 15, 2003, from http://www.bly.com/Pages/documents/CEPARTLISTEN1.DOC

Bovee, C. L., Thill, J. V., & Schatzman, B. E. (2003). *Business communication today* (7th ed.). Upper Saddle River, NJ: Prentice Hall.

Brantley, C. P., & Miller, M. G. (2002). *Effective communication for colleges* (9th ed.). Cincinnati, OH: South-Western/Thomson Learning.

Burley-Allen, M. (1995). *Listening: The forgotten skill* (2nd ed.). New York: John Wiley & Sons, Inc.

Chambers, W., & Asher, S. (1998, February). *Bottom line listening.* Retrieved November 1, 2003, from http://www.winstonbrill.com/bril001/html/article_index/articles/301-350/article323_body.html

Chan-Herur, K. (1994*). Communicating with customers around the world: A practical guide to effective cross-cultural business communication.* San Francisco: AuMonde International Publishing Company.

Chen, G., & Starosta, W. (1998). *Foundations of intercultural communication.* Needham Heights, MA: Allyn and Bacon.

Collins, P. (1997). *Say it with power and confidence.* Upper Saddle River, NJ: Prentice Hall.

Davis, B., & Walker, J. (2000, October). *Communicating with international students.* Paper presented at the meeting of the Association for Business Communication, Atlanta, GA.

Foster, D. (2000). *The global etiquette guide to Asia.* New York: John Wiley & Sons.

Galle, W. P., Jr., Nelson, B. H., Luse, D. W., & Villere, M. F. (1996). *Business communication.* Chicago: Irwin Publishers.

Harris, P. R., & Moran, R. T. (2000). *Managing cultural differences* (5th ed.). Houston, TX: Gulf Publishing Company.

Johnson, I. W., Pearce, C. G., Tuten, T. L., & Sinclair, L. (2003). Self-imposed silence and perceived listening effectiveness. *Business Communication Quarterly, 66,* 23-45.

Johnson, K. (1996). *Effective listening skills.* Retrieved August 4, 2003, from http://www.itmweb.com/essay514.htm

Kline, J. A. (2003). *Listening effectively: Achieving high standards in communication.* Upper Saddle River, NJ: Prentice Hall.

Lehman, C. M., & Dufrene, D. D. (2002). *Business communication* (13th ed.). Cincinnati, OH: South-Western/Thomson Learning.

Mentoring skills: Communication. (1998). Retrieved January 13, 2004, from http://www.uscg.mil/hq/g-w/g-wt/g-251/comm.htm

Murray, E. C. (2003, September). The pleasure of active listening. *Escala, 170,* 41-48.

Raudsepp, E. (n.d.). *Hone listening skills to boost your career.* Retrieved August 21, 2003, from http://www.careerjournal.com/myc/climbing/20021224-raudsepp.html?home _bricks

Schoombie, B. (1999, October 12). *Learning to listen.* Retrieved August 4, 2003, from http://www.suite101.com/print_article.cfm/4655/26005

Smith, C. (1992). *How can parents model good listening skills?* Retrieved January 15, 2004, from http://www.kidsource.com/kidsource/content2/How_Can_Parents_Model.html

Terpstra, V., & David, K. (1991). *The cultural environment of international business* (3rd ed.). Cincinnati, OH: South-Western Publishing Co.

The top seven mistakes poor listeners make. (n.d.). *MLM sales coach newsletter.* Retrieved November 7, 2003, from http://www.mlmu.com/archive/news/mlmsc0201.shtml

Thomlison, T. D. (1991). Intercultual listening. In D. Borisoff & M. Purdy (Eds.). *Listening in everyday life: A personal and professional approach* (pp. 87-137). Lanham, MD: University Press of America, Inc.

Three secrets of great listening. (2004, January). *Communication Briefings, 23*(3), 6.

Varner, I. (2000, January). The theoretical foundation for intercultural business communication: A conceptual model. *The Journal of Business Communication, 37*(1), 39-57.

Walker, D. (n.d.). *Active listening for the classroom.* Retrieved August 23, 2003, from http://7-12educators.about.com/library/weekly/aa081700a.htm

Why we don't hear others. (n.d.). *Communication Briefings, 20*, 1.

Wilson, B. (n.d.). *Part I: Strategies for business listeners.* Retrieved October 20, 2003, from http://www.businesslistening.com/listeningskills-2.php

Winzurk, J. D. (2000). *Listening and observing.* Cincinnati, OH: South-Western/Thomson Learning.

Wolvin, A. D., & Coakley, C. G. (1991). A survey of the status of listening training in some Fortune 500 Corporations. *Communication Education, 40*, 152-164.

Speaking: Verbalizing Ideas Effectively

Allyson D. Saunders
Weber State University
Ogden, Utah

Colleen Vawdrey
Utah Valley State College
Orem, Utah

Oral communication skills are acknowledged to be among the most important skills for anyone in business. The ability to speak well is crucial to obtaining, keeping, and advancing in careers in business. Included with other technical, cognitive, and practical skills considered necessary for business students should be oral presentation skills. This chapter addresses the fundamentals of public speaking, from planning to presenting the message. Since public speaking invokes fear in most beginning speakers (Reece, 1999), this aspect is given special consideration. In addition, emphasis is given to the special concerns of international audiences, team presentations, and gender differences.

PLANNING THE MESSAGE

According to Bailey (2005), "Most presentations succeed or fail long before you stand up!" (p. 141). Planning is the first critical step in any oral presentation. One of the most important parts of planning is determining the purpose of the presentation. Speakers must decide whether the goal is to report, explain, persuade, or motivate the audience. The presentation must be developed with the audience in mind.

Analyze the Audience

Several factors are essential to consider when analyzing the audience. What does the audience already know about the topic? Is the audience already predisposed on the topic—does the audience object to the topic? How large will the audience be—is the audience too large to invite questions, or is the audience small enough to have an interactive presentation? What concerns does the audience have about the topic? How much information is essential to achieve the purpose? Does the audience speak the same language or will speakers need an interpreter? Does the audience understand the jargon in the presentation (Sorenson, Kennedy, & Ramirez, 1997)? Speakers should answer these questions for the specific situation as the presentation is being prepared.

Presenting to an all English-speaking audience is challenging enough, but what about an international audience? More likely than not, some members listening to the presentation will have cultural and language differences from the presenter. Too often, Americans believe that everyone is the same (or at least should function as Americans do). This arrogant attitude will not be successful in an attempt to communicate with those of other cultures.

Meadows (1990) compared the world to a village of just 1,000 people. The makeup would include 584 Asians, 124 Africans, 95 Europeans, 84 Latin Americans, 52 North Americans, 6 Australians and New Zealanders, and 55 people from the former Soviet republics. Along with a mix of countless cultures would be more than 200 languages. The challenges presented by this global group are numerous. Rarely would all these groups be attending one speech, but the assumption must be made that at least a few of each group will be among the listeners.

Understand Cultures

Speakers must be sensitive to the fact that language defines culture. Although the speakers will likely not know the cultural beliefs of each audience member, they must be cautious in not presenting anything that may be offensive to a listener. People interpret messages based on their own cultural filter of knowledge, experiences, and viewpoints. Other cultures do not necessarily share the American style of speaking, since it tends to be problem oriented, direct, explicit, personal, and informal (Johnson, 1997).

The more speakers know about other cultures, the more comfortable they will be in presenting to international audiences. Many companies send employees to work in other cultures but fail to include cross-culture training, believing that other people will communicate in similar ways (Stamps, 1996).

Humor is a difficult concept to convey with different cultures. According to Axtell (1993), humor is one of the seven deadliest sins of international miscommunication. Something that is funny in one culture may not be in another. Even within the same culture, the interpretation of humor changes over time. Experts suggest speakers avoid humor completely or poke fun at only themselves in a gentle way (Allee, n.d.).

DEVELOPING SUPPORTING MATERIALS

Visual aids, which may include electronic presentations, handouts, and props, should enhance the presentation and not overpower it. Visuals act as an aid, and not the whole focus of the presentation, by providing assistance for the audience rather than a script for the presenter.

The following guidelines for speakers will be helpful when developing and presenting with electronic aids:

- Avoid the temptation to include too many words on a slide. Each slide should be limited to 40 characters per line and a maximum of seven lines per slide (Ober, 2003).

- Keep bulleted items parallel.

- Ensure that the color projected on the computer matches that projected on the screen.

- Keep special effects simple, such as avoiding repetitive animations.

- Avoid transitional sound effects.

- Disable screen savers and energy-saving automatic shutdown features.

- Stand on the left side from the audience's point of view to avoid interfering with slides (*Visuals Can Power*, n.d.).

People are able to grasp concepts more quickly with pictures than with words. A presenter may use simple pictures such as graphs and charts, which don't need words to explain. If the audience needs an explanation to understand the graphic, then the graphic should be simplified (*Visuals Can Power*, n.d.).

Handouts are a standard part of a presentation and provide a review/permanent record of the material or complex information that would be ineffective on a slide. If an electronic presentation is given, handouts can include miniature slides; however, not all slides need to be used in the handouts. Special care must be taken to ensure that mis-communication does not occur with jargon, acronyms, or terms unique to one language. Handouts should be given at the end of the presentation in order to keep the audience's attention, except when the information is essential for the audience to discuss during the presentation (Ober, 2003).

PREPARING THE MESSAGE

Although the words are essential to the message, 93% of the understanding comes from the way the message is presented; verbal is 7%; vocal is 38%; and visual is 55% of the total understanding (Allee, n.d.). After speakers know what the audience should learn, they can then begin developing the presentation. The speech should be divided into three parts. The adage of "tell them what you're going to tell them, tell them, and then tell them what you told them" works well in organizing the order of the presentation (*Small Business Presentations*, n.d.).

Because the key points are emphasized three times in the presentation, success in attaining the purpose of the presentation is more likely. The practice of using three examples, words, or ideas may have a psychological basis. Using three items seems to be more effective in remembering than using two or four (*Small Business Presentations*, n.d.).

In order to immerse the audience in the topic, speakers must first get the people's attention. This attention-getter must be related to the topic and may include a greeting, a shocking statement, or an anecdote (*Small Business Presentations*, n.d.). The closing should be just as powerful as the beginning by relating the key points to the attention-getter and motivating the audience to action.

PRESENTING THE MESSAGE

Presenting the message involves speaking to the audience and understanding the culture. Care must be taken to watch the audience for clues and to use simple language in delivering the message. Because so much of the message is visual and verbal, speakers must also dress the part, practice well, apply appropriate voice techniques, and watch for nonverbal cues (Allee, n.d.).

Speak to the Audience

Speakers can keep the audience's attention and maintain more credibility by speaking directly to the group. Notes should be used only as a quick reminder for the next topic. Speakers who read from notes frequently lose their audience. However, some cross-cultural audiences may view presentations that are given from notes only and not read as a form of disrespect and believe that the speakers did not prepare the remarks fully (Ober, 2003).

Eye contact with individuals is essential to keeping the audience part of the presentation. Speakers should focus on the audience by using "you-oriented" words rather than "I-oriented" words. One public speaking institute suggests using some kind of attention-gaining device every 2 to 4 minutes. Attention-getting devices include the following:

- Using a prop

- Telling a story to relate a point

- Asking questions of the audience

- Involving a member of the audience (Advanced Public Speaking Institute, n.d.)

Understand Cultural Speaking Norms for Groups

When groups are involved in oral interaction, the participants need to be aware of and sensitive to other cultural norms. Although considered impolite in the United States, people from Middle Eastern cultures may interrupt speakers before they finish speaking.

From the listeners' viewpoint, this action is encouraged as a sign of involvement in the conversation. On the other hand, Asians may remain very quiet, since that culture believes that subordinates should never challenge the viewpoint of a superior. Mexican listeners believe that negotiation to "win" a point is completely appropriate (Johnson, 1997).

A good piece of advice is to make learning about other people's cultures an ongoing endeavor. The more that is learned, the more confident speakers are that they will positively impact the audience (Johnson, 1997).

Watch for Clues from the Audience

As in any other situation, speakers should connect with the audience. Finding someone familiar with the culture differences will help speakers understand the audience needs. For example, Japanese listeners will commonly close their eyes and nod their heads up and down slightly. That does not mean the speaker is putting them to sleep; that is the culture norm to show concentration and attentiveness (Advanced Public Speaking Institute, n.d.).

Use Simple Language

Good advice when speaking to any group is to use simple words that the audience will understand. This concept is even more important in cross-cultural settings. Many English words may have a different meaning when translated. For example, "mad" usually means angry in the United States but means "insane" to a British audience (*What to Know*, n.d.).

English, as any other language, has idiomatic expressions that do not translate from one language to another, such as "all ears," "tickled pink," or "driving me nuts." Using these "colorful" expressions may cause more confusion than expected in a global audience. Having someone else specifically listen for these phrases in the speech will be useful during practice sessions so that they can be eliminated.

Dress the Part

The audience will arrive at a quick first impression based on the speaker's appearance, which for the audience is an indication of the speaker's credibility. Speakers are generally more confident when they dress well. A poor first impression due to inappropriate dress may negate an otherwise effective speech. Speakers' dress can say volumes and can cause the audience to make judgments on speakers' professionalism, level of sophistication, intelligence, as well as credibility. To create a positive first impression, speakers should dress one level above the audience (Executive Communications Group, n.d.). A polished appearance can help lead to a polished presentation.

Practice, Practice, Practice

Nothing can substitute for practice, practice, and more practice. Speakers must know the topic and, as much as possible, simulate the actual speaking experience by trying the microphone, speaking behind the podium, and using the presentation equipment. Speaker volume must be adjusted based on the room size, acoustics, and the audience size.

Breaking a long presentation into chunks of 3 to 5 minutes will make practice more manageable. Practicing an hour presentation can be overwhelming, but practicing 3- to 5-minute chunks is possible (Advanced Public Speaking Institute, n.d.).

Voice Techniques

Interesting speakers use a variety of volume, pitch, and speed. Most audiences in the United States are more likely to enjoy and remember a talk that is presented in a simple, conversational manner. Some of the elements that transform a formal presentation into a conversational presentation include simple gesturing and purposeful moving around the room. Using a full range of accents and dynamics increases the effectiveness of the presenter. Emphasizing appropriate words and controlling silences to allow for thoughtful repose are other ways to seize and hold the audience's attention (Harris, 1994).

Presenters must speak at a comfortable pace for the audience. The tendency for some speakers, knowing they have an international audience, is to believe that speaking louder will make the communication more understandable. The audience may have a challenge with English but not with hearing. That inclination may be offensive to these listeners (*What to Know*, n.d.). However, speakers should talk slowly and clearly using short, simple sentences (Ober, 2003).

Nonverbal Aspects

Nonverbal messages should enhance the verbal message. When nonverbal gestures overpower or contradict the verbal message, the presentation is less powerful. According to the authors' experience with student speakers, some common pitfalls to avoid are clicking a pen, sticking hands in pockets, swaying back and forth, playing with hair, and overusing hands. These habits are especially important with a global audience, since nonverbal gestures differ from culture to culture (Ober, 2003).

Axtell (1998) describes the head and face as the most expressive parts of speakers' nonverbal messages. Nodding the head up and down signals "yes" in some cultures but means "no" in others. When speakers try to use the nonverbal cues of the audience's culture, the audience may still be confused as to which culture is being represented and what the speaker is trying to say.

Eye contact differs from culture to culture significantly. For example, Americans use eye contact to show confidence. Hispanic women hold eye contact longer than other cultures. Asians tend to avoid direct eye contact, especially with people of higher authority. Middle Easterners are expected to maintain eye contact to avoid appearing disinterested. However, the one universally understood gesture is smiling, even though some 1,814,400 different smiles exist (Axtell, 1998).

In order to exhibit confidence and keep the audience from focusing on the nonverbal behavior, the authors recommend that speakers apply the following techniques:

- Keep both feet planted on the floor.

- Place hands on the podium or clasped together loosely.

- Avoid playing with objects.

- Pull hair back to avoid dangling hair.

Speakers often fail to notice their own inappropriate or annoying nonverbal gestures. Videotaping the presentation will allow speakers to notice any nonverbal gestures that could be annoying.

OVERCOMING ANXIETY

Studies agree that the number one fear for most people is public speaking, according to a Gallup poll of 3,000 Americans (Sawyer, 1993) and Book of Lists (Rolls, 1998). The idea is even a topic for comedians. Jerry Seinfeld noted,

> According to most studies, people's number one fear is public speaking. Number two is death. Death is number two? Does that seem right? To the average person that means that if they [sic] have to go to a funeral, they'd be better off in the casket than giving the eulogy (*Presentation Tips*, n.d.).

Why People Fear Speaking

Rolls (1998) uses McCroskey's apprehension identification theory. He categorizes people into two groups: trait communication apprehension (shyness) and state communication apprehension. Although the shy person may be nervous about a variety of situations and may live a large portion of his/her life in a state of apprehension, more common is the person who becomes anxious before and even during a presentation. This fear may result from several factors.

Lack of experience. The more practice speakers get at presenting, the better they become. However, if fear causes a person to avoid speaking, the practice can't happen. The cycle becomes one of repeated failure. Fear seems to affect women more than men. One study found that female executives experience high levels of speech anxiety (35%), whereas the male executives were less anxious (11%) about making speeches (Weisul, 2002). Another study by Behnke and Sawyer (2000) reinforced the same premise: that females exhibit a higher degree of anxiety during each stage of the process of public speaking.

Preparation. According to Daly, Vangelisti, Neel, and Cavanaugh (1989), half of the top 10 preperformance concerns of students were related to preparation. Anxiety had a negative effect on students' preparation, but when preparation began, students were able to overcome the initial apprehension to some degree.

Perception. Many beginning speakers believe they are the only ones who feel anxiety. If these speakers could realize that everyone feels some anxiety, they may be able to lessen their own. Feeling part of a group, talking about their anxiety, and comparing notes with others can be a strong coping mechanism for fear (Daly, Vangelisti, Neel, & Cavanaugh, 1989).

Standing out. Being the center of attention makes people worry about the little things—less than perfect clothing, a bad hair day, or any one of a dozen other "imperfections" that may increase the anxiety. These situations detract from the message itself and may cause speakers to lose focus on the important points in making a successful presentation (Daly, Vangelisti, Neel, & Cavanaugh, 1989).

When Anxiety Occurs

For some, anxiety sets in the moment speakers are asked to speak. For others, it starts during the preparation stage. By the time the person reaches the podium, anxiety has occurred for perhaps all speakers to some degree. In a study by Behnke and Sawyer (1999), they found that the greatest anxiety for students occurred just prior to giving the speech. That finding is not surprising, but the most revealing fact was that the second greatest amount of anxiety occurred when the speaking assignment was given. Giving students work time immediately following the announcement of the assignment may help reduce the beginning anxiety level.

Writers' block is a common phobia for written communication; this oral anxiety may appropriately be called "speaker's block." If it occurs before the speech is even prepared, the result is procrastination and, in turn, more anxiety. A study by Daly, Vangelisti, and Weber (1995) found that more anxious individuals are less likely to engage in the preparation process. They seem to spend more time "lost" in the process and fail to focus on organizing content, audience analysis, and visual aids.

Anxiety at the time of the presentation is highest for most people (Daly, Vangelisti, and Weber, 1995). If the introduction is successful, the anxiety usually subsides. Therefore, practicing the beginning, perhaps to the point of memorization, and having a strong introduction to the speech should help alleviate anxiety and allow the presentation to be successful.

How Fear Is Overcome

Although speakers are ultimately responsible for reducing their fear, teachers can provide suggestions and aid students in overcoming the apprehension. Kelly and Keaten (2000) suggest several ideas for teachers. Providing feedback during preparation and practice sessions can be helpful since a grade is not attached. Uncertainty about the assignment is reduced by showing examples that can help students feel more confident and less apprehensive. Creating flexible assignment options (from highly structured for very anxious students to loosely structured for more confident students) can provide assistance to students on their own need level.

Relaxing. Breathing deeply, evenly, and slowly for several minutes can help reduce anxiety prior to speaking. Experienced speakers even suggest taking a few deep breaths in the 30 seconds before beginning to speak and even verbalizing "relax" during the process (*12 Ways*, n.d.).

Using eye contact. Many beginning speakers believe looking at the audience will make them even more nervous, but experts say that looking listeners in the eye actually reduces stage fright (Allee, n.d.).

Visualizing success. Professor Harold Hill in *The Music Man* taught his band using the "Think Method." Although intended as a scam, the point can be very successful. People who see themselves giving a successful presentation can help ensure that outcome. During practice sessions, speakers should anticipate positive audience reaction and successful expectations. Although this method cannot take the place of preparation, it will be an effective complement. A study by Ayres and Hopf (1989) compared communication apprehension of students who were given visualization techniques to build confidence with those who were not. This visualization was determined to be an effective classroom tool that reduced anxiety.

Other successful strategies include pretending the speech is a chat with a group of friends, picturing the audience members in their underwear, and concentrating on past public speaking successes (Advanced Public Speaking Institute, n.d.).

The solution to speaking anxiety is not simple. Because the fear is so common, educators must not ignore it. Instead they must continue to help students deal with and reduce this anxiety. Since people are different, no one strategy will work for all; but with a variety of tools available, teachers can work toward finding the right combination for each student.

PRESENTING AS A TEAM

Giving a presentation with a team rather than alone includes many of the same principles. However, some additional considerations should be noted when the presentation involves more than one person.

Team Planning

Developing the purpose and analyzing the audience needs are obviously similar. Organizing the content and preparing the speech have some advantages with a team, since the workload can be divided among the members. Initial feelings about the process may lead speakers to believe a team process will be easier and less work. Upon further reflection about the process, the team members will realize that some compromises must be made. Different team members have different perceptions about the content and different approaches to preparation. Appointing a team leader may be critical to the success of the presentation (*When It's Time*, n.d.).

In addition, extra effort must be made to ensure the team members make the transitions smoothly. Making the presentation appear integrated and not several individual speeches combined requires planning and preparation beyond that of an individual speech (Flett, 1998).

Team Presentation

Simply determining the order of presentation is not enough. The team needs to practice together so the presentation moves logically and smoothly from one speaker to the next. Timing the presentation during the practice sessions will ensure the last member has adequate time to present his/her information. Building a bridge that links one member's information to the next will help the integration process (*When It's Time*, n.d.).

When presenting as a team, all members must realize they are "on stage" throughout the presentation. The audience will focus primarily on the current presenter but will also look at other team members. They must appear to be as interested in other team members as they want the audience to be (Flett, 1998).

Participation in team projects is a good way to help students prepare for those same collaborative experiences that will come in the business world. Learning to resolve differences, to work with others, and to compromise are implicit additions to the speaking process that are evident through team-speaking experiences.

GENDER DIFFERENCES

Communication between genders can often present interesting challenges. Men and women tend to view communication principles differently. As indicated previously, females seem to have more anxiety when speaking than males. One explanation is explored by Jamieson (1988). Historically, silence was required of women. An "unquiet" woman was punished on the dunking stool, and more "witches" were convicted of "assaultive speech" than any other crime. Also during this period, women were banned on all stages of public speech.

Obviously, the situation has changed. But the characteristics of the two groups remain different. Men typically view oral communication in a factual and analytical way, whereas women are typically more narrative and emotional. Men tend to emphasize independence, while women use language to create connections. Basically, two styles seem to prevail in these oral communication interactions. The "Information Style" is usually associated with men, and the "Relationship Style" is usually associated with women (Tysom, n.d.).

The following strategies may prove successful in communicating with members of the opposite gender.

When women communicate with men, they should apply the following techniques:

- Speak up and not allow themselves to be interrupted.

- Avoid using tag endings that make them sound unsure of themselves, such as, "Is that okay, or isn't it?"

- Focus on avoiding unnecessary details (storytelling).

- Monitor their body language and facial expressions, paying attention to giggling or smiling when not appropriate.

- Don't take male comments too seriously. Business matters should remain separate from personal feelings. (Tysom, n.d.)

When men communicate with women, they should apply the following techniques:

- Focus on being polite, using "please" and "thank you" when making a request.

- Avoid monopolizing the conversation, speaking for women, or interrupting them.

- Control any outbursts or anger or frustration that may make women uncomfortable.

- Pay attention when women are speaking, using good eye contact and "I'm listening," sounds and language.

- Encourage women to speak more succinctly by asking questions or bringing them back to the point. (Tysom, n.d.)

Understanding the perspective and implementing some strategies of the other gender will go a long way toward making the interactions more successful. Cross-gender communication can sometimes be just as challenging as cross-cultural communication.

SUMMARY
Successful presentations start with planning the message. Determining the purpose and analyzing the audience, including the culture and gender differences, will focus the presentation. Supporting materials, including handouts and electronic aids, should then be developed to enhance the verbal message. Once the message is prepared and practiced, speakers are ready to present. Anxiety issues, which are more prevalent at the beginning of the presentation, will be reduced by dressing appropriately and having a strong introduction.

Audience interaction is critical to ensuring the intended message is received. Good voice techniques and appropriate nonverbal messages create interest and keep the attention of the audience. Team presentations are effective when interest is created with a variety of presenters, but the parts of the presentation must merge well together.

A unique aspect of speaking is understanding the differences of gender and culture and the unique cues that audiences give. In essence, understanding and connecting with the audience, preparation, and a strong delivery can ensure a successful presentation.

REFERENCES

12 ways to build confidence speaking. (n.d.). Retrieved September 27, 2004, from http://wittcom.com

Advanced Public Speaking Institute. (n.d.). *Public speaking.* Retrieved September 22, 2004, from http://www.public-speaking.org

Allee, S. (n.d.). *Speech tips.* Retrieved September 22, 2004, from http://sheilaallee.com

Axtell, R. E. (1993). *Do's and taboos around the world.* New York: John Wiley & Sons, Inc.

Axtell, R. E. (1998). *Gestures: The do's and taboos of body language around the world.* New York: John Wiley & Sons, Inc.

Ayres, J., & Hopf, T. S. (1989). Visualization: Is it more than extra-attention? *Communication Education, 38,* 1-5.

Bailey, E. P. (2005). *Writing & speaking at work: A practical guide for business communication.* Upper Saddle River, NJ: Pearson/Prentice Hall.

Behnke, R. R., & Sawyer, C. R. (1999). Milestones of anticipatory public speaking anxiety. *Communication Education, 48,* 165-172.

Behnke, R. R., & Sawyer, C. R. (2000). Anticipatory anxiety patterns for male and female public speakers. *Communication Education, 49,* 187-195.

Daly, J. A., Vangelisti, A. L., Neel, H. L., & Cavanaugh, P. D. (1989). Pre-performance concerns associated with public speaking anxiety. *Communication Quarterly, 37,* 39-53.

Daly, J. A., Vangelisti, A. L., & Weber, D. J. (1995, December). Speech anxiety affects how people prepare speeches: A protocol analysis of the preparation processes of speakers. *Communication Monographs, 62,* 383-397.

Executive Communications Group. *Executive presentations.* (n.d.). Retrieved December 21, 2004, from http://ecglink.com

Flett, N. (1998). Ensure you're all on the same team. *Management, 45*(2), 14.

Harris, R. (1994). Practically perfect presentations. *Training and Development, 48*(7), 55-57.

Jamieson, K. H. (1988). *Eloquence in an electronic age: The transformation of political speechmaking.* New York: Oxford University Press.

Johnson, E. (1997). Cultural norms affect oral communication in the classroom. *New Directions for Teaching and Learning, 70,* 47-52.

Kelly, L., & Keaten, J. A. (2000). Treating communication anxiety: Implications of the communibiological paradigm. *Communication Education, 49,* 45-57.

Meadows, D. H. (1990, May 31). State of the village report (Syndicated Column). *The Global Citizen, 38*(2), 177-178.

Ober, S. (2003). *Contemporary business communication*. Boston: Houghton Mifflin Company.

Presentation tips. (n.d.). Retrieved September 27, 2004, from http://www.wittcom.com

Reece, P. (1999). The number one fear: Public speaking and the university student. In K. Martin, N. Stanley, & N. Davison. (Eds.). *Teaching in the disciplines/learning in context* (pp. 341-347). Perth, Australia: The University of Western Australia.

Rolls, J. A. (1998). Facing the fears associated with professional speaking. *Business Communication Quarterly, 61*(2), 103-106.

Sawyer, M. (1993). In a manner of (public) speaking. *Library Journal, 118*(8), 45-48.

Small business presentations. (n.d.). Retrieved December 21, 2004, from http://www.businesstown.com/presentations/present-tell.asp

Sorenson, R., Kennedy, G., & Ramirez, I. (1997). *Business and management communication: A guide book*. Upper Saddle River, NJ: Prentice Hall.

Stamps, D. (1996). Welcome to America: Watch out for culture shock. *Training, 33*(11), 22-30.

Tysom, C. (n.d.). *Business communication—bridging the gender gap*. Retrieved September 22, 2004, from http://www.tysom.com.au/articles.html

Visuals can power your presentation—if you know how to use them. (n.d.). Retrieved September 22, 2004, from http://totalcommunicator.com/vol2_1/visuals_article.html

Weisul, K. (2002, April 8). Does giving a speech spook women more? *Business Week, 3777*, 12.

What to know when you're speaking to an international audience. (n.d.). Retrieved September 22, 2004, from http://totalcommunicator.com/vol2_2/interaudience.html

When it's time to present as a team. (n.d.). Retrieved September 22, 2004, from http://totalcommunicator.com/vol2_1/team_article.html

Reading: The Key to Knowledge Acquisition

Cheryl D. Wiedmaier
University of Central Arkansas
Conway, Arkansas

Jeff L. Whittingham
University of Central Arkansas
Conway, Arkansas

In 1991, former U.S. Secretary of Labor Lynn Martin charged the Secretary's Commission on Achieving Necessary Skills (SCANS) with the task of preparing a report that identified the basic skills needed by U.S. workers. In the report, reading was determined to be one of the foundation skills, and a *reader* was defined on the SCANS 2000: The Workforce Skills Web site as one who...

> ...locates, understands, and interprets written information in prose and documents—including manuals, graphs, and schedules—to perform tasks; learns from text by determining the main idea or essential message; identifies relevant details, facts, and specifications; infers or locates the meaning of unknown or technical vocabulary; and judges the accuracy, appropriateness, style, and plausibility of reports, proposals, or theories of other writers. (2001, para. F1).

It is just as important today, if not more so, for students to develop reading skills that enable them to be productive workers and continue learning after they leave the classroom. Not only are reading skills valuable to students in the classroom, but almost every job today—entry-level or higher—requires some type of reading. Even though a job description may not specifically state "reading" as a required skill, reading is usually a foundational or basic skill (along with writing, arithmetic, speaking, and listening) needed in order to perform job tasks. As such, content area teachers need to reinforce reading techniques and strategies in their classrooms that will enable students to use reading skills for success in school, in the workplace, in a global society, and in meeting the challenges of everyday living. This chapter explores reading and information skills needed in the 21st century workplace and presents reading techniques that teachers may introduce and reinforce in their classrooms in order to help students master those skills. Written messages in paper and electronic forms are encountered in every workplace. As businesses and organizations become more global, workers will be required to use their reading skills to gather information from documents sent by various sources, including sources from other countries. Documents will also be acquired in different mediums, including e-mail, fax, and Web pages. Workers who have mastered reading skills will be valuable to employers who rely upon written documents to conduct day-to-day business activities.

WORKPLACE SKILLS
Reading in the Workplace

Rush, Moe, and Storlie (as cited in Roe, Stoodt, & Burns, 1995) provided the following list of general reading tasks required of business education students and workers in the business world:

1. Reading and implementing directions/instructions

2. Identifying main ideas and details in various reading materials

3. Skimming and/or scanning to locate needed information or to locate materials needed in problem solving and report writing

4. Reading newspapers, magazines, and professional journals to learn about current trends in the business world

5. Reading and implementing memo contents

6. Reading and responding to business letters

7. Reading invoices for accuracy

8. Reading computer printouts to locate information

9. Reading reference materials such as interest tables, financial handbooks, and handbooks of business mathematics

10. Reading and interpreting textbooks in order to complete class assignments that enable students to learn business skills

11. Reading technical vocabulary (pp. 476-477)

Job descriptions retrieved from the Occupational Information Network Web site (2003), O*NET® OnLine, provided job-specific details on topics such as job tasks, knowledge required, basic skills and functional skills required, generalized work activities of a job, work style characteristics, and physical and social factors. The job description for a bank teller, for example, lists work activities such as "prepare and verify cashier's checks, obtain and process information required for provision of services, and process and maintain records of customer loans" (2003, pp. 1-2). Reading comprehension is ranked sixth and written comprehension is ranked ninth in required skills and abilities. In comparison, the job description for a fast food cook ranked reading comprehension as third and written comprehension as second in required skills and abilities. Reading skills, therefore, are important to jobs in all areas, not just in the business world.

Not only is reading considered a basic skill required for success in today's workplace, but also reading will continue to be important as workers face challenges imposed by changes in their lives and their work in a global society. Rothwell (2002) identified workplace learning as essential to successful individuals and organizations. Although many workers will be asked to participate in job training as job requirements change, Rothwell (2002) suggested that workers will also themselves seek training to help manage these changes. Educators, therefore, should equip students with skills to prepare them for continuous learning, and the teaching of reading skills is an important part of this preparation.

Rothwell (2002) categorizes the 21st century worker as a free agent learner who "takes the initiative to learn on [his or her] own" (p. 39). Free agent learners look for the information they need when they need it, persistently searching through multiple sources for the information they need, and are self-motivated to achieve their own purposes. Organizations will continue to see an increasing number of free agent learners, and workers must assume some of the characteristics of the free agent learner in order to be successful in the workplace (Rothwell, 2002). Reading skills will be essential for this type of worker/learner.

Reading in the Information Age
According to Moursund (Robyler, 2003), technology literacy, information literacy, and visual literacy are three competencies needed by any citizen living in the Information Age.

Technology literacy, the ability to use technology tools efficiently, is now required in order to obtain employment in many fields. The previously mentioned O*Net Online description for a bank teller includes "interacting with computers as a required work activity and knowledge of computers and electronics and of telecommunications as required knowledge" (2003, pp. 2-3, 9). Groups such as the International Society for Technology in Education (ISTE) and the National Council for the Accreditation of Teacher Education (NCATE) have worked together to develop required technology standards for teachers and students. The National Educational Technology Standards for Students includes profiles of standards for various age groups. The profile for students in grades 9-12 includes 10 standards to be achieved prior to completing grade 12. Standard

5 listed on this profile states, "Use technology tools and resources for managing and communicating personal/professional information (e.g., finances, schedules, addresses, purchases, correspondence)" (2004, p. 5). The standards are available at http:// cnets.iste.org/ ncate/.

Information literacy is defined as "the ability to gather information from multiple sources, select relevant material, and organize it into a form that will allow the user to make decisions or take specific actions" (Shelly, Cashman, Gunter, & Gunter, 2002, p. 1.06). Information literacy also includes reading skills necessary for students and workers to gather and select materials.

Visual literacy includes skills that "enable [adults] to accurately interpret the visuals necessary for functioning effectively in our society" (Lever-Duffy, McDonald, & Mizell, 2003, p. 285). Visual literacy includes interpreting and understanding messages such as those found in charts, graphs, tables, and symbols used in today's society.

Students and workers are inundated with vast amounts of data and information. When given a research assignment or faced with a problem or situation needing explanation, students and workers generally turn to the Internet for help in identifying sources of information. In order to locate relevant and useful information, students must develop reading skills, as well as those skills described as technology, information, and visual literacy. These skills are among those most needed in the 21st century workplace.

MESSAGE ACQUISITION
Whether reading in the educational or workplace setting, students must be able to understand the material they read and be able to obtain the appropriate meaning from the message. This section presents techniques used to develop content-related vocabulary (including prereading, postreading, and independent reading activities), reading for details, and reading for directions.

Developing Content-Related Vocabulary
A solid foundation in content vocabulary is necessary for students to progress to future instruction. Teachers must integrate vocabulary instruction and vocabulary-building strategies into their content-specific lessons with global examples wherever possible. Every discipline has a unique vocabulary that must be learned and understood in order for students to comprehend the readings for their subject area courses. As students enter the workforce, they will most likely encounter new terminology specific to the jobs or careers they choose and cultures of individuals with whom they interact. Therefore, business educators should help students develop content-specific vocabulary in the business classroom as well as help students learn to analyze new words they may encounter in the workplace. The following techniques may be used to facilitate vocabulary building.

Prereading activities: Connecting new words to what students already know. Kane (2003) describes three types of vocabulary. *General* vocabulary words are words used in everyday language. *Content-specific* words or special vocabulary may be used in everyday language but take on a different meaning in the content area; for example, "*culture* in biology, *latitude* in geography, *congestion* in medicine, or *confirm* in religion" (p. 125). *Technical* vocabulary contains words used in specific fields—for example, technical vocabulary in accounting may include words such as accrual account, accumulated depreciation, current ratio, and cost of goods sold.

Vacca and Vacca (1999) present these five techniques to help students determine what they already know about new words and concepts: word exploration, brainstorming, list-group-label, word sorts, and knowledge ratings. Making these connections will aid students in understanding material and overcoming anxieties when encountering new material.

Word exploration. Word exploration allows students to examine what they may already know about a topic or concept. Students are asked to freewrite in a journal for no more than five minutes about a topic or concept suggested by the teacher. Spelling, punctuation, and grammar are not graded—students simply write about what they know or can connect to the assigned topic or concept.

Brainstorming. Although brainstorming is used quite often in classrooms to generate ideas, this technique may also be used to allow students to discover what they already know about a new topic or concept. Teachers introduce a key concept from the material to be studied and allow students to work in small groups to create a list of words related to the concept. Brainstorming in this fashion allows the teacher and students to determine what is already known about the topic/concept.

List-group-label. The list of words created in the brainstorming session may then be grouped into logical arrangements. Once groups of words are determined, students label each group. The teacher may ask students to predict what will be studied, based on the word list.

Word sorts. Students are given a list of key words from the unit of study and are asked to sort them into logical groups of two or more using cards or worksheets. The teacher may use the closed sort method in which students are given the main categories, allowing them to sort the words based on common criterion. The open sort method asks students to explore meanings and relationships of key words without using main categories provided by the teacher, as in the closed sort method.

Knowledge ratings. Knowledge ratings present key words in a survey format. Students are asked to analyze their knowledge of these words by rating their understanding of each word (e.g., can define, have seen/heard, not familiar). The teacher may then lead a discussion asking students to identify the hardest words, easiest words, most common words, etc. This can be applied to general subjects as well as job-specific terminology.

Post-reading activities: Applying and clarifying new words. Vacca and Vacca (1999) and Gunning (2003) suggested the activities of concept circles and word analogies to guide students in applying what has been learned to the learning environment. These techniques can help students to extend their vocabulary and concept development.

Concept circles. Concept circles may be used to help students relate words conceptually to one another. Concept circles may be used in a variety of ways, including the following:

- Place words and phrases in sections of the circle and ask students to identify the relationships between the words and phrases placed in the circle sections.

- Instruct students to shade a section of a circle containing a word or phrase that does not relate to the words or phrases in the other sections. Students then explain why the remaining sections are related.

- Leave one or two sections of the circle blank and instruct students to fill in the blank sections with words or phrases relating to those listed in the other sections.

Word analogies. Word analogies allow students to understand new words and concepts by relating them to those they already know. Students not only will learn new words and concepts, but they will also likely remember them when relationships are built. Greenwood (2004) asserted that students will create their own word analogies after they are familiar with the process. Vacca and Vacca (1999) listed the following types of analogies, each presented with an example statement and the correct answer provided in parentheses.

- Part to whole—asset : balance sheet :: _____ : income statement (revenue)

- Person to situation—Steve Wozniak : Apple Computers :: _____ : Microsoft (Bill Gates)

- Cause and effect—Internet : paperless messages :: chip miniaturization : _____ (portable computers)

- Synonym—liability : debt :: _____ : net worth (owner's equity)

- Antonym—debit : credit :: revenue : _____ (expenses)

- Geography—Little Rock : Arkansas :: Jefferson City : _____ (Missouri)

- Measurement—ohms : resistance :: _____ : power (watts)

- Time—MHz : GHz :: Mbps : _____ (Gbps)

The word analogy statements may be formatted in different ways. The statements are read as follows: asset is to balance sheet as _____ is to income statement. A statement may be listed with word choices provided to the students in a word list or as part of the analogy statement. For example, the asset : balance sheet statement could be written as the following:

- asset : balance sheet :: _____ : income statement (liabilities, expenses, owner's equity).

On their own: Learning words independently. Students will not learn all the words they need to know in the classroom. As they enter the workforce, they will encounter new words. Gunning (2003) and Kane (2003) suggested that students learn how to use word analysis, context clues, reference materials and trade books, reading for details, and reading for directions as techniques for acquiring new words on their own.

Word analysis. The use of morphemes, words broken into meaningful segments, contributes to students' word analysis. Morphemes include root words, prefixes, and suffixes.

Learning the history and derivations of words (especially Greek and Latin etymology) can also help students increase their vocabularies. This knowledge can be interesting as well as helpful to students in learning vocabularies across all content areas. Teaching students to analyze words and break words into smaller segments will not guarantee they will always determine the correct meaning. However, this strategy may be taught in conjunction with others to help students analyze new words.

Context clues. Authors often provide context clues for their readers. Kane (2003) listed the following three strategies used for introducing vocabulary in context:

- Introduce the new concept or word, but do not define it until later in the reading material.

- Introduce the new concept or word and then supply an example, but not the specific definition.

- Introduce the new concept or word without providing a definition or example, but present the word in context within the passage.

Students should be taught these strategies so that they can use them as they read material containing new words.

Reference materials and trade books. When students are only required to use reference materials in a simplistic way—copying definitions of given terms verbatim, for example, they often form a negative attitude about using them. Students need to know that reference materials such as textbook glossaries, dictionaries, and atlases can be useful tools to aid them in their reading and comprehension of global terms. Many of these resources are available online for easy access.

Whereas textbooks are written to be sold and used in school systems, trade books are written for the general public and may be found in libraries. Roe et al. (1995) explained that trade books include information about new products, materials, and techniques. A teacher may find these publications useful in developing students' reading interests and abilities, as they are typically written at a higher reading level than textbooks.

Reading for Details
Roe et al. (1995) described how main ideas and details work together in informative writings. "The main idea of a paragraph is the big idea that the author develops and supports with details throughout the paragraph" (pp. 78-79). Details are further defined as "the smaller pieces of information or ideas that are used to support the 'big idea'" (p. 79). Whether perusing a textbook or a written report, readers will need to determine the main ideas and details of their readings.

Students can learn to determine the main ideas and supporting details of content reading by restating main ideas in their own words and finding the key words in sentences that point to these ideas. Roe et al. (1995) suggested directing students to (1) locate the key words in sentences and paragraphs and (2) compose a sentence summarizing the relationships among the key words.

Another technique suggested by Roe et al. (1995) included categorization of details. Students are directed to (1) identify the key words in a given paragraph and (2) categorize the details as important or unimportant to communicating the main idea. Students are then asked to justify their categorizations of these details.

Reading for Directions
Interpreting written directions is another important task that students and workers must be able to complete. In addition to the ability to read, Roe et. al. (1995) identified two skills required in order to follow written directions—the ability to identify details and the ability to identify sequence. Reading for directions requires that students and workers read at a slower rate and read word for word. Rereading the material may also be necessary in order to follow each step listed. The following procedure for reading directions was presented by Roe et al. (1995):

1. Read the directions from beginning to end to get an overview of the task to be performed.

2. Study any accompanying pictorial aids that may help in understanding one or more of the steps or in picturing the desired end result.

3. Read the directions carefully, visualizing each step to be performed.

4. Read with an open mind, disregarding any preconceived ideas about the procedure involved.

5. Take note of such key words as *first*, *second*, *next*, *last*, and *finally*. Let these words help you picture the order of activities to be performed.

6. Read each step again, just before you actually perform it.

7. Carry out the steps in proper order. (p. 156)

The consequences of not following the directions in step-by-step fashion are immediate and observable; therefore, Roe et al. (1995) suggested that students answer the following questions when reading directions:

1. What am I trying to do? (What is the task?)

2. What materials are required?

3. Do I understand all of the terms/words used in these directions?

4. What is the sequence of steps?

5. Have I omitted anything?

6. Am I ready to perform the task?

7. Was I successful in accomplishing the task? (p. 461)

This section presented content-related vocabulary building techniques, as well as techniques to obtain important details from written messages and to follow written directions. Content-related vocabulary is very important to message acquisition in the classroom as well as in the workplace. Pre-reading and post-reading vocabulary building activities may be used by the teacher for classroom reading while the independent vocabulary learning techniques may be used by the student in the classroom or in the workplace. Determining important details from a written message and following written directions are skills students will find necessary in completing classroom assignments as well as work assignments in a global society.

SPECIALIZED READING SKILLS
Assisting students with development of their reading skills is a critical role for all teachers, not just reading teachers. In addition to the techniques described for helping students to develop skill in understanding the message, some specialized reading skills will assist them in their business-related reading. These skimming and scanning techniques

are particularly helpful to students in the workplace who must read and quickly assess the value and disposition of what they have read.

Skimming and Scanning Techniques

Various authors have identified techniques that help students to develop more specialized reading skills. These techniques enable students to gain an overview of a reading assignment so that they more readily can grasp the meaning of what they have read; for example, teachers can help students learn how to skim and/or scan content to improve comprehension. Some of these skimming and scanning techniques also can help students to be more "efficient" readers, as they identify what text will need close attention in subsequent readings. Techniques for specialized reading skills are identified as previewing, which incorporates scanning and skimming; in-the-middle skimming; the Z technique; the underline technique; and overviewing.

Previewing. A powerful pre-reading skill used by efficient readers is previewing. Previewing the text gives students an idea of content and is an important factor for increasing comprehension. There are two methods of previewing, scanning and skimming (Hurst, Wilson, Camp, & Cramer, 2002).

Scanning. Scanning is reading to find specific information (Roe et al., 1995). To scan a text the student looks over the material quickly while searching for precise material. This skill is useful for specific tasks such as searching for telephone numbers in a telephone book. The reader does not read each name listed, but rather, looks for one specific name (Hurst et al., 2002).

Skimming. Skimming is used to get a quick overview of full text material and as a warm-up approach to an actual reading event. Warming-up for reading is similar to the warm-up process undertaken by athletes before a strenuous physical event and can be just as important for reading success. Efficient readers use skimming to warm up their minds and assess such components as purpose, readability, and audience. Skimming focuses attention on the special features of the section such as subheadings, boldface, italicizing, illustrations, maps, charts, graphs, tables, and lists. At the same time it allows the reader to begin the process of understanding the overall content of the text. Skimming is not simply a matter of quickly looking over a page of text. It is a skill that can be practiced through one of the following techniques.

In-the-middle technique. To master the in-the-middle skimming technique, the reader reads the sentences immediately following the title of a piece of text and then visually follows the tip of the index finger as it moves down the middle of the page. Readers must resist the temptation to follow the familiar left-to-right pattern of traditional reading and instead focus on the center of each column of print. This technique allows readers to assess the general topic, the layout, and the length of the reading selection. Readers may begin to practice this approach by using it to first skim newspaper or magazine articles and then expanding its use to more content-laden material.

The Z technique. Another approach to skimming is the Z technique. The Z technique is useful in skimming pages with wide columns or full pages of text. Readers allow their eyes to sweep across the page from left to right and then back to the left in a Z pattern without pausing. This pattern is repeated three to six times with readers spending not more than five seconds per page. Readers often feel nervous when using this technique due to perceived omissions in content. They must be reminded that the technique is designed to glean a general impression of the passage to help in setting purpose and to determine the author's intended audience. When using the Z technique, readers should watch for important repeated words or phrases that are clues to the central meaning of the text.

The underline technique. The underline technique of skimming can be used for quickly reading content text. Using the underline technique, the reader quickly moves the index finger, or all four fingers held together, without interruption from the left to the right margin under each line of print. This allows the reader to view every word in order, but increases speed by prohibiting the eyes from lingering on any specific word or words. While reading, the reader looks for groups of meaningful words rather than slowing down to look at individual words (Cohen & Poppino, 1984).

Overviewing. Harvey and Goudvis (2000) described a skimming technique developed by comprehension researcher Jan Dole called the overviewing technique. They suggested that the reader be exposed to mini-lessons on topics such as activating prior knowledge, noting characteristics of text length and structure, noting important headings and subheadings, determining what to pay attention to, determining what to read and in what order, determining what to ignore, deciding to quit reading because the text does not have relevant information, and deciding if the text is worth reading more carefully. A careful overview of text may save time for readers presented with difficult text selections. The ability to overview eliminates the reader's need to read everything while searching only for specific information.

Reading Rates

A factor in reading skill is the rate at which a person reads. Reading rate is not just a matter of "faster" reading; the speed of reading should be matched to the purpose for reading. Various authors have discussed ways to increase reading rate and ways to read all types of content from various media. Students may benefit from determining their reading rate with various types of content. As they understand that reading rate will vary, depending on the purpose of their reading, they will be able to adjust their reading rate to different types of information.

Increasing reading rate. The question of how fast a person should read is not easily answered. Readers approach written text with many purposes, ranging from slowly reading directions or savoring a favorite author to quickly skimming an article for information. Whatever the reading rate, it is most often driven by the purpose and guided by common sense. It does not make sense to speed read when the result has little value; however, many occasions require faster reading (Cohen & Poppino, 1984). The ability to assess the appropriate reading speed is called flexibility of rate. Flexible readers take their cue from the purpose of reading and self-monitor to adjust their own reading rate (Roe et al., 1995). In essence, the question of how fast a person should read is answered individually and related directly to the purpose of reading (Cohen & Poppino, 1984). The importance of reading rate, however, should not be downplayed. Rasinski (2000) believes that, although reading rate is only one piece of the puzzle, it is a very important part of diagnosing and assessing overall reading performance.

Readability. In addition to learning the skills required for reading, students should experience reading from all media they will encounter in the workplace. Twenty-first century workers read from the printed page, computer screens, and handheld device screens; and workers in the business world read documents that range from letters and memos, to manuals and handbooks, to reports and charts (Roe et al., 1995). The readability levels of these documents vary from average to high levels.

Readability is related directly to reading rate. Efficient readers assess the readability of written text during skimming. As readers skim text, they determine its difficulty. For example, if students are familiar with or specifically interested in the text, then after a skimming exercise, they might decide on a quick reading rate for the material. At the same time, if students are unfamiliar with the text, skimming might reveal the need to perform a slow and thorough reading. Switching reading rates based on readability, even within one reading event, is a technique often used by efficient readers. Inefficient readers often read material at a consistently slow pace (Cohen & Poppino, 1984).

According to Harvey and Goudvis (2000), readability of written text is an important consideration when increasing reading skill or reading rate. They further suggested that readers be exposed to books on three reading levels: easy, just right, and challenging. Easy books are described as those containing words and ideas familiar to the reader; just right books are described as books containing words and ideas that are mostly familiar to the reader; and challenging books are those in which there are many words and ideas the reader does not understand. Readers consistently assigned challenging books often become discouraged and stop reading, just as readers given only easy books fail to be challenged and lose interest in reading. A healthy balance of all three readability levels is prescribed to maintain interest and increase reading skills. Allington (2002) advocated the use of a multisource and multileveled curriculum to avoid the reading difficulty problems students might encounter with traditional content-area texts.

Charting reading rate. Cohen & Poppino (1984) suggested that readers practice skimming while reading fiction as an exercise to increase reading rate for nonfiction or content text. Additionally, readers should chart their reading rate over time to determine progress. To determine reading rate, the reader reads a passage for five minutes. Next, the reader determines the average number of words per line multiplied by the number of lines read, and then divided by five, or the number of minutes spent in reading. This figure gives readers a rough estimate of words read per minute (wpm). Readers interested in increasing their reading rate should calculate their wpm rate and chart it over time, attempting to increase their rate with each subsequent reading. The reading rate may be computed with this formula:

- $\dfrac{\text{Average Words Per Line} \ \text{X} \ \text{Number Lines Read}}{\text{Minutes Spent Reading}}$ = Words Per Minute (WPM)

Reading rate is an important factor in achieving overall reading success. For a successful reading event to occur, content students need to determine the difficulty of the text and match their reading rate accordingly. This may be achieved either through internal self-monitoring or through the use of a reading rate formula. Regardless, it is important to remember that common sense is the best guide in determining the appropriate speed to read content material.

SUMMARY

Reading is a basic workplace skill that will continue to play an important role in the success of today's workers in a global society. Teachers should prepare students for the workplace by equipping them with necessary skills. Students should develop message acquisition skills and build content-related vocabulary skills through prereading, postreading, and independent reading activities to enable students to derive meaning from unfamiliar words encountered in content- and work-related materials. Message acquisition skills include learning to read for details and for instructions.

Specialized reading skills are also needed to help students becomes more efficient readers. These skills include skimming techniques that enable students to get a quick overview of the material's purpose, content, and audience, while scanning techniques enable students to read materials quickly to identify specific information. Another important factor for reading success is reading rate. Students should determine the difficulty of the material to be read and match their reading rate accordingly.

Developing reading skills is not just a responsibility of the reading teacher. Content area teachers, including business education teachers, should promote the acquisition of reading and vocabulary techniques that will enable students to be successful in school, in the workplace, in their personal lives, and in a global society. These skills help students to acquire skills necessary for workers in the 21st century workplace and required of productive citizens in the Information Age.

REFERENCES
Allington, R. L. (2002). You can't learn much from books you can't read. *Educational Leadership, 60*(3), 16-19.

Cohen, E. C., & Poppino, M. A. (1984). *Reading faster for ideas.* New York: Holt, Rinehart and Winston.

Greenwood, S. (2004). Content matters: Building vocabulary and conceptual understanding in the subject areas. *Middle School Journal, 35*(3), 27-34.

Gunning, T. G. (2003). *Building literacy in the content areas.* Boston: Allyn and Bacon.

Harvey, S., & Goudvis, A. (2000). *Strategies that work: Teaching comprehension to enhance understanding.* York, ME: Stenhouse.

Hurst, B., Wilson, C., Camp, D., & Cramer, G. (2002). *Creating independent readers: Developing word recognition skills in k-12 classrooms.* Scottsdale, AZ: Holcomb Hathaway Publishers.

Kane, S. (2003). *Literacy and learning in the content areas.* Scottsdale, AZ: Holcomb Hathaway Publishers.

Lever-Duffy, J., McDonald, J. B., & Mizell, A. P. (2003). *Teaching and learning with technology.* Boston: Allyn and Bacon.

Roblyer, M. D. (2003). *Integrating educational technology into teaching* (3rd ed.). Upper Saddle River, NJ: Merrill Prentice Hall.

Roe, B. D., Stoodt, B. D., & Burns, P. C. (1995). *Secondary schools reading instruction: The content areas* (5th ed.). Boston: Houghton Mifflin Company.

Rothwell, W. J. (2002). *The workplace learner: How to align training initiatives with individual learning competencies.* New York: American Management Association.

SCANS 2000: The Workforce Skills Website. (2001). SCANS skills—Detailed list. Retrieved January 28, 2004, from http://www.scans.jhu.edu/NS/HTML/SkillsDet.htm.

Shelly, G. B., Cashman, T. J., Gunter, R. E., & Gunter, G. A. (2002). *Teachers discovering computers: Integrating technology in the classroom* (2nd ed.). Boston: Course Technology.

Vacca, R. T., & Vacca, J. L. (1999). *Content area reading: Literacy and learning across the curriculum* (6th ed.). New York: Addison Wesley Longman, Inc.

Writing: Transmitting Ideas with Words

Susan Jaderstrom
Santa Rosa Junior College
Petaluma, California

Clear, concise, written communication is vitally important in today's fast-paced global business environment. Online communication technology allows people from different cultural backgrounds to communicate directly and quickly with each other. As business becomes more intercultural, business educators must integrate intercultural written communication into business classes and teach writing strategies that produce professional, effective results with a variety of different workplace documents. This chapter includes research on written communication and provides teaching suggestions on writing for today's global business environment.

IMPORTANCE OF WRITTEN COMMUNICATION

More high school students are enrolling in challenging mathematics and science courses, and fewer students are enrolling in English composition (The College Board, 2002). Recent analyses indicate that more than 50% of first-year California college students cannot write papers relatively free of language errors (ICAS, 2002). During the years 1998-2002, Public Agenda's *Reality Check* found that more than 73% of employers say that employees have just fair or poor skills in grammar, spelling, and writing (Reality Check, 2002). In 2003, The National Commission on Writing in America's Schools and Colleges described writing as the neglected "R" and stated, "Writing today is not a frill for the few, but an essential skill for the many" (p. i).

E-mail has become an essential part of 57 million Americans' work lives, which is more than 60% of those employed in the United States (Pew Internet & American Life, 2002). According to the International Data Corporation (IDC), a global market intelligence and advisory firm, the total number of e-mail messages sent daily will exceed 60 billion worldwide by 2006 (Johnston, 2002). A growing number of high-tech and other white-collar jobs are moving to other parts of the world in a trend called "offshoring" (Gallagher, 2004). "Offshoring" is hiring overseas employees to do work instead of having the work done in the United States. Gallagher further states that the person at the end of the telephone or e-mail could be overseas, which means that communication with that worker will be an integral part of the workplace.

Instructors must analyze curriculum to make certain that the writing strategies adequately reflect workplace writing and the globalization of business. Curriculum should include correct grammar, spelling, and writing skills. Instructors must also teach students appropriate writing skills for the global environment. Because of the projected increase in e-mail communications and overseas job "offshoring," all business instructors must teach the proper methods of communicating by e-mail.

NECESSARY SKILLS FOR WRITING

To be effective writers, business students must be skilled in grammar, capitalization, and punctuation; proficient using computer software; aware of cultural differences; and familiar with memo, e-mail, letter, and report formats.

Grammar, Capitalization, and Punctuation

Most students learn grammar in elementary and middle school. When students reach high school, English teachers emphasize other aspects of writing instead of traditional grammar and usage. Teaching grammar and punctuation to younger students who use text or instant messaging is a challenge because these students develop a style of written communication that is inappropriate for business writing. This style generally includes little or no attention to spelling, grammar, capitalization, or punctuation; the substitution of acronyms and abbreviations for common phrases; the use of emoticons, which are symbolic smiley faces that represent the mood of the sender; and incomplete or run-on sentences.

Some community colleges have business English courses, which emphasize grammar and writing. In colleges that do not have business English courses, business communication instructors are teaching rules for grammar and punctuation in their courses (Anderson & Seshadri, 2003).

Research by Anderson and Seshadri (2003) concludes that students in college business communication courses, who did grammar exercises as outside class assignments unrelated to their writing, could not identify grammar, punctuation, and spelling errors in sentences any better than students who did not do extra exercises. Gilsdorf and Leonard (2001) surveyed corporate executives and instructors and compiled a list of the most distracting writing errors. The research indicated that educated readers are seriously bothered by errors that have an impact on readability such as sentence fragments, run-on sentences, unpunctuated parenthetical expressions, dangling modifiers, and apostrophes in plural nouns. Gilsdorf and Leonard believe that teachers should persist in efforts to correct sentence structure problems to improve readability.

Sitler (2001) suggests two approaches to teaching grammar in written documents. One approach is a student-led short lesson on a point of grammar or style. Another approach is recording the pattern of errors for each student and making the students responsible for finding and fixing those errors. Some instructors apply the "mailability" scale (can this document be sent to a customer?) when grading. One suggestion for college-level students is to return a paper that contains more than three spelling, grammar, and punctuation errors without a grade. The returned paper, if correctly revised, receives one letter grade lower than if it had been error-free on the first submission. If the revised paper still contains errors, the student receives an "F" (Anderson & Seshadri, 2003).

Teaching students to write short, simple, and concise sentences, which are easier for international readers to translate, eliminates many punctuation problems. Students should rewrite a sentence if they do not know how to punctuate it. Many times students neglect to capitalize properly, which may or may not be deliberate (Mallon & Oppenheim, 2002). Instructors need to emphasize the capitalization of proper nouns especially in e-mail messages.

Computer Software Proficiency

Given the penetration of computers in business and the high levels of Internet access, knowledge of computer and computer software is necessary for every business student. Business writing tools include knowledge of word processing, spreadsheet, database, and presentation graphics software; proficiency in using the Internet and search engines; and experience with e-mail programs.

Although word processing software does not automatically improve the quality or quantity of writing, students who use word processors tend to enjoy writing more (Roberston, 1997). Spell checkers are good at flagging misspelled or repeated words but will not recognize "I am resigning my position for personnel problems" as incorrect. Grammar checkers cannot distinguish between the correct use of "which" or "that." International readers will struggle translating misspelled words or incorrect grammar. Conscientious instructors make students aware of the limitations of grammar and spell checkers by developing exercises that purposely emphasize problems with relying upon these tools too heavily. Despite the limitations of these tools, students should utilize both spelling and grammar checkers in their writing.

Cultural Differences

Business writing must focus on intercultural business, and business issues need to be integrated with business strategies and corporate culture (Varner, 2001). Varner discusses current events at the beginning of every class because these events help students see beneath the tourist aspects of culture. By incorporating current events, students begin to recognize the impact of culture on business and their writing.

A good introduction for intercultural writing is to share some American communication failures in marketing to other countries. For example, KFC's "finger-lickin' good" slogan translated to "eat your fingers off" in Chinese, and the Chevy Nova never sold well in Spanish-speaking countries because "No va" translates to "it doesn't go" in Spanish (The University of Texas, n.d.). After discussing these blunders, teachers can ask students for recommendations to avoid making similar mistakes in their writing.

Creating a map showing foreign investments or international partnerships in the local community, county, or state can illustrate to students how global communication may affect local employees (Okula, 2004). When teaching cross-cultural communication, instructors should avoid making cultural profiles of nationalities such as European or Asian. Cultures may show general tendencies, but not all groups in a culture have the same characteristics (Varner, 2001). Writing assignments should encourage students to actively learn more about international business and other countries; and the writing assignments should focus on logical, factual information (Ranney & McNeilly, 1996). A valuable teaching resource is researching the *The World Factbook* (2003) on the Central Intelligence Agency (CIA) Web site, which contains facts about geography, people, government, economy, communications, transportation, and transnational issues in countries around the world (http://www.cia.gov/cia/publications/factbook/docs/profileguide.html).

An example of a meaningful intercultural written assignment is giving students an existing brochure and asking them to revise it for people whose first language is Spanish (DeVoss, Jasken, & Hayden, 2002). Another example of a written assignment is redesigning a portion of a technical manual for a specific intercultural audience, which involves researching a variety of factors such as income, population, Internet access, and literacy skills. By designing documents, students become familiar with formulating questions about other cultures and completing research before writing.

Encouraging students to examine their own stereotypes is important but sometimes risky, difficult to teach, and uncomfortable in the classroom. Assumptions about other cultures run deep and inevitably affect communication. To improve intercultural communications, instructors need to help students question cultural biases in relation to other cultures both within and outside the United States (DeVoss et al., 2002). A good discussion starting point on American multiculturalism is a multiple-choice quiz that asks questions based upon local or state statistics. Gorski (2003) developed a cultural awareness online quiz and lesson plans that instructors can use in the classroom.

Communication Formats

A variety of assignments using memo, letter, and report formats is important in helping students feel comfortable with on-the-job documents. One of the key ways that writers in the workplace learn to write is through the processing of document modeling, which is analyzing documents on file and patterning their own writing after these documents (Mabrito, 1999). Mabrito suggests that students bring in examples of international documents from their own workplaces, which are more familiar and more important to students than generic textbook examples, for discussion and analysis. If students are not working, instructors can provide samples of previous students' written work to help in modeling. Students can write a similar document using the document modeling strategy.

Students should also have opportunities to write business e-mail messages. Although e-mail is an essential business communication tool, many business students take it casually. Some students believe that misspellings, capitalization errors, and punctuation problems are not important when writing e-mail. A study by Microsoft Network (MSN) found that 16% of 18-24 year olds sign all of their e-mails "love and kisses" even if they are writing to their employer (Mallon & Oppenheim, 2002).

Students should compose using computer software programs and the spelling and grammar tools available on the software. Students should be aware of cultural differences and be able to select the appropriate communication format. No matter whether a student is writing an e-mail or another kind of written document, accurate grammar, spelling, and punctuation are important.

THE WRITING PROCESS FOR MEMOS, LETTERS, REPORTS, AND E-MAIL

Writers can follow the logical steps of prewriting, brainstorming, writing and organizing, revising for style, and proofreading to produce memos, letters, reports, and e-mail. According to Linkins (2003), the suggested percentage of time spent on each writing step is as follows (p. 24):

- Prewriting   12.5%

- Brainstorming   25.0%

- Writing and organizing   25.0%

- Revising for style   25.0%

- Proofreading   12.5%

Prewriting

When given a writing assignment, most students sit down at the computer and start keyboarding. This approach leads to rambling thoughts that may make the finished product difficult for readers to understand. All students need to answer some basic questions before beginning to write:

1. Who is my audience? Who is the primary audience and who else will read the document? Is my audience inside or outside of the organization? Am I writing to superiors, subordinates, or peers? Am I known to my audience? How much does this person know about the topic? Are the readers domestic or international? Does a language barrier exist? When writing e-mail, students need to ask the following additional questions: Is e-mail the appropriate medium? Is the person in a

different time zone or country, which makes a phone call difficult? Do the readers use e-mail frequently? Does the recipient procrastinate? Is e-mail part of the corporate culture? Does it matter if the e-mail is forwarded to others without permission? Is it important to have a written record? Could the e-mail message be misunderstood?

2. What is my purpose? Do I have a general purpose or a specific purpose?

3. What action do I want my reader to take?

4. What is in it for the reader?

After analyzing the prewriting questions, a one-sentence statement is composed, which tells the reader the topic, who is affected, and what will and/or should happen. Everything in the document should support or clarify the one-sentence statement.

Brainstorming
After writing the clear one-sentence statement, brainstorming or "fast writing" occurs. Brainstorming is the process of recording ideas and facts without sorting or evaluating them. The goal is to record as many ideas as possible, while keeping in mind the cultural background of the reader. For example, writing to group-oriented cultures involves relating to the welfare of the organization, the community, or the readers' families (Thrush, 2000).

Writing and Organizing
After brainstorming, the student determines the type of document and begins writing. Teaching students the appropriateness of using e-mail versus the other forms of written and verbal communication is a necessary part of the business curriculum. A teaching strategy is giving students a variety of situations and having them choose among the various communication formats.

All written content should refer back to the one-sentence statement. Each e-mail message, however, should contain only one main point. The goal in writing is to be clear and concise using short, simple words. When writing e-mail, informative subject lines are vital. Students need practice creating subject lines and using verbs if reader action is needed such as "Comment on the Attached" (Munter, 2003). Teaching subject lines also includes placing the most important words first, since this is what readers see in the inbox. Because no official standards exist for business e-mail, instructors can teach general standards such as openings and closings.

When writing to an international audience, students must be very careful about using analogies and examples. If the reader is unfamiliar with the subject of the example, the analogy is meaningless. Teaching students to avoid words with multiple meanings is also important. Words with multiple meanings include "close," "object," or "present," which cause problems in comprehension and translation. Other cultures are not as heavily oriented toward profit making as American firms; therefore, costs and other financial considerations may not be as important in communicating (Thrush, 2000). When writing, students need to identify and analyze contradictions introduced by culture and translation. In addition, students need practice adapting English concepts into equivalent concepts in other cultures.

Revising for Style

Most writers revise first for content, then for style, and finally for correctness (Ober, 2001). Revising for style includes accurate and complete writing with short, simple words and the elimination of all contractions, clutter, jargon, ambiguity, and bias. The average sentence in a memo, letter, or report should have fewer than 20 words, and each paragraph should support one idea consistently and logically and be no more than 60 to 80 words (Ober, 2001). At this point, checking readability statistics, which are readily available in word processing programs, is necessary.

Because readers glance quickly over e-mail, students need experience writing in short, simple sentences and short paragraphs, placing the main point of each paragraph first. Research by Mallon and Oppenheim (2002) indicates that the personal business e-mail averages 15 words per sentence with the total message approximately 145 words. The rest of the e-mail message repeats, rephrases, and reiterates the first paragraph. A hurried e-mail reader is more likely to delete an incoherent, lengthy e-mail than to spend the time deciphering the meaning of the e-mail message (Flynn & Flynn, 2003). Teachers need to help students avoid ending the e-mail with unnecessary phrases such as, "I hope that this answered your question" (Munter, 2003).

Students should avoid graphics if the picture is unfamiliar to the reader. For example, Macintosh computers use the trash can icon for deleting files. While that icon is readily identifiable in the United States, few other countries have a similar trash can (Thrush, 2000). A teaching strategy is to create a collage of international symbols and American graphics and have students determine which images are global. Symbols can be found from public spaces in major international cities and from international industry standards (Hoft, 2002).

Colors have different meanings in different cultures. Highlighting in red in the United States is common; however, in parts of Africa, dark red is a color of mourning or can be blasphemous. In China, Japan, and much of Asia, red is a lucky color. First place ribbons in Great Britain are green as opposed to blue in the United States (Thrush, 2000). Students should avoid colors entirely when writing unless they thoroughly research the cultural background of the reader.

Proofreading

After organizing the content and checking for style, the final proofreading occurs. Proofreading checks for grammar and spelling errors and compares facts and figures. Often instructors develop assignments including incorrect dollar amounts or words that sound or look alike such as "do" and "due" or "loose" and "lose" to emphasize the importance of proofreading. Also included in the assignment can be the differences between the British and American spellings of words such as "analyze" and "analyse" and "check" and "cheque." Canadians, Australians, and many others often follow patterns somewhere between American English and British English. The School of Computing and Information Technology, University of Wolverhampton, United Kingdom, has a Web page devoted to the differences among English spellings, which is http://www.scit.wlv.ac.uk/~jphb/american.html (Green, 2003).

Students may be familiar with the proofreading techniques for printed copies, but they also need techniques to improve their proofreading of electronic material. Some of these techniques involve proofreading in blocks or paragraphs, using the eraser side of a pencil as a pointer on the screen, and taking frequent breaks. Students need to be taught to look for spacing inconsistencies and make certain that the material makes sense.

The most important part of editing an e-mail message is to eliminate long, wordy sentences that do not reinforce the main point of the paragraph. Too many e-mail writers overuse exclamation points or include excessive punctuation such as the ellipsis (Mallon, 2002).

For important e-mail, students need to know how to compose in a word processing program and then select, copy, and paste the text into an e-mail program. Important e-mail messages should take the same amount of time that is typically put into traditional written documents because careful writing, revising, and editing are necessary. A delay in sending an e-mail for a day or so is very important for sensitive and important documents. Sometimes printing e-mail before sending it helps in the proofreading process. To avoid embarrassing mistakes, students should slow down, take time to revise, evaluate, and proofread a message.

No e-mail should leave a computer without using the e-mail spell-checking feature, which is an automatic setting on many e-mail programs. Routine messages can be sent after checking spelling and pausing to reflect upon the appropriateness of the message. Students must also give careful consideration to sending attachments. Of primary importance is whether the reader can open the attachment. In addition, some servers block attachments because of viruses. Classroom discussion should also include e-mail and attachment confidentiality, the encrypting of files, and digital and electronic signatures.

Writers must determine the type of message to send depending upon the preference of the reader. The writing process for memos, letters, e-mail, and reports involves knowing the steps of prewriting, brainstorming, writing and organizing, revising for style, and proofreading. During each one of these steps, the writer must consider the cultural background of the reader and compose messages that clearly communicate the message and that are easily translated by the reader.

WRITING FOR INTERCULTURAL AUDIENCES

No matter whether the message is e-mail, letter, or other type of written document, awareness of intercultural issues is important. This awareness involves being conscious of the differences in the use of the English language; using an appropriate writing style; writing in either formal or informal tone; acknowledging holidays; determining when to use the active and passive voices; avoiding slang; and using understandable date formats, time references, and measurements.

The English Language

According to Dieu (2004), English is spoken as a native language by approximately 375 million people and as a second language by nearly the same number of speakers in the world. Speakers of English as a second language will soon outnumber those who speak it as a first language. Around 750 million people are believed to speak English as a foreign language. One out of four of the world's population speaks English to some level of competence (Dieu, 2004).

The British business community has its own set of rules that are tempered by both custom and attitude for using the English language for business communication (Scott, 1998). British English is traditionally more formal and proper than American English. Mallon and Oppenheim (2002) point out that British English has become less standardized and prescriptive since the beginning of the twenty-first century. Mallon and Oppenheim suggest that this change may be occurring because the Internet reflects the American culture, and the American language of e-mail may be affecting the e-mail language of other cultures. France, for example, bans the use of the word "e-mail" in all government ministries, documents, publications, or Web sites (Keaton, 2003).

Students who learned American English should familiarize themselves with the British usage of words. For example, in British English, "mail" is "post" and a "pharmacist" is a "chemist." Jones (2001) provides a list of these common words that instructors can use to illustrate the differences in usage.

Americans learn to vary their writing style by using synonyms. However, using different terms to refer to the same thing confuses readers translating English. For example, synonyms for the word "directions" could be "instructions," "guidelines," "information," "directives," or "commands." Providing exercises with a variety of synonyms and having students use one term consistently will help students develop clear international communication.

Writing Style

In addition to the differences in cultural English, a difference exists in writing style. Writing style is the tone in a piece of writing, and the tone determines what a reader reads into the words and sentences (Campbell, 1998). A study by Park, Dillon, and Mitchell (1998) discovered that although South Korean business people regularly write business documents in English, the writers might continue to use the rhetorical patterns of their native languages. Whereas Americans are logical and sequential, Koreans tend to be more emotion-driven and more sensitive to the personal tone of the message (Park et al., 1998).

In an international business writing class with students from Belgium, Finland, and the United States, Connor, Davis, De Rycker, Phillips, and Verckens (1997) discovered that students writing in English from all three countries tended to write in a similar manner. The instructors speculate that this similarity existed because cultural expectations were a part of the course and that students adjusted their writing toward the norms of the other countries. Connor et al. (1997) suggest that students studying other cultures as a part of their writing classes tend to write in a more "international" style, which contains fewer national features so that the writing can be received well globally.

Informal vs. Formal

American messages are sometimes too direct for individuals in cultures where it is important to get to know a person before doing business. Readers from Latin or Asian cultures, for example, tend to be more interested in long-term relations with reliable people than in products or profits for their own sake (Campbell, 1998). Campbell (1998) suggests writing opening paragraphs that establish common ground and show an understanding of the reader. The following is an example of an opening to a Chinese reader, "I hope that you have had a safe journey home and that you have found family in good health. The Midwestern part of our country that you graciously visited continues to have wet weather."

Teaching students to write in a formal tone will help avoid offending others or showing ignorance toward another culture. Many American writers use first names when corresponding. When communicating internationally, students should use last names, titles, and other indications of rank and status. In many countries, the title is more important than the name.

International Holidays

Students need to be aware of international holidays and not assume that all countries are aware of American holidays. Students can research public holidays, bank holidays, national days, election days, school holidays, and celebrations at http://www.national-holidays.com (Jumez, n.d.). In addition, not all countries have a Monday through Friday work week. In many Islamic countries, Friday is the day of rest and the week starts on Saturday. In Israel, Sunday is the start of the week, and most people take off Friday and Saturday (Morrison & Conaway, 2004).

Jargon, Clichés, Slang, and Humor

Many American writers use jargon, clichés, and slang terms such as "bean counter" for an accountant or "freebie" for something that is free. International readers do not understand all American terms. To help students become aware of slang, teachers can direct them to a resource for writers to the International slang word and phrase dictionary (n.d.) at http://www.online-library.org/help/slang.shtml. Students can also rewrite sentences such as, "We will give it our best shot," or "We don't want to put our eggs in one basket" with concise, clear language.

Humor typically does not translate well. Students should be aware that international readers might be trying to translate writing using an English dictionary. International readers may not want to admit their confusion when translating unfamiliar phrases or technical words.

"You" Attitude

Most communication textbooks stress using the "you attitude" when writing. However, in some Asian countries, the reader prefers, "Would this plan interest your company?" instead of the question, "Would this plan interest you?" (DeVries, 1994). In some cultures, what the company thinks is more important than what the individual thinks. In addition, students need to analyze situations conveying negative information such as disagreeing or pointing out mistakes without the "you" attitude.

Active and Passive Voice

Business writing typically uses the active voice (a form of *to be* with the past-participle *ed* or *en* except irregular verbs). The active voice takes fewer words, is easier to read, and is more precise and strong. Students need help writing in the active voice and determining when the passive voice is appropriate. The passive voice softens the impact of negative news. For example, the following active sentence is in the "you" voice, "Your payment is 30 days late. You need to send your payment within two days to avoid a service charge." Students can convey the same information by avoiding the "you" voice and using passive tense in a sentence such as, "The payment has not been received in our office. Please send the payment within two days to avoid a service charge."

Dates, Measurements, and Time

The following are suggestions to avoid problems with dates, measurements, and time when writing internationally:

- Write out a date. Instead of writing 6/15/05, write out June 15, 2005, or 15 June 2005. Do not use seasons (for example, summer) since the northern and southern hemisphere experience the seasons at different times of the year.

- Use the 24-hour military clock for time outside of the United States. For example, "The time of the phone call will be 18:00 your time on 15 June 2005." When using times for domestic communication, indicate the time zones. For example, "The time of the phone call will be 2:30 p.m. Eastern Standard Time (EST) on June 15, 2005."

- Use metric measurements for international communication. Use the metric measure followed by the American measurement in parentheses. For example, "The office is approximately 8.04 kilometers (5 miles) from the airport." An online converter is available at www.onlineconversion.com (Fogt, 2003).

Writing for intercultural audiences involves being aware of the differences in the English language used by other cultures, using an appropriate writing style for the culture, and communicating clearly and precisely by avoiding references to American holidays and language. Americans tend to be more informal; however, international writing tends to be more formal. Students need to be aware of when to use the "you" attitude, the active and passive voices, and the formats for international dates, times, and measurements,

SUMMARY

Online communication technology, e-mail messages, and "offshoring" of jobs to other countries encourage people from different cultural backgrounds to communicate with each other. Because business writing is vitally important in today's global environment, classroom instruction must focus on intercultural business. Teachers need to use strategies for integrating grammar, spelling, and punctuation instruction within their courses. The writing process of prewriting, brainstorming, writing and organizing, revising for style, and proofreading a wide variety of written documents is essential to effective communication. Business students need to analyze when to use and how to write a variety of e-mail messages, memos, letters, and reports to different audiences. Familiarity with spelling and usage of different English patterns is an important aspect of effective communication. Researching the cultural background of the reader determines the type of writing style to use to best communicate messages. Students need to be reminded that the use of American words, slang, and jargon in their writing can hinder effective communication. Writing emphasis must be on clear, concise communication that is easily interpreted by English readers around the world whose first language is not English.

REFERENCES

Anderson, K., & Seshadri, S. (2003). I did, but I still don't get it. *Proceedings of the 2003 Association for Business Communication Annual Convention.* Retrieved January 25, 2004, from http://www.businesscommunication.org/conventions/Proceedings/2003/PDF/12ABC03.pdf

Campbell, C. (1998, February 20). *Beyond language: Cultural predispositions in business correspondence.* Paper presented at Region 5 STC Conference, Fort Worth, Texas. Retrieved May 25, 2004, from http://www.nmt.edu/~cpc/internationalethos.html

Central Intelligence Agency. (2003, October 23). *The world factbook.* Retrieved January 25, 2004, from http://www.cia.gov/cia/publications/factbook/docs/profileguide.html

The College Board. (2002). *Ten-year trend in SAT Scores indicates increased emphasis on math is yielding results; reading and writing are causes for concern.* Princeton, NJ: College Entrance Examination Board.

Connor, U., Davis, K., De Rycker, T., Phillips, E., & Verckens, J. (1997). An international course in international business writing: Belgium, Finland, the United States [Electronic version]. *Business Communication Quarterly, 60*(4), 63-75.

DeVries, M. (1994). *Internationally yours.* Boston: Houghton Mifflin.

Dieu, B. (2004, January 4). *Some facts and figures about the English language.* Foreign Language Department, Curso Experimental Bilingue, São Paulo, Brazil. Retrieved January 25, 2004, from http://the_english_dept.tripod.com/esc.html

Devoss, D., Jasken, J., & Hayden, D. (2002). Teaching intracultural and intercultural communication: A critique and suggested method [Electronic version]. *Journal of Business and Technical Communication, 16*(1), 69-95.

Flynn, N., & Flynn T. (2003). *Writing effective e-mail.* Menlo Park, CA: Crisp Learning.

Fogt, R. (2003). *Onlineconversion.com.* Retrieved January 15, 2004, from http://www.onlineconversion.com

Gallagher, N. (2004, January 15). 1,760 Sonoma County jobs emigrate. *The Press Democrat,* p. A1.

Gilsdorf, J. & Leonard, D. (2001). Big stuff, little stuff: A decennial measurement of executives' and academics' reactions to questionable usage elements [Electronic version]. *The Journal of Business Communication, 38*(4), 439-476.

Gorski, P. (2003). Multicultural awareness quiz. *McGraw-Hill multicultural supersite intercultural activities.* Retrieved January 25, 2004, from http://www.mhhe.com/socscience/education/multi/activities/awarenessquiz.html

Green, M. (2003, September 26). *WWlib - Notes on American English.* The School of Computing and Information Technology, University of Wolverhampton, Wolverhampton, WV1 1EQ, United Kingdom. Retrieved January 21, 2004, from http://www.scit.wlv.ac.uk/~jphb/american.html

Hoft, N. (2002, March 26). *What are the most important skills for creating international technical communication?* Presentation to the Orlando Chapter of the Society for Technical Communication. Retrieved May 25, 2004, from http://www.world-ready.com/stcorlando.htm

ICAS. (2002). *Literacy: A statement of competencies expected of students entering California's public colleges and universities.* Intersegmental Committee of the Academic Senates of the California Community Colleges, the California State University, and the University of California, 2002. Sacramento.

International slang word and phrase dictionary. (n.d.) *On-line library.org.* Retrieved January 22, 2004, from http://www.online-library.org/help/slang.shtml

Johnston, G. (2002, September 28). You've got mail: 60 billion a day by 2006. *Computerworld.* Retrieved January 9, 2004, from http://www.computerworld.com/softwaretopics/ software/groupware/story/0,10801,74682,00.html

Jones, S. (2001). *Common words in American and British English.* Retrieved May 25, 2004, from Department of Applied Linguistics & ESL, Georgia State University. Web site: http://www.gsu.edu/~wwwesl/egw/jones/words.htm

Jumez, J. (n.d.). *Bank holidays of the world.* Retrieved January 22, 2004, from http://www.national-holidays.com

Keaton, J. (2003, July19). Forget 'e-mail,' s'il vous plait. *Seattle Post-Intelligencer.* Retrieved January 22, 2004, from http://seattlepi.nwsource.com/national/131503_email19.html

Linkins, J. (2003). The pen and the sword: How to make the writing process work for you [Electronic version]. *The FBI Law Enforcement Bulletin, 72*(2), 20-24.

Lost in translation. (n.d.) Retrieved January 26, 2004, from the University of Texas, Department of Advertising Web site: http://advertising.utexas.edu/research/humor/lost.html

Mabrito, M. (1999) From workplace to classroom: Teaching professional writing [Electronic version]. *Business Communication Quarterly, 62*(3), 10-106.

Mallon, R., & Oppenheim, C. (2002). Style used in electronic mail. *Aslib Proceedings 54*(1), 8. Bradord: Cambridge University Press.

Morrison, T., & Conaway, W. (2004). *The world's many calendars.* Retrieved May 25, 2004, from http://www.getcustoms.com/2004GTC/Articles/iw1199.html

Munter, M. (2003). Business e-mail: Guidelines for users [Electronic version]. *Business Communication Quarterly, 66*(1), 26-41.

The National Commission of Writing in America's Schools and Colleges, College Entrance Examination Board. (2003). *The neglected "R": The need for a writing revolution.* Retrieved January 9, 2004, from http://www.writingcommission.org/

Ober, S. (2001). *Contemporary Business Communication* (4th ed.). Boston: Houghton Mifflin.

Okula, S. (2004). Step up to the soft skills. *Keying In, 14*(3), 6.

Park, M., Dillon, T., Mitchell, K. (1998). Korean business letters: Strategies for effective complaints in cross-cultural communication [Electronic version]. *The Journal of Business Communication, 35*(3), 328-346.

Pew Internet & American Life. (2002, December 8). *E-mail at work.* Retrieved January 9, 2004, from http://www.pewinternet.org/reports/

Public Agenda Online (2002). *Reality check 2002.* . Retrieved January 9, 2004, from http://www.publicagenda.org/specials/rcheck2002/reality5.htm

Ranney, F., & McNeilly, K. (1996). International business writing projects: Learning content through process [Electronic version]. *Business Communication Quarterly, 69*(1), 9-27.

Roberston, K. (1997). *Microcomputers in teaching.* Retrieved January 9, 2004, from http://www.ou.edu/class/eipt3113/wp.html

The School of Computing and Information Technology, University of Wolverhampton, United Kingdom. (n.d.). Retrieved January 9, 2004, from http://www.scit.wlv.ac.uk/~jphb/ american.html

Scott, J. (1998). Dear ??? Understanding British forms of address [Electronic version]. *Business Communication Quarterly, 61*(3), 50-62.

Sitler, H. C. (2001). Solutions to mechanical errors in writing: Usage scans and fix-it pages [Electronic version]. *Teaching English in the Two-year College, 29*(1), 72-76.

Thrush, E. (2000, January 22). *Writing for an international audience.* Retrieved May 24, 2004, from http://www.suite101.com/article.cfm/5381/32233

Varner, I. (2001). Teaching intercultural management communication: Where are we? Where do we go? *Business Communication Quarterly, 64*(1), 99.

Numeracy and Computing: Making Sense of Data

Carol Blaszczynski
California State University, Los Angeles
Los Angeles, California

Numeracy, the mathematical counterpart of literacy, empowers people in their roles as global citizens, consumers, employees, employers, and investors. Through computing, various types of divergent information are communicated. This chapter addresses the role of numeracy and computation skill in making sense of data, numbers, part-whole relationships, computational methods, money, time, measurement, numerical data depicted graphically, and statistical ideas. The chapter concludes with a section that presents teaching ideas.

NUMERACY AND COMPUTATION SKILL

This section discusses the role of numeracy and computation as foundational skills, the *National Standards for Business Education's* endorsement of computational skills, and the rich cultural heritage of numerical concepts.

Numeracy and Computation as Foundational Skills

Numeracy, also known as quantitative literacy, may be defined as "the quantitative reasoning capabilities required of citizens in today's information age" (Steen, 2004, n.p.). Why is numeracy so important? The Vice President for Public Leadership of the Educational Testing Service (ETS), Anthony Carnevale, stated "mathematics is the biggest barrier to upward mobility in educational attainment" (Steen, 2004, n.p.). Mathematics mastery is not only a gateway to college, but also a filter for occupational opportunity and higher earnings (Department of Education, 1997). Numeracy and computation skill enhance the ability of people to make informed decisions in their various roles in organizations and marketplaces.

National Standards for Business Education

The *National Standards for Business Education*, developed by the National Business Education Association (NBEA) (2001), promote computation skill development at all levels of business instruction. The standards for computation encompass six specific areas: mathematical foundations; number relationships and operations; patterns, functions, and algebra; measurement; statistics and probability; and problem-solving applications. Computation skills, as defined by the standards, are more than simply the skills required to make precise, quantitative calculations. Indeed, they are "the skills that encompass the ability to solve mathematical problems, analyze and interpret data, and apply sound decision-making skills" (NBEA, 2001, p. 48).

Cultural Heritage of Numerical Concepts

Numerical concepts are steeped in the rich cultural heritage from which they were developed. Activities common among all societies, both past and present (Bishop, 1988), include locating, counting, measuring, explaining, designing, and playing. The mathematics of cultural groups is also known as ethnomathematics (Shirley, 1996).

Over 4,000 years ago the Mesopotamians used money, calculated simple and compound interest, and developed and followed accounting methods. Among the oldest discovered writings are business records (Brinkworth, 1994). From the Roman era up to the Renaissance, Latin served as the dominant language of commerce (Brinkworth, 1994). In fact, *Liber Abaci*, written by Fibonacci in 1228, illustrated mercantile applications of algebra and arithmetic and facilitated the rise of Hindu-Arabic calculation notation, the number system used today. In the tenth century Arabs in the business community used finger-reckoning (finger math) arithmetic for commerce (O'Connor & Robertson, 1999).

Beginning accounting students, for example, learn that basic bookkeeping concepts were developed by Luca Pacioli, a monk, in Italy about 1490 (Flescher, n.d.; Smith, 2002). Brother Pacioli published these concepts in the book *Summa de Arithmetica, Geometria, Propotioni et Propotionalita* (*Everything About Arithmetic, Geometry, and Proportion*). Furthermore, many of these concepts form the cornerstone of basic accounting practice today.

Each culture has developed a number system to count or quantify amounts. This development is an important concept for businesses and consumers. Although the *National Standards for Business Education* (NBEA, 2001) emphasize the need for accuracy and precision in number usage, many times numbers are actually estimates. In accounting, for example, depreciation amounts are based upon estimates. The useful life of an asset is estimated according to guidelines used in various industries, and the amount of trade or salvage value is also an estimate.

Thus, while "mathematics is the only language shared by all human beings regardless of culture, religion or gender" (Annenberg/CPB, n.d.), each culture has contributed a rich heritage of mathematics development. While accuracy and precision are hallmarks of numeracy in a global society, the role of estimates in business mathematics applications should not be ignored. One aspect of numeracy and computing for a global society is part-whole relationships.

PART-WHOLE RELATIONSHIPS

While quantities or amounts are often referred to using whole numbers, many instances require that the parts of a whole be expressed. Two major ways to express parts of the whole are as percentages and as ratios and proportions.

Percentages are easy to express, since percentage means per hundred. Numbers are commonly expressed as percentages to make for easier comparisons between and among raw data.

Ratios are common in accounting and financial analyses. For example, it is commonplace to calculate the current ratio in accounting; that is, current assets divided by current liabilities. Besides computing the ratio, a person must understand what the ratio means. The current ratio indicates the ability of the business to meet its short-term obligations through short-term assets. One useful guideline for assessing the current ratio is that it should be approximately 2 to 1. However, what is considered to be a healthy current ratio may vary from industry to industry (American Express Company, 2003). Interestingly enough, ratios may also be written as proportions. For example, the ratio 2/1 can be written as a proportion of 2:1.

Thus, expressions of part-whole relationships are needed when amounts or quantities are not whole numbers. Percentages, ratios, and proportions are ways of expressing part-whole relationships. How, then, are whole numbers expressed?

NUMBERS

In this section written numerals (data formats) and number systems are addressed.

Written Numerals (Data Formats)

Correct data formats vary from country to country, including formats for dates, time, currency, and the writing of large numbers (Guffey, 2003). The data format for writing large numbers is the same for both the United States and the United Kingdom: 9,677,222.33. The opposite is true for Portugal, Germany, and France, where a comma rather than a period is used to separate cents from dollars. Periods are used rather than commas to separate hundreds from thousands and hundred thousands from millions: 9.677.222,33

General rules for citing numbers (Guffey, 2003) include (a) using figures to cite numbers (i.e., 12) rather than spelling the amount (i.e., twelve), if the number is greater

Table 1. A Comparison of the American and British Systems for Writing Large Numbers

Number of zeros	American system	British system
9	billion	milliard
12	trillion	billion
15	quadrillion	—
18	quintillion	trillion

Note. The American system for writing large numbers is used by the United States, the United Kingdom, Brazil, Canada, Greece, and Puerto Rico. While the American system is used by Italy, Russia, and Turkey, in those countries 10^9 is known as a "milliard." The British system is used by Austria, Denmark, Finland, France, Germany, Hungary, Norway, Sweden, the Netherlands, French-speaking Canada, Spain, the Spanish-speaking countries of Central and South America (except Puerto Rico), Portugal, and Poland. The languages of Croatian, Czech, Serbian, and Slovak also use the British system for writing large numbers (Sizes, Inc., 2004).

than ten; (b) making a practice of converting dollar figures into local currency, and (c) refraining from using a figure to express months of a year.

Numbers over one million are known by different names in different countries. Most countries follow one of two naming conventions: the American system or the British system. Interestingly, while the American system stems from the former French system, the French have switched to the British system (OnlineConversion.com, n.d.). A comparison of the two systems is presented in Table 1. Careful global business communicators will consult this table when preparing global communications involving large numbers expressed partially in word form.

Software programs allow users to format numbers in the correct style for the culture or country of the intended recipient. A measurement converter smart tag for Office XP is downloadable from the Microsoft Web site at http://www.microsoft.com/downloads. This smart tag has the ability to convert measurement units from one system to another within documents created in Word. In fact, the smart tag locates common international measurement units within the document and tags them. The user can click the smart tag to convert a measurement from one international unit to another. Furthermore, measurement units can also be added, and conversion rules can be edited (Microsoft, 2004). Data recognized by Word have a purple dotted underline beneath them to indicate a smart tag. To determine the actions that can be taken with a smart tag, move the insertion point over the smart tag indicator text. When a Smart Tag Actions button appears, click on the button to view an actions menu (Microsoft Word Help, n.d.).

Spreadsheet software allows for the formatting of dates and times for many countries. This formatting can be accomplished by going to the format menu, selecting cells, clicking on date or time under the number category tab, and then selecting the locale appropriate for the audience or by consulting the online help feature of Microsoft Excel.

An alternative to these recommendations for number formats is to employ the International Organization for Standardization (ISO) standards for formatting dates and time. The International Organization for Standardization, comprising the national standards institutes of about 150 countries, has developed standards to be used globally (International Organization for Standardization, 2004).

ISO 8601 suggests numerical date and time representations on an internationally accepted basis (International Organization for Standardization, 2003). Calendar day, the commonest date representation, would take the format of YYYY-MM-DD. In this data format, YYYY represents the Gregorian calendar year, MM represents the month (January is 01 and December is 12), and DD represents the day in the month, ranging from 01 to 31. For example, 2005-07-01 represents the first day of July in 2005. This representation system avoids common problems such as determining whether 4-6-2005 is April 6, 2005, or June 4, 2005. Thus, businesses educators should consider teaching ISO standards to improve the clarity of messages sent to all receivers regardless of their country.

Number Systems

The Roman numeral system made addition and subtraction easy; however, multiplication and division were cumbersome. One major drawback of the Roman numeral system was the absence of zero. The origin of zero is uncertain. While the concept of zero has been attributed to India circa 650 A.D., other sources indicate that the Incas used zero at an earlier date (O'Connor & Robertson, 2000a). Unfortunately, the use of zero was not disseminated to other cultures by the Incas.

Like the Incas, the Mayans developed a base 20 numeral system (O'Connor & Robertson, 2000b). Most likely, the base 20 stemmed from ancient people using both their toes and fingers for counting. A base number system is a characteristic that influences place value or positional notation. The decimal system is base ten. The powers of 10 (exponents) establish place value: hundreds, tens, ones, tenths, hundredths, and so on. Exponents are superscript numbers to the right of the number that denote its power. Using the previous example, hundreds are 10^2, tens are 10^1, ones are 10^0, tenths are 10^{-1}, and hundredths are 10^{-2} (Guedj, 1997).

The Hindu-Arabic number system is named after the Hindus, who may have invented it, and after the Arabs, who disseminated the system to Western Europe. The earliest examples of our present number symbols are found on some stone columns erected in India circa 250 B.C. (dePillis, 2002). These specimens contain no zero and do not use positional notations.

Thus, written numerals (data formats) and number systems facilitate standard global communication of computation results. But what methods are used to perform computations?

COMPUTATIONAL METHODS

People perform calculations in different fashions: in their heads or mentally, using pencil and paper, using manipulatives, using a calculator, and using a computer (NBEA, 2001). The calculation progression is not universal. Some cultures use manipulatives in problem solving before those in the United States do. Each of these methods will be discussed in the following paragraphs.

It is important to be able to solve simple calculations in one's head. Often students are encouraged to estimate answers before performing complex calculations or computations. Frequently, those estimations are done mentally. The usefulness of mental computations cannot be overrated. Business educators should encourage students to estimate answers prior to solving problems (see Blaszczynski, 2001; James, 2003; Tobias, 1993). John Allen Paulos (1988) asserted, "If people were more capable of estimation and simple calculation, many obvious inferences would be drawn (or not), and fewer ridiculous notions would be entertained" (p. 13).

Manipulatives are physical objects that aid students in visualizing relationships and applications (Utah State University, 2003). Further, computer-based manipulatives can be used to enrich learning and increase interactivity. In some cultures students may learn to perform calculations using the Japanese soroban, Slovanic abacus, or Chinese rods or other types of mechanical devices, helping to reinforce concepts and to visualize the problem (Nelson, 1992). When numbers are larger, the use of pencil and paper allows recording more complex problems that would tax memory load. Once students learn through the media of paper and pencil, they can then advance to using more sophisticated tools, such as calculators and computers.

Calculators are ubiquitous tools in contemporary society. As a matter of fact, shopping carts in some Wal-Mart stores come equipped with calculators on the handlebars, allowing shoppers to estimate their total bill quickly and accurately. Nevertheless, despite the prevalence of calculators, one should not assume that people understand how to use them effectively. Some people will input numbers inaccurately, causing erroneous results. Instruction in calculator usage is important to ensure that the benefits of the technology are realized. Thus, estimating answers prior to using a calculator is a recommended practice (James, 2003; Tobias, 1993).

Calculator use enhances cognitive gains in visualization, number sense, and conceptual development (NCTM, 2002). Technological tools, such as calculators and computer software, facilitate students' development of higher-order thinking, including reasoning, problem solving, problem posing, decision making, and reflection (NCTM, 2003). Moving beyond calculator usage, many people use a computer to perform calculations. For example, if a person is using the computer for word processing and needs a calculator, the computer user will oftentimes turn to a utility such as the calculator accessory to perform a quick calculation. For more sophisticated calculations, however, most computer users turn to Microsoft Excel. Many lessons plans (Association of Teachers of Mathematics, n.d.) and books have been written for utilizing Excel to perform calculations ranging from the simple to the complex.

The importance of accuracy in calculations is illustrated by the following anecdote. A clerical error cost Trans Alta Corp., Canada's biggest investor-owned power generator, the equivalent of US $24 million (Schmidt, 2003). This error stemmed from an erroneous amount entered into a spreadsheet cell. As a result of this error, an office of 24 employees was closed.

Thus, regardless of the computational strategy used, accuracy in computing is critical. Business educators should encourage students to develop different strategies to solve problems, including mental calculation, pencil and paper, manipulatives, calculators, numeric keypads, and computers. Developing the ability to use different methods increases appreciation for diverse strategies used by various cultures. Many of these computational strategies are used when computing money exchanges.

MONEY

Money is a means of exchange for products and services provided by individuals, businesses, and governments. Each nation has its own money denominations and currency, which increases the complexity of travel and of conducting business in and with people from other nations. Exchanging and converting money among the different denominations can become quite complex.

Web sites are available that provide currency exchange information such as www.oanda. com/convert/classic, www.x-rates.com/calculator.html, and finance.yahoo.com/m3?u. Members of a global society need to be conversant with the various money denominations and be comfortable with currency conversions.

Thus, money allows products and services to be exchanged and is measured by denominations in currencies of different countries. Calculators can enhance money exchange. Another dimension of global communication is the measurement of time.

TIME

Two major aspects of time include international time and the type of calendar a culture uses to keep track of the passage of time.

International Time

There are 24 time zones or meridians around the globe. Military time is measured using a 24-hour clock and referred to as Zulu time or zero meridian time (Timeanddate.com, n.d.a). Military time is also known as Coordinated Universal Time (UTC) based on Greenwich Mean Time (GMT) (Timeanddate.com, n.d.). To plan video or phone conferences at culturally acceptable times around the world, one can use a world clock planner, such as the one available at the web site, www.timeanddate.com/ world clock/meeting.html.

Calendars

Different calendars have existed over the centuries. Calendars may be lunar, solar, or luni-solar (Meyer, 2003). The lunar calendar is based on moon cycles, while the solar calendar is based on seasonal cycles. The Muslim calendar used throughout the Islamic world is strictly lunar. On the other hand, the Gregorian calendar is solely solar. The Gregorian calendar serves as the official calendar of the United States and many other nations (Ascher, 2002). Luni-solar calendars attempt to serve as both lunar and solar calendars. The Jewish calendar is luni-solar and coordinates religious observances (Ascher, 2002). Some years must have 13 months, while others must have 12 months. Approximately every third year a leap month is included because 12 months have approximately 11 days greater than the tropical year (Webexhibits.org, n.d.).

Many people live with different calendars—ones specific to their cultural or religious groups and calendars specific to their nations. As Ascher (2002) asserted, "Within one's own life, the actual challenge of living under multiple calendars is the challenge of reconciling the different cultural priorities expressed in each" (p. 54).

Thus, time is measured by an international clock and various calendars. But how are weights, areas, volumes, distances, and temperatures measured?

MEASUREMENT

The metric system has been promoted by the National Council for Teachers of Mathematics (NCTM) as a principal system of mathematics instruction. According to the NCTM's position statement (2000),

> On an international level in the scientific and industrial worlds, the metric system is a standard system of measurement . . . To compete in a world that already functions with the system, our students also need to be competent with the metric system (n.p.).

The measurement achievement standard of the *National Standards for Business Education* is "Use common international standards of measurement when solving problems" (NBEA, 2001, p. 49). The standard involves identifying and converting measurements for countries outside the United States using conversion calculators on the Internet and estimating and converting U.S. units of measurement to metric measurements.

The English measurement system originated from the thirteenth century and was selected by the U.S. Congress about 1790. The General Conference on Weights and Measures in 1960 recommended worldwide adoption of a simplified metric system version, the International System of Units (SI). The United Kingdom switched to the metric system in 1996. The U.S. stock exchanges switched from fractional to decimal share-price trading in April 2001, while Canadian stock exchanges began using the decimal share-price system in April 1996. All products labeled in Europe need to have SI units before 2010. Dual labeling will not be permitted. The European Union Commission extended this directive for ten years to permit more time for organizational compliance to allow metric-only measurements for consumer products with labeling (U.S. Metric Association, 2004). Currently, only three nations have not adopted the metric system: the United States, Liberia, and Burma.

Thus, the metric system is a standard global measurement system that allows various cultures to communicate with ease. But how can measurement and other computational results be represented graphically?

GRAPHICAL IDEAS

While a picture may be worth a thousand words, the picture may not reveal the appropriate words. Graphical displays have the potential to enlighten readers with the elegant depiction of relationships, trends, and significance. Conversely, poorly constructed graphical displays can be worse than having no graphical display whatsoever. Edward Tufte, author of *The Visual Display of Quantitative Information*, refers to visuals with elements that are confusing as "chartjunk." Examples of chartjunk include excess ticks, redundant data representation, and busy grid lines (Tufte, 1983).

Tufte is an outspoken critic of such computer programs as PowerPoint because of the poor renderings produced by the graphical templates native to the program. According to Tufte (2003), "Presentations largely stand or fall on the quality, relevance, and integrity of the content." Further, "If your words or images are not on point, making them dance in color won't make them relevant. Audience boredom is usually a content failure, not a decoration failure" (p. 3). Those outside the U.S. believe that the reliance of Americans on special effects is overdone, and they prefer simplicity (Allee, 2002).

DuFrene and Lehman (2004) advocated using five strategies for building professional PowerPoint presentations: develop a consistent design that evokes the presentation's tone; develop simple content supportive of the presenter; incorporate multimedia effects in moderation; supplement spoken transitions using slides that proceed logically through the presentation; and use flexible, interactive design elements. The following chapter about visualizing addresses the better use of graphic communication.

Thus, simple, consistent design and logical presentation enhance graphical ideas. Graphical displays communicate summary results or trends to an audience. Another aspect of numeracy and computation that presents summary data is statistical ideas.

STATISTICAL IDEAS

Statistical ideas are the backbone of research studies conducted to provide generalizations of results. Studies that follow rigorous statistical methods have the possibility of unearthing results that may impact policy and practice positively. Statistical concepts and their symbols are universal among nations and possess the ability to communicate across cultures quickly and efficiently. The statistical ideas are discussed in the following paragraphs.

Three measures of central tendency describe how distributions may be characterized. These measures include the mean, the median, and the mode. Simply put, the mean is the simple average of the distribution; that is, the sum of the values in the distribution divided by the number of values in the distribution. Perhaps this is the most commonly reported statistic; indeed, it is most likely the one with which most citizens have the greatest familiarity. The second measure is the median, the value that appears in the middle of the ordered distribution. If a distribution comprises 11 values, the value that appears in the middle (the sixth item) would be the median. In cases where there is an even number of values in a distribution, the two items in the middle of the distribution are averaged. For example, the sixth and seventh values in a distribution of 12 items would be averaged to determine the median. The median is an important measure because it is not affected by outliers, extreme values in a distribution. The third measure of central tendency is the mode, which is the most frequently appearing value in a distribution. Distributions can have multiple modes. To give the best picture of a distribution, most researchers report more than one measure of central tendency to provide the most relevant data for readers and decision makers (Carroll & Carroll, 2002).

Besides reporting measures of central tendency, measures of dispersion should be reported. Three measures of dispersion include the range, the variance, and the standard deviation. The range is calculated by subtracting the lowest value in a distribution from the highest value in a distribution. The variance reveals how the data are spread around the center of the distribution (Carroll & Carroll, 2002). The last measure of variability, the standard deviation, is obtained by squaring the value of the variance. Both the standard deviation and the variance use all the values in the data set and are more accurate descriptions of dispersion than the range.

While the tenets of statistics are logical, they are not necessarily followed universally by researchers. As a result, consumers of research studies need to read critically to be sure that statistics are employed judiciously. If researchers or reporters fail to report statistics accurately, then the results can be misrepresented or distorted.

Thus, statistical symbols and concepts are powerful and aid communication across cultures. Measures of central tendency and measures of dispersion provide information about a distribution that enhances interpretation for decision making. Teaching activities for statistical ideas and other aspects of numeracy and computation are included in the next section.

TEACHING IDEAS
Activities and ideas for teaching numeracy and computing are presented in this section.

Measurement Ideas

Many sources exist for teaching computation. Among them are an abundance of Web sites for teaching measurement (see The United States Metric Association, 2002a, 2002b, 2003, 2004). In addition, strategies that can be used to commemorate Metric Week, celebrated during the week of October 10, can be found at the U.S. Metric Association's Web site, http://lamar. colostate.edu/~hillger/ideas.htm. Visual learners may find the Antoine frame-of-reference method useful since it uses everyday items as references for the size of metric measurements. For example, a meter is approximately equivalent to a yardstick plus a piece of chalk (United States Metric Association, 2002a).

Stock Market Exchange Project

Many aspects of computing are involved in the stock market exchange project. Some of these aspects are converting currency, writing ISO date formats, using a spreadsheet, calculating statistics, creating a graphic aid, and writing a clear explanation of the project results.

Ask students to record the market gain or loss for four different stock exchanges: the New York Stock Exchange, the Toronto Stock Exchange, the London Stock Exchange, and the Tokyo Stock Exchange. Students should record data points for four consecutive weeks using ISO date formats for the four exchanges using a web site such as Yahoo Finance at http://finance.yahoo.com. Students should record (a) the amount of the gain or loss; (b) the gain or loss amount converted to U.S. dollars to facilitate comparison by using a money converter, such as the Full Universal Currency Converter at http://www.xe.com/ucc/full.shtml; and (c) the percentage of gain or loss. The data recording can be done on a worksheet or using an Excel spreadsheet. At the end of the four weeks, students calculate the average weekly gain or loss for each of the stock exchanges. Graphic aids can be created to summarize the month's activity for the four stock exchanges. In a short memo report, students can then interpret the changes and identify any trends among the four stock exchanges. This activity can be adjusted for the instructional level and the sophistication of the students.

Data Analysis Activity

The following activity can be used to develop numeracy and data interpretation skills. Provide students with data about worldwide obesity incidence in various countries using the Web site http://www.iotf.org/media/globalprev.htm.

The first data set should include the following countries: Argentina, Canada, Cuba, Cyprus, England, Estonia, Ireland, Luxembourg, Nauru, Slovakia, and Switzerland. Each of these countries, with the exception of England, has higher reported obesity rates for men than for women. The second data set should include these countries: Barbados, China, Germany, Japan, Mexico, Samoa, Saudi Arabia, Scotland, South Africa, and the United States. In each of these countries women have a higher reported rate of obesity than do men. Ask students to calculate measures of central tendency and dispersion. The following questions should be answered by students.

1. Based on the first set of obesity data, to which group—men or women—would you most likely market products and services for fitness and weight loss? Why?

2. Based on the second set of obesity data, to which group—men or women—would you most likely market products and services for fitness and weight loss? Why?

3. When the data sets are combined, to which group—men or women—would you most likely market products and services for fitness and weight loss? Why? Further, what generalization(s) can you make about the countries with high obesity rates? (Are they located in particular parts of the world? Are they developed or developing nations?)

4. The data reported on the Web site were collected in different years. What impact might this have on the data? In addition, some of these data were gathered through self-reports of individuals. In your opinion, how reliable are the self-reported data? Another potential problem with the data is that they were collected from different age groups and were not consistent from country to country. What impact does this inconsistent data-collection technique have on the comparability of the data?

Other ideas for teaching computation may be found in the 2003 National Business Education Association *Yearbook* chapter about accounting and business computation (Blaszczynski, 2003).

Thus, business educators can use various ideas to teach numeracy and computing.

SUMMARY
Across cultures people share the language of mathematics that is employed in numeracy and computation. Mathematics has the potential to communicate with greater accuracy and precision than written and spoken language.

Business educators can arm students with an arsenal of computation strategies that can be used to solve problems mentally, with manipulatives, on paper, and with the aid of technology such as calculators and computers. Finely tuned numeracy and computation skills develop in students an appreciation for the power and elegance of numbers and their varied forms to communicate across cultures in a data-driven world. Both the presentation of numerical data graphically and the communication of statistical ideas provide summary data for decision making. The concept of measurement is a principal theme in numeracy and computation. Across cultures money, clock time, and calendar time are measured differently. On the other hand, the metric system provides a standard system for communicating about temperature and dimensions.

Teaching activities for numeracy and computation should provide active learning to promote skill development through writing, collecting data, and reflecting. Business educators can use Web resources to design activities based on current events, as suggested by some of the teaching activities described in this chapter. Interactive assignments create excitement in students about the power and relevance of numeracy and computation in global communication.

REFERENCES

Allee, S. (2002). *Crafting a speech to a global audience.* Retrieved April 30, 2004, from http://www.sheilaalle.com/speechtips/speak111801/.htm

American Express Company. (2003). *Current ratio: Financial formulas from American Express.* Retrieved March 15, 2004, from http://home3.americanexpress.com/smallbusiness/tool/ratios/currentratio.asp

Annenberg/CPB. (n.d.). *Math in daily life: How do numbers affect everyday decisions?* Retrieved April 30, 2004, from http://www.learner.org/exhibits/dailymath/language.html

Ascher, M. (2002). *Mathematics elsewhere: An exploration of ideas across cultures.* Princeton, NJ: Princeton University Press.

Association of Teachers of Mathematics. (n.d.). *Excel spreadsheet files—animal game.* Retrieved February 9, 2004, from http://www.atm.org.uk/resources/Excel.html

Bishop, A. (1988). Mathematics education in its cultural context. *Educational Studies in Mathematics, 19,* 179-191.

Blaszczynski, C. (2001). Stamping out business math illiteracy. *The Delta Pi Epsilon Journal, 43*(1), 1-5.

Blaszczynski, C. (2003). Accounting and business computation. In M. H. Rader (Ed.), *Effective methods of teaching business education in the 21st-century: National Business Education Association yearbook, no. 41* (pp. 166-185). Reston, VA: National Business Education Association.

Brinkworth, P. (1994). The making of mathematics: A matter of interest. *The Australian Mathematics Teacher, 50*(1), 5.

Carroll, S. R., & Carroll, D. J. (2002). *Statistics made simple for school leaders.* Lanham, MD: The Scarecrow Press, Inc.

Department of Education. (1997). *Mathematics equals opportunity.* White paper prepared for Secretary of Education Richard W. Riley. Retrieved October 29, 2003, from http://www.ed.gov/pubs/math/index.html

dePillis, J. (2002). *777 mathematical conversation starters.* Washington, DC: Mathematical Association of America.

DuFrene, D. D., & Lehman, C. M. (2004). Concept, content, construction, and contingencies: Getting the horse before the PowerPoint cart. *Business Communication Quarterly, 67*(1), 84-91.

Flescher, F. (n.d.). *Luca Pacioli: The father of accounting.* Retrieved January 27, 2004, from http://members.tripod.com/~FlynF/pacioli.htm

Guedj, D. (1997). *Numbers: The universal language.* New York: Harry N. Abrams, Inc.

Guffey, M. E. (2003). *Business communication: Process and product* (4th ed.). Mason, OH: South-Western.

International Organization for Standardization. (2003). *Numeric representation of teaching time.* Retrieved February 17, 2004, from http://www.iso/ch/iso/en/prods-services/popstds/datesandtime.html

International Organization for Standardization. (2004). *About ISO-introduction.* Retrieved February 17, 2004, from http://www.iso/en/iso/en/aboutiso/introduction/index.html

James, M. L. (2003). Strategies for detecting and correcting errors in accounting problems. *Business Education Forum, 58*(1), 20-22.

Meyer, P. (2003). *Types of calendars.* Retrieved March 15, 2004, from http://www.hermetic.ch./cal_stylestud/lunarcal/types.htm

Microsoft. (2004). *Download details measurement converter smart tag.* Retrieved January 13, 2004, from http://microsoft/com/downloads

Microsoft Word Help. (n.d.). *About smart tags.*

National Business Education Association. (2001). *National standards for business education: What America's students should know and be able to do in business.* Reston, VA: Author.

National Council of Teachers of Mathematics. (2000, March). *Position statement: Metrication.* Retrieved November 4, 2001, from http://www.NCTM.org/about/position_statements/position_statement_09.htm

National Council of Teachers of Mathematics. (2002, October). *Position statement: Calculators* and the education of youth. Retrieved April 30, 2004, from http://www.NCTM.org/about/position_statements/position_statement_01.htm

National Council of Teachers of Mathematics. (2003, October). *Position statement: The use of technology in the learning and teaching of mathematics.* Retrieved April 30, 2004, from http://www.NCTM.org/about/position_statements/position_statement_13.htm

Nelson, D. (1992). Ten key areas of the curriculum. In D. Nelson, G. G. Joseph, & J. Williams (Eds.), *Multicultural mathematics* (pp. 42-84). Oxford, United Kingdom: Oxford University Press.

O' Connor, J. J., & Robertson, E. F. (1999). *Arabic mathematics: Forgotten brilliance?* Retrieved October 29, 2003, from http://www-groups.dcs.st-and.ac.uk/~history/HistTopics/Arabic-mathematics.html

O' Connor, J. J., & Robertson, E. F. (2000a). *A history of zero.* Retrieved October 29, 2003, from http://www-groups.dcs.st- and.ac.uk/~history/HistTopics/zero.html

O' Connor, J. J., & Robertson, E. F. (2000b). *Mayan mathematics.* Retrieved October 29, 2003, from http://www-groups.dcs.st- and.ac.uk/~history/HistTopics/Mayan-mathematics.html

OnlineConversion.com. (n.d.). *Denominations above one million.* Retrieved February 9, 2004, from http://www.online conversion.com/large_numbers.htm

Paulos, J. A. (1988). *Beyond innumeracy: Mathematical illiteracy and its consequences.* New York: Hill and Wang.

Schmidt, L. (2003, July 25). TransAlta closes U.S. trading office. *Edmonton Journal,* p. F2.

Shirley, L. (1996). Using ethnomathematics to find multicultural mathematical connections. In P. A. House & A. F. Cox (Eds.), *Connecting mathematics across the curriculum: 1995 yearbook* (pp. 35-43). Reston, VA: National Council of Teachers of Mathematics.

Sizes, Inc. (2004). *Names of big numbers.* Retrieved April 30, 2004, from http://www.sizes.com/numbers/big_num.Name.htm

Smith, L. M. (2002). *Luca Pacioli: The father of accounting.* Retrieved January 27, 2004, from http://acct.tamu.edu/Smith/ethics/pacioli.htm

Steen, L. A. (2004). Quantitative literacy: Why numeracy matters for schools and colleges. In *MAA online*. Retrieved February 13, 2004, from http://www. maa.org/features/ QL.html

Timeanddate.com. (n.d.a). *Military/NATO/lettertimezones*. Retrieved November 7, 2003, from http://www.timeanddate.com/library/abbreviations/timezones/military/

Timeanddate.com. (n.d.b). *Time zone abbreviations*. Retrieved November 7, 2003, from http://www.timeanddate.com/library/abbreviations/timezones/

Timeanddate.com. (n.d.c). *The world clock meeting planner*. Retrieved November 7, 2003, from http://www.timeanddate.com/worldclock/meeting.htm/

Tobias, S. (1993). *Overcoming math anxiety* (rev. ed.). New York: W. W. Norton & Company, Inc.

Tufte, E. R. (2003). PowerPoint is evil. [Electronic version]. *Wired Magazine*. Retrieved February 10, 2004, from http://www.wired.com/wired/archive/11.09/ppt2_pr.html

Tufte, E. R. (1983). *The visual display of quantitative information*. Cheshire, CT: Graphics Press.

U. S. Metric Association. (2002a). *Antoine frame-of-reference method... familiar-item examples*. Retrieved October 29, 2003, from http://lamar.colostate.edu/~hillger/ frame.htm

U. S. Metric Association. (2002b). *Tips to educators for teaching the metric system*. Retrieved February 9, 2004, from http://lamar.colostate.edu/~hillger/week.htm

U. S. Metric Association. (2003). *Ideas for a school's celebrating National Metric Week*. Retrieved February 9, 2004, from http://lamar.colostate.edu/~hillger/ideas.htm

U. S. Metric Association. (2004). *Metric usage and metrication in other countries*. Retrieved October 29, 2003, from http://lamar.colostate.edu/~hillger/internat.htm

Utah State University. (2003). *National library of virtual manipulatives for interactive mathematics: Project information*. Retrieved May 30, 2004, from http://matti.usu.edu/ nlvm/projinfo.html

Webexhibits.org. (n.d.). *The Jewish calendar*. Retrieved April 30, 2004, from http:// webexhibits.org/calendars/calendar-jewish.html

Visualizing: Conveying Information Graphically in a Global Business Environment

Martha H. Rader
Arizona State University
Tempe, Arizona

Graphic design has evolved from its roots in the early printing industry to the creation and publication of contemporary business documents with the use of technology. Well-designed business publications contain the essential elements of visual design, including relevance, consistency, proportion, direction, and design restraint. The effective use of typography, illustrations, and color gives publications a professional appearance. This chapter describes the various types of graphic technology used to present information to a global audience and discusses the challenges associated with using graphics in multicultural environments.

THE EVOLUTION OF GRAPHIC DESIGN

Graphics are symbols such as letters of the alphabet or illustrations such as road signs whose context, position, and location connote a particular meaning (Hollis, 1994). Graphics generally combine both words (text) and images (descriptive illustrations) to convey messages. *Graphic design* involves planning and creating the visual presentation of verbal information. Other terms for graphic design include visual communication, visual design (McCoy, 2001), commercial art (an earlier term) (Hollis, 1994), and desktop publishing (Parker & Berry, 1998).

Historical Foundations

Graphic design in the United States evolved from the process of book printing in Europe (McCoy, 2001). An early printing press with movable type invented by Johann Gutenberg in Mainz, Germany, in 1436-37 revolutionized the printing process (Chernow & Vallasi, 1975). Prior to that time, books and other manuscripts were laboriously handwritten by scribes (Helba, 2003a). The famous Gutenberg Bible was printed in Latin in the Rhine Valley in the 1450s, and the new printing process subsequently spread rapidly across Europe. More than 8 million books were printed between 1450 and 1500; during this period 1,125 printing shops are known to have existed in 259 cities across Europe (*Compton's Encyclopedia*, 1971).

The first iron printing press was built in England by the Earl of Stanhope in 1804. The first steam-powered cylinder presses were invented in England in 1814. Robert Miehle perfected the multicolor cylinder press in the 1880s in the United States. Printing was a cumbersome and expensive mechanical process that involved setting type by hand until Ottmar Mergenthaler, a naturalized American, invented the Linotype machine in 1890 (Helba, 2003a). The process of printing was greatly simplified when photo-typesetting technology was introduced in the 1960s (Thurm, 1998).

For the first five centuries after its invention, printing conveyed content primarily by the use of text (McCoy, 2001). Illustrations were seldom used because of technological and cost considerations. *Typography* (the lettering that was typeset) was considered to be message-neutral until the Italian Futurists, Russian Constructivists, German Bauhaus and Dadaism, and other early European 20th century design movements developed typographic forms that conveyed meaning visually as well as verbally (Heller & Pomeroy, 1997; Hollis, 1994). By the 1930s, the European Modernist movement influenced American graphic designers to emphasize visual images and condense text-heavy verbal descriptions in advertising (McCoy, 2001). In the 1950s and 1960s, the "picture is worth a thousand words" approach began to dominate business communication in the United States.

In the 1960s the "Swiss method," stressing the accuracy of information and unity of design throughout a company's publications, became popular. In the United States, corporations such as IBM and Container Corporation adopted this graphic style that focused on consistency of appearance characterized as a specific "company look." More recently, the Post-Modernism or Post-Structuralism approaches have emphasized content represented by images and typography that are intended to be both seen and interpreted. This type of design is more intellectually rigorous for the audience because it draws on humor, irony, and personal interpretation of the messages that are conveyed (McCoy, 2001).

Current Applications

Today graphic design is an essential part of the world of business communication, including marketing, advertising, public relations, and publishing. It involves the design not only of traditional business documents such as letters, memos, reports, brochures, newsletters, and magazines, but also includes the design of numerous other forms of business communication such as Web pages, signage, logos, business cards, posters, business forms, packaging, and product labels. Graphic design involves many activities such as planning the headlines and text for typesetting, choosing the typefaces, selecting the illustrations, designing the *layout* (placement on the page), and coordinating the production/printing process (Parker & Berry, 1998).

TECHNOLOGICAL INNOVATIONS

The development of microcomputers and accompanying software in the 1980s allowed users to produce business documents utilizing many design features that were previously too costly for general usage. Technological innovations included advanced word processing features, spreadsheet graphics software, presentation graphics software, desktop publishing software, photo enhancement software, illustration software, and Web page design software.

Word Processing Features

Word processing software offered users a variety of typefaces (fonts) and font sizes, and other special features for creating documents, including cut-and-paste, text wrap, automatic styles and formatting, pagination, centering, alignment, variable line spacing, columns, search-and-replace, and spelling/grammar checking. Advanced word-processing features included database and spreadsheet capabilities, color, drawing tools (lines, boxes, circles), automatic bulleting, and the importation of illustrations.

Microsoft OfficeXP includes language-specific features that allow the user to edit documents in more than 130 languages (Microsoft Global Development, 2004). Multilingual features include formatting requirements for specific languages, such as entering text from right to left. The user can easily key international characters, including punctuation marks, by using keyboard commands. For example, the Spanish punctuation mark "¿" can be keyed by using the command *alt + ctrl + shift +?*

Spreadsheet Graphics Software

Spreadsheet software such as Microsoft Excel allows users to perform mathematical calculations and automatically create tables and charts that contain or represent the resulting data graphically. Graphics that can be created by spreadsheet software include many types of line charts, bar charts, pie charts, and diagrams. Various types of graphics can easily be generated from spreadsheets and imported into word-processing documents to enhance the clarity and interest of business reports and other publications. Although the software generates standardized formats for charts and graphs, the designs can be customized to vary features such as typography, colors, shading, directionality, and headings.

Presentation Graphics Software

Presentation graphics software such as PowerPoint allows the user to create slide shows easily and quickly that are designed to accompany business presentations. The software provides standardized backgrounds, formats, headings, bullets, clip art, and special effects such as wipes, fades, and animation that a user can select to enhance a slide show. In addition, users can import customized spreadsheet graphics, illustrations, photographs, music, video, and other special effects.

Desktop Publishing Software

Desktop publishing software such as Adobe PageMaker, Quark XPress, and Microsoft Publisher are applications used primarily for page layout (Parsons, 1996). *Page layout* is the arrangement of graphic elements on the pages of a publication. Page layouts that are part of a large publication such as a book or catalog are assembled into *press layouts*. Desktop publishing software includes features that allow the user to manipulate or enhance the typography by adjusting the spacing between the letters (*kerning*) and tracking (*automatic kerning*), fine-tuning the vertical line spacing (*leading*), rotating type, creating type variations such as 3D and *reverse type* (white letters on a dark background), *screening* (shading), *cropping* (eliminating part of a graphic), and infinite variations of color. Desktop publishing software permits much more precise placement of text, graphics, boxes, *rules* (vertical and horizontal lines), amount of screening, color, and other features than those available in word-processing software.

Photo Enhancement Software

Photo enhancement software such as PhotoShop allows the user to edit graphics in many ways, including adjusting the clarity, color, contrast, size, shape, and content. The software allows the user to import graphics and convert graphic files from one format to another, rotate text and graphics, convert text to graphics files, design different backgrounds, and create three-dimensional and other special effects.

Illustration Software

Illustration software such as Adobe Illustrator and Macromedia FreeHand contains "tools" or special features that allow the user to create artwork electronically, including drawing, painting, and other types of illustrations. The illustration software includes electronic tools such as airbrushing, drawing lines and other shapes, drawing freehand line art, editing clip art, shading, adding *spot color* (one-color enhancements), and creating *four-color* (full color) illustrations. Adobe's new suite software In Design includes features of Illustrator and PhotoShop to enhance the basic features of PageMaker.

Web Design Software

Web design software such as Microsoft's FrontPage and Macromedia's Dreamweaver allow the user to design and create Web pages without being an expert in programming languages such as HTML or JavaScript. Web design software permits the user to create backgrounds, insert text and images, create hyperlinks and buttons, and insert enhancements such as animation and video clips. Specialized software such as Flash and Shockwave are available to enhance Web pages with advanced animation and video/audio editing features.

ELEMENTS OF VISUAL DESIGN

Effective, professional-looking business publications must include the essential elements of visual design. Essential elements include the following qualities: relevance, consistency, proportion, direction, and design restraint (Parker & Berry, 1998).

Relevance

Every design element on a page of a printed document should relate to the purpose of the message. The typeface, graphics, color, and paper should all fit together and complement one another in communicating the appropriate message to the receiver. For example, a contemporary typeface with a high-tech appearance would be more appropriate than an old-fashioned Roman typeface in a brochure about a new product such as high-definition television or the latest model of a high-performance sports car.

Consistency

Business communications should have consistency in the design and layout. Typeface, type size, margins, *gutters* (the spaces between columns), sizes of illustrations, spacing around graphics, borders, and repetition of graphic elements such as vertical/horizontal lines should be consistent throughout a publication. Some variety imparts interest, however, such as varying the placement of photographs and other illustrations from one page to another.

Proportion

The size of a graphic element should be based on its relative importance in the document and on the page. The size of an illustration, a typeface, and the thickness of a *rule* (line) convey a message about its importance. For example, a headline with a large typeface is perceived as being more important than a headline with a smaller typeface, and a large illustration is perceived as more important than a smaller one. For large typefaces, wide columns are more appropriate than narrow ones (Parker and Berry, 1998). Too much information crowded on a page detracts from its appearance. The effective use of white space enhances readability and creates a visually appealing layout for the page.

Direction

The arrangement of elements on a page should help guide the reader's eye on the page. The focal point of a message is generally in the upper left corner of the page. In English-language publications, items should be arranged on the page from top left to bottom right. In some foreign languages, however, the arrangement of items on the page is traditionally right to left. The directionality of lines in graphic images conveys an important part in a message. Horizontal lines are often viewed as passive, while vertical lines convey a dominant or positive message (Bradshaw, Rader, & Fuetterer, 1999). Diagonal lines convey a dynamic message, while curving lines suggest movement.

Design Restraint

The work of amateur desktop publishers can often be differentiated from that of professional graphic designers by a lack of design restraint. Use of too many different design elements such as typefaces, illustrations, and special effects (such as animations in PowerPoint presentations and Web pages) creates a cluttered, unprofessional look. Graphic designers should include illustrations to improve understanding, not simply to fill up a page.

TYPOGRAPHY

Typography (type design) is the most important visual element that influences a message. Effective typography separates professional publications from those that look amateurish (Helba, 2003a). Typographic choices should be appropriate for the context in which they are used, and above all, should be legible.

Type Families

A *typeface* is a particular design for type or type "family"; for example, Times New Roman, Arial, or Garamond. A *font* is a specific type style and size of a typeface family—for example, Arial bold 12. However, the terms "font" and "type" are often used interchangeably, although this practice is technically inaccurate.

Typeface families are classified as either serif or sans serif. *Serif* type has small cross-strokes at the top and ends of each *character* (letter or number), while *sans serif* type does not (Proot, 1996). Serif type is most appropriate for large blocks of text, while sans serif type is commonly used for headlines and other display type.

Type Architecture

Typefaces may be further grouped into classifications based on their *type architecture* (design characteristics) (Parker & Berry, 1998). Type architecture is determined by factors such as the shape of *counters* (the white space inside a character such as an "o"), *stress* (angle of a curved stroke) (Helba, 2002), shape of serifs (square versus rounded), *x-height* (the height of a lowercase "x" of a typeface), and vertical versus diagonal orientation. For example, serif typeface classifications include Old Style (e.g., Garamond, Palatino), Transitional (Times, Century Schoolbook), and Modern (Bodoni, Didot); sans serif classifications include Geometric (Avant Garde, Futura), Humanist (Frutiger, Optima), and Grotesque (Arial, Helvetica) (Helba, 2002; Matteson, 1996).

A sans serif typeface for a headline generally should match the design characteristics of the accompanying serif typeface of the text. Old Style and Traditional type classifications go well with Humanist type; Modern type looks best with Geometric type (Matteson, 1996).

Type Selection

The choice of a typeface depends on the nature of the message. A typeface can convey a tone or mood such as traditional or contemporary, masculine/feminine, dignified/whimsical, or ethnic/cultural. Type also can portray a specific period/historical setting such as Old West, Victorian, or Art Deco. Some specialized type transmits an international message by its similarity to Asian, Middle Eastern, or Greek characters, while other type is designed for children's publications or products, as shown in Illustration 1. Specialized typefaces are most appropriate for headlines, large displays, or accompanying company logos.

Typefaces are available for literally hundreds of languages, including Native American and other native languages throughout the world, American Sign Language, and ancient languages that are no longer spoken. Sources of language fonts are available at the following Web sites: www.dtcc.edu/~berlin/fonts.html, www.sil.org/computing/fonts, and www.freelang.net/fonts.

Illustration 1. Specialized Display Type

Literally thousands of variations of type are available at a relatively low cost in the United States, primarily because U.S. copyright law does not permit letterforms to be copyrighted. Only the software code that creates a font can be copyrighted in the United States. In other countries such as Britain and Germany, however, typefaces are protected by copyright law (Thurm, 1998).

Typography has trends, similar to those for cars and hairstyles. For example, Helvetica was the most popular typeface in the 1970s but today is considered as old-fashioned as a beehive hairstyle (Williams, 1995). Using an old-fashioned typeface makes a publication appear outdated.

Design restraint is essential when choosing fonts; novice desktop publishers tend to use too many fonts. As a rule of thumb, the number of fonts, including different sizes of the same typeface, should be limited to a maximum of three on a page (Matteson, 1996).

COLOR

The use of color in business publications and other documents has increased tremendously in recent years, largely because technological innovations have led to decreased cost. The use of color adds impact and is usually a desirable addition to a document if the printing budget permits it. Two-color printing (black plus one other color) is much less expensive than four-color.

Basics of Color

Colors impart various meanings, nuances, and moods. Certain colors are appropriate in particular documents and images, while others are not. Warm colors (yellow, red, and orange) are engaging and intense, while cool colors (blue, green, and purple) are generally more subdued and elegant (Parker & Berry, 1998). Warm colors are frequently used to accent the most important elements of a design, while cool colors are used for unified elements throughout the design of a document. Warm colors are a good choice for foreground colors, while cool colors are most appropriate for backgrounds (Bradshaw, Rader, & Fuetterer, 1999).

Effective color documents utilize a well-planned scheme for the selection of colors. Some colors look attractive in combination with other specific colors, while others do not. To avoid color clash, select colors that are analogous (next to one another) on a color wheel. A *color wheel* represents the three *primary colors* (red, blue, and yellow) in a triad at opposite sides of the wheel, with colors that result from mixing those colors (*secondary colors*) arranged in the circle on a continuum. Analogous colors (e.g., blue, teal, and green) work well together and give publications a unified appearance (Parker & Berry, 1998). To create contrast, use *complementary colors*, or colors that are located opposite one another on the color wheel.

International Implications of Color

Colors suggest many different meanings and associations that vary from one culture to another. Colors of everything in a society—clothing, automobiles, taxis, houses, can connote various meanings, from social status and gender to marital status and political party affiliation.

Colors may have various meanings, depending on the context. For example, in the United States, the color red can indicate a net loss of money (in a business report), Christmas cheer (in a Christmas card), love (in a Valentine), safety (fire engines, fire extinguishers, no-parking zones), and sex appeal (in a sports car or lipstick advertisement).

In Great Britain, red is the color of the monarchy and official government business, including judges' robes, carpeting in courts of law, military uniforms, mailboxes, telephone booths, and buses. Red also signifies blood; English physicians traditionally wore red cloaks until the late 19th century (Peterson & Cullen, 2000). Red is the color worn in fox hunting, and barbershop poles are red-and-white.

In China and Taiwan, printing in red indicates good fortune, joy, harmony, and fertility. Red is the traditional color for Chinese wedding dresses, the New Year, wrapping paper for New Year's gifts, and on the mainland is associated with communism. Red headlines are often used in Chinese newspapers and magazines. Exceptions to the usual positive associations for the color red are funeral notices, which are generally printed in red, and a name written in red, which indicates the termination of a relationship or the death of the named individual (Peterson & Cullen, 2000).

In Japan, red ink is also used to indicate the end of a relationship. However, red is also popular in Japan for television graphics, headlines, and other print materials. In Turkey, red signifies death (Copeland & Griggs, 1986, as reprinted in Usunier, 2000).

In business communication, careful selection of colors is essential in order to convey the intended message internationally. Examples of cultural connotations for various colors include femininity, which is portrayed by pink and other pastel colors in the United States but is symbolized by yellow in many other parts of the world. In the United States, the color green is associated with the outdoors, ecology, money, and Ireland/St. Patrick's

Day. Green is associated with disease in countries with dense jungles (Copeland & Griggs, 1986, as reprinted in Usunier, 2000), with germ-free sterility in Scandinavia, with the Islamic religion (in Arab countries), birth and youth (China), and New Year (in Italy, the season of Epiphany). In China, the combination of blue characters on a white background is used for funeral lanterns and is considered to be inappropriate for any other purpose (Peterson & Cullen, 2000).

Organizational Uses of Color

Companies use color to promote organizational and brand identity. For example, blue is the signature color of "Big Blue" IBM, and red is associated with Coca Cola throughout the world. The psychological impact of color is especially important in advertising. Darker shades project a dignified, conservative image, while warm colors (red, yellow, and orange) project action, youth, and excitement (Parsons, 1996). Color can be used to project a corporate image and unify the appearance of a company's publications.

Spot Color

Spot color is the use of a specific premixed ink color shown in a color chart—for example, Pantone Matching System (PMS) colors. Spot color is an inexpensive way to create a two-color publication, which adds interest to otherwise black-and-white publications. Color charts specify the saturation (brightness) as a percentage. Colors on a color wheel are 100% saturated; adding black decreases the amount of saturation and darkens the color (Parker & Berry, 1998). Spot colors can be used to enhance text such as headlines and other elements such as boxes, rules, information graphics, and clip art. More expensive *process colors* are used in printing full-color publications using dot patterns of the four basic colors of ink (cyan, magenta, yellow, and black).

Screening

Screening, or using a smaller percentage of a spot color to produce a lighter shade, creates the effect of using more than one color without incurring any additional printing cost. For example, a bright red color screened to 10% appears light pink. Screening can be used to produce two or more shades of the same color in order to enhance the appearance of a publication, to highlight the background of information in a box, and to differentiate information in a chart or graph. Page layout, illustration, and photo enhancement software include a feature allowing the user to screen colors.

ILLUSTRATIONS

Carefully chosen and well-placed illustrations can enhance the information, the appearance, and the effectiveness of business documents (Parker & Berry, 1998). Various types of illustrations include charts, tables, and diagrams generated by a spreadsheet program, clip art, image fonts, line art generated by illustration software, and photos.

Illustrations and Culture

Cultural and religious influences affect the use and selection of illustrations and other business data in various countries. "High-context" cultures believe that who communicates information, how it is communicated, and why it is communicated are more important than the actual information that is communicated (Jandt, 1998). In "low-context" cultures such as Germany, Britain, Sweden, and the United States, businesspeople rely on the use of facts and figures to make business decisions (Lewis, 2000). In many "high-context" cultures such as Italy, Latin America, Arab countries, and China, businesspeople make decisions based more on subjective factors such as personal relationships, intuition, emotions, and spirituality. Japan is an exception; it is a high-context society but data oriented in business decision making (Elashmawi & Harris, 1998). In certain parts of the world such as Asia, Brazil, and France, managers may ignore objective business reports and consult astrologers, spiritual advisors, or graphologists (handwriting analysts) to guide decision making (Schneider & Barsoux, 1997).

Use of photographs, gender roles, and representation of age groups varies widely in advertising from one country to another. In Saudi Arabia and other Islamic countries, the representation of human or animal figures in art is prohibited by the Koran (Peterson & Cullen, 2000). While advertisements in Saudi Arabia now depict people, women are modestly covered. In Japan, advertisements show groups of people more frequently than individuals or couples; in Western countries the reverse is true. Korean advertisements frequently depict elderly individuals, as their wisdom is venerated (Usunier, 2000).

Even images of plants and fruit have various meanings in different cultures. For example, in Japan a cherry tree is a national symbol. In China, images of pears, oranges, and peaches are frequently depicted because a pear symbolizes prosperity, an orange symbolizes happiness and good health, and a peach symbolizes longevity (Peterson & Cullen, 2000).

Spreadsheet Graphics

Less culture-bound than pictorial illustrations are *spreadsheet graphics,* which refer to illustrations containing numerical data or other visual information that is generated by spreadsheet software (Rader & Kurth, 1994). Spreadsheet applications can easily and inexpensively generate two-dimensional and three-dimensional charts and graphs for business documents and presentations, in black-and-white or full color. Spreadsheet graphics enhance narrative communications by simplifying and summarizing complex information, emphasizing special points, and improving the readability of statistical or financial information. Various kinds of spreadsheet graphics include tables, pie charts, simple bar charts, multiple bar charts, subdivided or stacked bar charts, single line graphs, multiple line graphs, and component-part line graphs.

Tables are composed of data arranged in columns and rows. Tables vary from short informal listings of non-numerical information to formal arrangements of detailed reference data. Although not a "visual" in the strictest sense, tables are the most detailed and most versatile graphic aid (Rader & Kurth, 1994).

Pie charts depict the percentage that component parts (slices) represent of a whole quantity (circle or pie). *Bar charts* are used to compare quantities of data by the length of equal-width bars. *Simple bar charts* represent varying quantities by showing horizontal or vertical bars that vary in length. *Vertical bar charts* generally depict time (years, months) on a horizontal axis and quantities on a vertical axis. In *horizontal bar charts*, the horizontal axis contains numerical values and the vertical axis depicts the titles of data categories (e.g., products, locations, demographics). *Multiple bar charts* depict two or three different data categories for a certain time period or category. For example, a financial report might include a multiple bar chart portraying the sales of two or three divisions over a five-year period. *Subdivided* or *stacked bar charts* divide a bar into sections to show the relationship of the parts to the whole.

Line graphs plot data on a grid over a particular time period. Types include single, multiple, and component-part line graphs. *Single line graphs* are used to plot a series of continuous data over a time period (Rader & Kurth, 1994). Time is plotted on the horizontal axis, and amounts are plotted on the vertical axis. *Multiple line graphs* plot two or more separate series of data on the same axis. *Component-part line graphs* are used to plot component parts of a single series of data. The separate parts of multiple line graphs and component-part line graphs are differentiated by color, shading, or crosshatching (Lesikar & Pettit, 1997).

Various kinds of diagrams include pictograms, organizational charts, flow charts, and schematics. *Pictograms* are images representing data vertically or horizontally, similar to bar charts (Rader & Kurth, 1994). For example, pictorial symbols such as stacks of coins might represent expenditures of money or the number of houses built. *Organizational charts* represent the structure of an organization by depicting departments or job titles and their relationship to one another. *Flow charts* depict the sequence of steps involved in the completion of a process or procedure. *Schematics* are cutaway drawings that show the workings of a mechanical process or machine.

Clip Art

Clip art is ready-made artwork. Twenty years ago clip art consisted of catalogs of ready-made illustrations that designers literally clipped out and pasted into publications. Today clip art consists primarily of images in computer file formats. Clip art files of thousands of images are available from publishers and can be purchased over the Internet. Some clip art is in the public domain and is available free on the Internet.

In international business communication, reports and other documents should contain clip art that is appropriate across cultures. Certain images have connotations that are inappropriate in some cultures. For example, an owl symbolizes wisdom in the United States but in India means bad luck; in Singapore a stork connotes maternal death rather than birth of a child; and in Japan a fox suggests witchcraft (Copeland & Griggs, 1986, as reprinted in Usunier, 2000).

The *resolution* of a clip-art image determines its clarity and quality. In *raster* images, the resolution is determined by the number of *bits* or *pixels* (closely spaced dots or tiny squares) per square inch (Helba, 2003a). The resolution of a raster image is measured in *dpi* (dots per inch) or *ppi* (pixels per inch). Images that are intended to be printed are measured in dots per inch; screen images are measured in pixels per inch. For best quality, the resolution of a raster image should equal the resolution of the output device (for example, 600 dpi). An image will appear blurred or "pixelated" if its resolution is too low for the printer. In *vector* graphics files, the image is created by a series of mathematical descriptors, or vectors. Resolution is not a problem with vector graphics, as the image automatically adjusts its resolution to the output device.

The most appropriate file formats for printed images include TIFF format for raster images, EPS format for vector images, and PDF format for either type of image. Other popular file formats for screen-resolution images used on Web pages include GIF, BMP, and JPEG; the resolution of these file formats is too low for high-quality printing.

Line Art

Many clip art images consist of simple line art. *Line art* is a raster image (rectangular array) consisting of solid areas or lines (Helba, 2003a). Line art can be created on a computer by using the shape or AutoShape tools in software such as PhotoShop, PageMaker, or MS Word. It can also be created by using the pencil tool in draw or illustration software. Line art is particularly effective for printing simple illustrations in one- and two-color documents. Novice desktop publishers often import line art from low-resolution GIF files from the Internet into printed documents with poor results.

Image Fonts

Image fonts contain frequently used symbols rather than letters of the alphabet. Image fonts are also known as pi fonts, symbols, or dingbats (Helba, 2003c). Popular image fonts include Wingdings, Zapf Dingbats, Symbol, Thingbats, Patterns One, Monotype Botanical, and Webdings (Helba, 2002). Image fonts can be used to generate simple one-color images instantly to highlight information in business publications and other documents. Some companies transfer their corporate logo to an image font to facilitate its frequent use in corporate documents (Helba, 2003c).

Photographs

Photographs provide powerful imagery, add impact, and convey realism in a way that text and line art cannot (Parker & Berry, 1998). The quality of a photograph is derived from numerous factors such as focus (sharp or blurred), contrast (difference between light and dark areas), brightness, and color.

Photographs may be imported into documents from digital cameras, from clip art collections, and by scanning conventional photos. Photo editing software such as PhotoShop allows the user to improve the quality of photographs by increasing or decreasing the brightness, retouch or erase areas, change the color, resize or crop the image, add a frame around the picture, combine elements from two or more sources into one photo, flip an image on its vertical or horizontal axis, apply a drop shadow or shadow masks, and create highlights and other special effects (Helba, 2003b).

Color photographs require four-color printing, which is a much more expensive process than printing in black-and-white. *Halftone screening* is used to print black-and-white photos inexpensively by representing light and dark tones by small and large dots.

Photo editing software can easily convert color or black-and-white photographs to print-ready halftone images.

TEACHING STRATEGIES AND RESOURCES

Graphic design principles can be included in business classes such as computer applications, word processing, desktop publishing, Web design, business communication, marketing, and e-commerce. These courses can incorporate units or lessons focusing on visual communication from an international perspective.

Teaching Strategies

Examples of assignments such as case studies and other Web-based research, group critiques, business reports, word processing projects, spreadsheet projects, and desktop publishing projects that allow business students to develop their creativity and technological expertise are listed below.

a. Examine the Web sites of two or three large corporations based in an Asian country such as Japan or Korea. Compare them to the Web sites of two or three similar U.S. companies. Discuss the design and cultural similarities and differences between the Asian and the American Web sites—for example, the use of color, images, and factual information.

b. Create an appropriate bar chart using Excel from data that is provided in table format. Print a copy of the bar chart. Then convert the dollars to British pounds and print the new bar chart. Finally, convert the original data to Japanese yen and print the new bar chart.

c. Design a business card, including an appropriate logo and fonts, for a fictional ethnic restaurant—for example, French, German, Greek, or Mexican. Then pair up with another student and critique each other's designs. Finally, revise the design based on the improvements suggested by your partner.

d. Design a three-panel brochure from a fictional travel agency that is advertising tours in other countries. Use the text that is provided by the teacher and import appropriate graphics from sources you find on the Internet.

e. Search for "free fonts" on the Internet. Print five examples of fonts with an international appearance—Japanese, African, Greek, Arabic, and Old English.

f. Search for "free clip art" on the Internet. Find a simple clip art image of a holiday that is unique to another country and print it.

g. Open Microsoft Word, and under the "Insert" menu, select "symbol." Change the font to Wingdings and/or Webdings, size 30. Find a Jewish symbol, a Chinese symbol, an image of the world, and a smile face. Print the four symbols on one page.

h. Pair up with another student who has some knowledge of another language such as French or Spanish. Key a sentence in that language, including appropriate punctuation marks. Use the Help feature in Microsoft Word to determine how to type the appropriate accent marks or other language symbols.

i. Form groups of three students. Examine an issue of a popular U. S. magazine such as *Esquire* or *Cosmopolitan* that contains many advertisements. Evaluate each advertisement for its appropriateness in other countries. Identify three examples of advertisements that are universally appropriate and three examples of advertisements that contain elements that would be inappropriate in international magazines. Discuss the reasons for your selections.

Resources

Excellent sources for desktop publishing and design include books by Parker and Berry (1998) and Peterson and Cullen (2000). The following magazines and Web sites are recommended resources for business educators seeking additional information about visual design.

- www.adobe.com/products/adobemag/pastissues.html (past issues of *Adobe Magazine*)

- www.allgraphicdesigns.com (compilation of graphics and desktop publishing resources)

- www.desktoppub.miningco.com/library/weekly/99082897.htm (desktop publishing lesson plans)

- www.dtpjournal.com (Web site for *Desktop Publishers Journal*, an excellent magazine)

- www.fontsite.com/Pages/RulesofType/ROT097.ht (the rules of typography)

- www.grantasticdesigns.com/glossary.html (glossary of graphic design and Web page design terms)

- www.informationdesign.org/archives/cat_visual_design.php (an index of the archives of the quarterly magazine *International Review of Graphic Design/ InfoDesign: Understanding by Design News*)

SUMMARY

Graphic design involves planning and creating the visual presentation of verbal information. Modern graphic design has evolved from the invention of the printing press to the creation and publication of contemporary business documents with the use of digital technology. Technological innovations include advanced word processing features, spreadsheet and presentation graphics, desktop publishing software, photo enhancement and illustration software, and Web page design.

The essential elements of visual design include relevance, consistency, proportion, direction, and design restraint. Typography is the most important element influencing the design of a message. Designers should have an understanding of type architecture and its role in the selection of type that conveys the appropriate design characteristics, tone, and historical setting. Colors should be carefully selected to convey the intended message and avoid cultural taboos. The meanings and connotations of colors vary widely among different cultures. Spot color and screening can add interest to publications inexpensively by using only two colors of ink.

Various types of illustrations, including spreadsheet graphics, tables, clip art, line art, image fonts, and photographs can enhance the information presented in business documents. Cultural and religious influence plays an important role in the use and selection of illustrations in different countries.

Various business education courses can incorporate units or lessons focusing on visual communication from an international perspective. Student-centered teaching strategies that involve individual and group student projects are particularly effective in developing students' creativity and technological expertise. Assignments involving Web-based research, group critiques, business reports, word processing projects, spreadsheet projects, and desktop publishing projects are suggested. Finally, a number of resources, including books, magazines, and Web sites are recommended.

REFERENCES

Bradshaw, R., Rader, M., & Fuetterer, K. (1999). *Building communication by design* [Electronic slideshow]. Tempe, AZ: Arizona State University.

Chernow, B. A., & Vallasi, G. A. (Eds.) (1975). *The Columbia encyclopedia* (5th ed., pp. 1165-1166). New York: Columbia University Press.

Compton's encyclopedia (1971). (Vol. 18, p. 504). Chicago: F. E. Compton.

Elashmawi, F., & Harris, P. (1998). *Multicultural management 2000: Essential cultural insights for global business success.* Houston, TX: Gulf Publishing Co.

Helba, S. (Ed.). (2003a). *Adobe InDesign 2: Introduction to electronic documents.* Upper Saddle River, NJ: Prentice Hall.

Helba, S. (Ed.) (2003b). *Adobe Photoshop: Introduction to digital images.* Upper Saddle River, NJ: Prentice Hall.

Helba, S. (Ed.). (2003c). *QuarkXPress 5: Introduction to electronic documents.* Upper Saddle River, NJ: Prentice Hall.

Helba, S. (Ed.). (2002). *Type companion for the digital artist*. Upper Saddle River, NJ: Prentice Hall.

Heller, S., & Pomeroy, K. (1997). *Design literacy: Understanding graphic design*. New York: Allworth Press.

Hollis, R. (1994). *Graphic design: A concise history*. New York: Thames & Hudson.

Jandt, F. (1998). *Intercultural communication: An introduction* (2nd ed.). Thousand Oaks, CA: Sage Publications.

Lesikar, R. V., & Pettit, J. D. (1997). *Report writing for business* (10th ed.). Homewood, IL: McGraw-Hill/Irwin.

Lewis, R. D. (2000). *When cultures collide: Managing successfully across cultures*. London: Nicholas Brealey Publishing.

Matteson, S. (1996, January 7). Mixing and matching typefaces. In *Monotype typography 101*. Retrieved March 15, 1996, from http://www.monotype.com/html/type/type101.html

McCoy, K. (2001). American graphic design expression: The evolution of American typography. In S. Heller & G. Ballance (Eds.), *Graphic design history* (pp. 3-18). New York: Allworth Press.

Microsoft Global Development (2004). Retrieved May 22, 2004, from http://www.microsoft .com/globaldev/DrIntl/faqs/winxp.mspx

Parker, R. C., & Berry, P. (1998). *Looking good in print* (4th ed.). Scottsdale, AZ: The Coriolis Group.

Parsons, B. (1996). *Graphic design with PageMaker*. Albany, NY: Delmar Publishers.

Peterson, L. K., & Cullen, C. D. (2000). *Global graphics: Color: A guide to design with color for an international market*. Gloucester, MA: Rockport Publishers.

Proot, K. G. (1996). *Adobe PageMaker 6 for the Macintosh*. Cambridge, MA: Course Technology.

Rader, M. H., & Kurth, L.A. (1994). *Business communication: With contemporary issues and microcomputer applications* (2nd ed.). Cincinnati, OH: South-Western Publishing Co.

Schneider, S. C., & Barsoux, J. L. (1997). *Managing across cultures*. London: Prentice Hall Europe.

Thurm, S. (1998, July 15). Copy this typeface? Court ruling counsels caution. *The Wall Street Journal*, pp. B1, B6.

Usunier, J. C. *Marketing across cultures* (3rd ed.). Harlow, England: Pearson/Prentice Hall, 2000.

Williams, R. (1995, July/August). Thirteen telltale signs. *Adobe Magazine*, 41-43.

Intercultural Communication: Bridging Cultural Differences

Lillian H. Chaney
University of Memphis
Memphis, Tennessee

Jeanette S. Martin
University of Mississippi
Oxford, Mississippi

Intercultural communication, as first defined by Edward T. Hall in 1959, is communication between persons of different cultures (Chaney & Martin, 2004). Culture plays an important role in people's lives; it provides structure and makes life easier and less confusing. While numerous definitions of culture have been proposed over the years, the following definition emphasizing the link between culture and communication was advanced by Marsella (as cited in Samovar & Porter, 2001): "Culture is shared learned behavior which is transmitted from one generation to another for purposes of promoting individual and social survival, adaptation, and growth and development" (p. 33). This chapter addresses ways to identify cultural differences, develop strategies for minimizing cultural differences, explore cultural programming, and use resources to promote cultural understanding.

IDENTIFYING CULTURAL DIFFERENCES

Individuals differ in numerous ways – by ethnicity and by whether the culture is individualistic or collectivistic, masculine or feminine, or low- or high-context. In addition, differences in what is considered truth and people's perceptions of attitudes and behaviors of persons from other cultures must be considered in intercultural interactions.

Ethnicity

Ethnicity refers to identifying people as members of the same ethnic group. An ethnic group has these ingredients: It is perceived to be different according to race, national origin, religion, or language from other people in a society; group members view themselves as different; and members share activities characteristic of their ethnic group

(Yinger, 1994). In addition to race, national origin, religion, and language, ethnicity may also be apparent through differences in customs, appearance, rituals, and food choice. Problems arise in interactions with other people when they are categorized on the basis of ethnicity. However, in some cases people wish to have their ethnicity recognized, especially when they perceive it to be important to the interaction. European Americans, for example, may not identify with their ethnic group. However, non-European Americans, such as Japanese Americans, African Americans, and Mexican Americans, often do prefer to identify with their ethnic group. Communicating effectively with others includes recognizing and respecting their ethnic identities, including the use of labels they may prefer, e.g., Latino vs. Mexican American (Gudykunst, 2004).

Individualism-Collectivism

Individualism is the belief that more emphasis should be placed on the individual than on the group. Self-interest and taking responsibility for one's own actions and destinies are characteristics of people in individualistic cultures. Collectivism is the belief that more emphasis should be placed on the group; cooperation, conformity, and interdependence are characteristic of people in collectivistic cultures (Gudykunst, 2004).

According to Hofstede's (1991) research, the United States ranks first in individualism, followed by Australia, Great Britain, Canada, and The Netherlands. U.S. persons consider self-reliance important, since they were taught from childhood to think for themselves, to make their own choices and decisions, and to live with the consequences of their actions. In individualistic cultures children are expected to be self-supporting by the age of 18 or 20 and to live independently of their parents (Chaney & Martin, 2004).

People from collectivistic cultures, such as Japan and China, place emphasis on the group rather than on the individual. The Japanese proverb, "The nail that sticks up gets knocked down," expresses the belief that no one should stand out from the group—that the group is more important. People from collectivistic cultures place greater importance on conforming to one's family, including respecting parents' opinions, than do people from individualistic cultures (Gudykunst, 2004).

Masculine-Feminine Cultures

Masculine cultures, according to Hofstede (1991), are "societies in which social gender roles are clearly distinct (namely, men are supposed to be assertive, tough, and focused on material success, whereas women are supposed to be more modest, tender, and concerned with the quality of life)" (p. 82). Characteristics of cultures that are primarily masculine include an emphasis on achievements, economic growth, and business performance; sex roles are complementary; and people live to work. Examples of masculine cultures include Japan, Austria, and Venezuela.

Feminine cultures are "societies in which social gender roles overlap (i.e., both men and women are supposed to be modest, tender, and concerned with the quality of life)" (Hofstede, 1991, pp. 82-83). In cultures that are primarily feminine, sex roles are flexible and people work to live; the emphasis is on the surroundings and on nurturing over achievements. Examples of feminine cultures are Sweden, Norway, and the Netherlands. According to Hofstede's (1991) study of 50 countries and three regions, the United States ranked fifteenth on masculinity.

Low- and High-Context Communication

Low-context communication, according to Ting-Toomey (1999), "refers to communication patterns of direct verbal mode, straight talk, nonverbal immediacy, and sender-oriented value" (p. 209). In low-context communication, people state what they expect or want; they prefer that people be very direct. On the other hand, high-context communication "refers to communication patterns of indirect verbal mode, ambiguous talk, nonverbal subtleties, and interpreter-sensitive value" (Ting-Toomey, 1999, p. 209). In high-context communication, nonverbal aspects of the message are important. One must be able to read between the lines to understand the intended meaning of a message. Stated succinctly, high-context communication is indirect and nonverbal; low-context communication is direct and verbal. When there is perceived incongruence between the verbal and nonverbal message in both low- and high-context cultures, nonverbal signals are more likely to be believed. Cultures that are collectivistic, such as the Japanese, tend to use high-context communication, while individualistic cultures, such as Americans in the United States, generally use low-context communication (Chaney & Martin, 2004).

Truth and Trust

Cultural variations exist in what is considered truth. Truth, in the United States, comes from objective observations; it must be verifiable. Statistics are often used to support or establish something as fact. Other cultures, though, have different conceptions of truth. While U.S. persons use objective facts, in many other cultures they may rely on religious beliefs or subjective opinions to determine what is considered truth. In Latin American countries, the Catholic Church is looked to as a source of truth; likewise, in Middle Eastern countries religion is a main source of truth, and objective facts would not overrule their religion. In countries such as China, however, the source of truth is the Chinese people's faith in the governmental party (Samovar & Porter, 2001).

Trust can also be an issue in interactions with other cultures, especially during negotiations. Trust can be based on mutual respect and friendship. Adhering to conditions of a written contract when negotiating with other countries can also be a basis for trust. The United States is considered a high-trust culture in its business transactions, while China, Hong Kong, Taiwan, France, and Italy are considered low-trust cultures. High-trust cultures have had better success in creating large organizations, while low-trust cultures, which have difficulty trusting people who are not related to them, tend to have more small family businesses. When considering cultural differences, truth and trust must be included as factors in interactions with people of other cultures (Samovar & Porter, 2001).

Perceptions and Attributions

Perceptions, which occur unconsciously, involve one's "awareness of what is taking place in the environment" (Gudykunst, 2004, p. 159). People constantly form judgments about the intentions and motives of persons from other cultures when interacting with them. Stereotypes of people from other cultures have an impact upon how the other person is perceived. These perceptions vary based on gender, experience, ethnicity, and culture. Perceptions are usually biased based on experiences, moods, and emotional states, as well as on expectations. Perceptions of others, often formed on such nonverbal cues as facial expressions and manner of speaking, may include that a certain person is an extrovert or is emotionally unstable; such perceptions are often accurate unless they are biased. These biases can be overcome by looking for exceptions and becoming consciously aware that previously held stereotypes of others may lead to inaccurate assumptions and explanations of the behaviors of others (Gudykunst, 2004).

Attribution is "the ability to look at social behavior from another culture's view" (Chaney & Martin, 2004, p. 49). Individual attributions involve comparing one person's behavior with others and trying to determine the extent to which a consensus exists when examining the object of the behavior as well as the context of the behavior. When the behavior of strangers is consistent with stereotypes, people tend to attribute their behavior to their culture or ethnicity, but when the behavior of strangers is inconsistent with stereotypes, attributions are based on person-based characteristics such as their personalities (Gudykunst, 2004).

The ability to perceive emotions, respond to the emotion, cognitively understand and reason about the emotion, and consciously control one's response to another person's emotions is called emotional intelligence, practical intelligence, or common sense (Mayer, Salovey, & Caruso, 2000). Goleman (1995) made the theory of emotional intelligence famous by interpreting it for the business world. The important concept about emotional intelligence is that it can be learned, but some people have a higher affinity for learning emotional intelligence, just as some people have higher intelligence quotients than others (Lane, 2000). Because one's perceptive abilities are used to recognize the meaning behind people's emotions, a person could also use emotional intelligence to perceive cultural differences, thus allowing one to develop cultural intelligence about a culture that is different from one's native culture.

Identifying cultural differences involves examining ethnicity, as well as whether the culture is individualistic or collectivistic, masculine or feminine, or low- or high-context. In addition, an examination of cultural variations in how truth is perceived, as well as how perceptions vary can be useful in identifying cultural differences. People often differ in their ability to recognize differences due to their emotional competencies.

DEVELOPING STRATEGIES FOR MINIMIZING CULTURAL DIFFERENCES

When people live in another culture for an extended period of time, they have choices to make concerning how much of the new culture they are going to accept and to what extent the new culture will override, complement, or be rejected based on values and behaviors of the home culture.

Enculturation

When one grows up in a culture, he or she learns how to understand people through what is said and done. This socialization process is called enculturation, or how people learn their own culture. Enculturation happens through interaction, observation, and imitation of events. Some cultures are more open than others, and individuals differ considerably within cultures. In many Arab cultures it would be considered rude to ask about someone's wife and children; in Mexico, however, people are expected to learn about each other's families (Chaney & Martin, 2004).

Adaptation

These three dimensions influence adaptation: language differences, physical differences, and psychological differences between the native culture and the new culture (Borden, 1991). Normally when people enter a new culture, they do not want to abandon their past; therefore, they acculturate the ideas from the new culture into their old culture. If people from different cultures assimilate a significant number of cultural traits from each other, they will develop a cultural synergy and create a stronger overriding culture that is merged from the two separate cultures. Corporate cultures are often a synergy of different cultures. People who grow up with more than one culture are generally more multicultural (Chaney & Martin, 2004) and have an advantage in the workplace. They are qualified to fill positions that involve interacting with persons from varied backgrounds—jobs such as those in law enforcement, health care, or travel.

According to Hall (as cited in Samovar & Porter, 2001), when people "touch a culture in one place, everything else is affected" (p. 45). For example, the civil rights movement in the United States changed many U.S. attitudes, values, and behaviors, such as housing patterns, work discrimination, service discrimination, education systems, and the legal system. When people reach past their own cultural characteristics, they decide whether they can adapt and have a foot in two different worlds, or whether they will maintain their cultural characteristics and not adapt (Samovar & Porter, 2001).

The challenges of adaptation include ethnocentrism (the belief that one's own cultural background is correct), language differences, acquisition of knowledge about the host culture, and immersion in the host culture. The simple acts of learning about oneself, learning a few words in the host culture's language, and researching the host culture are important before going to live in that culture. Once in the host culture, one needs to listen, observe, and interact in order to learn the rituals of the culture (Samovar & Porter, 2001).

Acculturation

When entering a new culture, the person has to make adjustments and adapt to it; this is called acculturation. Acculturation is necessary because culture is habitual, and people tend to dislike change. While acculturation generally happens between a dominant culture and one that is not as dominant in the world, either culture can borrow from the other. When one culture borrows something from another culture, it is called diffusion (Samovar & Porter, 2001). Cultures in general resist major alterations. The French, for example, try to place limits on allowing words from other languages to be brought into their language because they want to keep their language pure and free of such diffusion.

The four strategies of acculturation are assimilation, integration, separation, and deculturation. Depending on people's needs and how similar or dissimilar the new culture is to their native culture, they will unconsciously choose one of these dimensions in order to be psychologically balanced and live happily in the second culture (Alkhazraji, 1997; Berry, 1983). Alkhazraji's (1997) study of Muslims in the United States showed that they tended to prefer separation or integration (i.e., part separation, part assimilation) as their acculturation mode. Many could change their work culture but not their home culture because of their strong religious values and beliefs.

Assimilation occurs when a person completely accepts the new culture as his or her culture and replaces the old culture with the new culture (Berry, 1983). Alkhazraji (1997) found that Muslims who were willing to assimilate tended to have college or graduate degrees, saw more professional opportunity in the United States, and often felt that the Islamic work culture was not correctly implemented in their own country.

Integration occurs when the person becomes an integral part of the new culture, perhaps through working and sending their children to public schools; however, they keep their cultural integrity at home (Berry, 1983). Alkhazraji (1997) found that while the participants were willing to accept U.S. organizational cultures, certain values of their native culture were sufficiently important to Muslims to retain, such as stopping work to pray.

Separation happens when people maintain their native culture in all aspects without becoming involved in the new culture (Berry, 1983). The Muslims participating in Alkhazraji's (1997) study who chose separation were U.S. born, highly religious, and did not perceive the discrepancy between their beliefs and the majority. They chose to maintain their ethnic identity and traditions and made no attempt to establish a relation-ship with the dominant system.

Deculturation happens when persons do not accept the new culture but lose their original culture in the process (Berry, 1983). In Alkhazraji's (1997) study, deculturation was the second most common mode of acculturation chosen. These Muslims were a mixture of U.S. and non-U.S. born respondents who varied in their religiosity. A great deal of acculturative stress occurred within this group. It was hypothesized that this group may be discriminated against, which delays assimilation.

In summary, strategies to minimize cultural differences include enculturation, adapta-tion, and acculturation. The person's interaction with the dominant culture and his or her personal needs determine which strategy the person will choose.

EXPLORING CULTURAL PROGRAMMING

After cultural differences are identified and strategies are developed for minimizing these differences, an examination should be made of one's own cultural programming. The process of exploring one's cultural programming involves examining a) stereotypes of people of other cultures, ethnocentric attitudes, and cultural mindsets; b) norms, rules, roles, and networks that influence encoding and decoding of messages; c) subcultures and subgroups; and d) public and private self.

Stereotypes

Stereotypes are "perceptions about certain groups of people or nationalities" (Chaney & Martin, 2004, p. 6). These stereotypes are sometimes based on limited exposure or observations and can be positive or negative, accurate or inaccurate. People make stereotypical statements that apply to an entire group without taking into account individual differences. For example, a positive stereotype of U.S. persons is that they are generous; a negative stereotype of U.S. individuals is that they are impatient (Axtell, 1994). Further, variations in stereotypical behavior can be seen between one region of a country and another. Thus, making generalizations about groups of people can be unwise, since there will always be some people who simply do not fit the stereotypical mold others may hold of their culture. Another consideration is that a person's behavior may vary based on the situation and circumstances (Thiederman, 1991).

Stereotypes also exist for persons of other cultures. When Axtell (1994) asked U.S. persons who conduct business with people of other countries to provide one-word descriptors of people of various cultures based on their experiences, their descriptions were both positive and negative. The British, for example, were perceived as polite, reserved, and formal; the French were viewed as arrogant, rude, and gourmet; Italians were described as emotional, demonstrative, and talkative; and Asians were viewed as polite, intelligent, and xenophobic (possessing a fear of strangers/foreigners). Applying such stereotypes to all persons of a particular culture is unwise, as such perceptions can have a negative impact on the ability to view persons as individuals rather than as members of a cultural group.

Ethnocentrism, Cultural Relativism, and Mindsets

Ethnocentrism is the belief that one's own culture or group is superior to that of others. Ethnocentrists believe that their values, customs, and language are correct and those of other cultures or groups are incorrect or, at the very least, quaint. Some ethnocentrism is natural and unavoidable; most people prefer their own culture and their own behaviors and tend to evaluate others based on a self-referential criterion, or on what they already know (Gudykunst, 2004; Thiederman, 1991).

Cultural relativism is the opposite of ethnocentrism. According to Gudykunst (2004), "Cultural relativism involves trying to understand strangers' behaviors in the context of the cultures or groups of strangers engaging in the behaviors" (p. 131). People have difficulty understanding the behavior of strangers when using their own ethnic frames of reference. The higher one's level of ethnocentricity, the greater the anxiety level when interacting with strangers and the greater the difficulty in accurately predicting and explaining the behavior of strangers. People who are culturally relative, on the other hand, attempt to understand strangers' behaviors from the other's perspective and can usually predict and explain more accurately the behaviors of strangers (Gudykunst, 2004).

Ethnocentrism has been referred to as one type of "mindset" (Fisher, 1997). Mindsets, according to Chaney and Martin (2004), are "ways of being that allow us to see, perceive, and reason through our own cultural awareness" (p. 9). Since people learn through cultural upbringing to be either open-minded or close-minded to the mores of other cultures, people can alter their mindsets to become more accepting of the values and beliefs of people of other cultures. U.S. mindsets include the idea that the United States is a superior nation. This sense of superiority is evidenced by the way U.S. persons use the term *American* to mean people of the United States, when in reality, people of North, South, and Central America are also Americans.

Norms, Rules, Roles, and Networks
Norms, rules, roles, and networks are situational factors that influence encoding and decoding of messages within a culture. "Norms are culturally ingrained principles of correct and incorrect behaviors that, if broken, carry a form of overt or covert penalty" (Chaney & Martin, 2004, p. 10). Norms reflect moral and ethical principles that provide guidelines for how people should behave (Gudykunst, 2004). In contrast, rules do not have a basis in morality; they are statements of expected behaviors formed to clarify cloudy areas and the consequences of failing to follow the guidelines. A role includes behavioral expectations that accompany a position in a group (Gudykunst & Ting-Toomey, 1988). Roles are, of course, affected by norms and rules. Networks involve an exchange of assistance; they are formed on the bases of friendship, similar interests, and the need to belong. These networks are actually subgroups. Since in many cultures people prefer to conduct business with those they know, developing networks is important for doing business in multicultural environments.

Subcultures and Subgroups
Subcultures are "collections of people who possess conscious membership in identifi-able units of an encompassing, larger cultural unit" (Klopf, 1997, p. 36). They have traits that set them apart from the dominant culture, or macroculture. The U.S. macroculture, which comprises 75% of the population, is made up of people of European, Latin American, and Middle Eastern origin. The largest U.S. subcultures include people of African descent (about 12% of the population) and people of Asian descent (almost 4% of the population) (*CultureGrams 2004: USA*, 2003). In addition to ethnicity and race, subcultures in the United States may be categorized by age, religion, and sexual prefer-ences. The term *subcultures* may also be used to refer to a city, a university, or a business. To meet the definition of a subculture, three criteria should be met: First, the group members are self-identifiable; that is, group members wish to be considered a part of the group. Second, group members exhibit behavior that is characteristic of the group. Third, the dominant culture recognizes the smaller group as a subculture and has given it

a name; e.g., university freshmen (Klopf, 1997). A term used more recently for subcultures is "cocultures," because of the possible implication that members of subcultures or nondominant groups are inadequate or perhaps inferior (Samovar & Porter, 2001).

Subgroups, while part of the macroculture, "are groups with whom the macroculture does not agree and with whom it has problems communicating" (Chaney & Martin, 2004, p. 11). Communication difficulties arise from the fact that the communication style of persons in subgroups is quite different from that of the dominant culture. Prostitutes, youth gangs, and prison populations are examples of subgroups. The vocabularies of members of the subgroups, referred to as "cant," make it difficult for members of the macroculture and subcultures to understand the intended meanings of the words used by subgroups (Samovar & Porter, 2001).

Public and Private Self

Cultural differences exist with respect to the extent to which people are willing to share information with others. Information related to the public self typically includes discussions about work and political and social issues. Information related to one's private self includes such topics as marital status, sexual preference, and criminal record (Chaney & Martin, 2004).

One depiction of a person's inner self is the Johari Window, named for its creators, Joseph and Harrington (Luft, 1984). The four windowpanes are labeled arena, blind spot, hidden, and unknown. The arena represents information that is known to the person and to others; it is information a person is willing to share. A person with a large arena pane is willing to share more information than one with a small arena pane. The second pane represents the person's blind spot; this is information known to others but not to oneself. The third pane represents information that is hidden; this is information known to the person but not known by others. The fourth pane represents what is unknown by others and by oneself.

The Johari Window can be translated into one's public self and private self. In the Japanese culture, for example, the public self is rather small while the private self is large. In the United States, people exhibit a larger public self and a small private self. Because U.S. persons have a larger public self, people of other cultures have said that U.S. persons are too explicit, too outgoing, and too friendly. People of the United States are more inclined to reveal their feelings and express their opinions than are people from Asian cultures. Even within a culture, however, people vary in the degree to which they are willing to share information with outsiders (Barnlund, 1989).

Cultural Programming Theories

Four theories of how mindful intercultural communication develops have been advanced as follows: uncertainty reduction theory, expectancy violations theory, systems theory, and identity negotiation theory.

Uncertainty reduction theory is a cognitive response to lessen the anxiety that people experience when communicating with people whose culture is different from their own. As one learns more about a culture or an individual within the culture, the less uncertainty and anxiety are a problem. The problem occurs when anxiety is higher than is comfortable because one might become panicked and unable to accurately interpret or predict another person's behavior (Gudykunst, 2004). Hofstede (1991) found that people with weak uncertainty avoidance find it easier to overlook differences between themselves and people from a different culture. However, people with strong uncertainty avoidance would want to specialize, would prefer clear instructions, and would want to avoid conflict and competition.

Expectancy violation theory (EVT) approaches intercultural communication from the standpoint that it is important to understand one's own and the other person's expectancies and cultural boundaries. One's expectancies are learned, socially normative behaviors for the community in which one lives. As a person has more interaction with another culture, he/she will shift from a reliance on learned data to an emphasis on psychological data that has been learned through intercultural interactions. Deviant behavior is tolerated more in low uncertainty avoidance cultures and less in high uncertainty avoidance cultures. Because behavior that is unexpected is novel, it causes people to process the information from the behavior more finely. Because intercultural communication interactions are heterogeneous in nature, they will be more prone to violation of what is expected. These differences often end in misunderstandings and unclear communication (Burgoon, 1995).

Systems theory, based on Kim's research (2001), uses a systems approach to look at the interface between the host culture and the home culture on a newcomer's ability to adapt to a new culture. She sees adaptation not as a distinct phenomenon, but as an everyday activity of all people to fit into the environment in which they live. Adaptation is considered a psychic evolution process between change and stability. The more one adapts to the new environment, the smaller the severity of the fluctuation between change and stability becomes. Systems theory considers adaptation a problem to be solved through education and growth within the community. The system revolves around the idea of a person's cultivating an adaptive personality.

Identity negotiation theory is based on understanding identity security and its vulnerability in intercultural encounters. The three tenets of this approach to intercultural communication are that people bring their identity (culture) to all communication encounters, that people must understand and be able to perceive the cultural norms that are endorsed and considered critical by another culture, and that with identity security one becomes vulnerable when interacting with someone in another culture. This theory considers the wants and needs of the individual and is an integrative theory drawing on research in social psychology, sociology, and communication (Ting-Toomey, 1999).

In summary, an exploration of cultural programming involves examining stereotypes of people of other cultures; of ethnocentric attitudes and cultural mindsets; of norms, rules, roles, and networks that influence communication; of subcultures and subgroups; and of public and private self. In addition, cultural programming theories provide an understanding of how intercultural communication develops.

USING RESOURCES THAT PROMOTE CULTURAL UNDERSTANDING

Resource materials that are available for those interested in bridging cultural differences include electronic media, experiential activities and simulations, reference books, and Web sites.

Electronic Media

Videos can be used effectively to supplement lectures and to add interest to class discussions. Examples of videos currently available are the following:

- *Working with Japan* (1992), a six-part series covering preparation, negotiation, business entertaining, women in business, and managing the relationship. Available from Big World Media.

- *Doing Business in Asia* (1990), four videocassettes, each containing a case study on Japan, Hong Kong, Taiwan, and South Korea. Originally prepared by Northwest Airlines, these videos are now available from Big World Media.

- *Doing Business in Latin America* (1997), a series of videos on the countries of Argentina, Brazil, Chile, and Mexico. Available from Big World Media.

- *Doing Business in Southeast Asia* (1998), a series of videos on the countries of Malaysia, Singapore, and Indonesia. Available from Big World Media. (A booklet describing other videos available from Big World Media may be secured from www.bigworldmedia.com.)

- *Cultural Diversity* (1992), deals with ethnic and cultural diversity in the workplace – with a focus on French and U.S. employees. Available from Intercultural Press.

Experiential Activities and Simulations

Activities related to understanding cultural differences that would be useful for trainers and educators include Stringer and Cassiday's (2003) *52 Activities for Exploring Values Differences,* Seelye's (1996) *Experiential Activities for Intercultural Learning, Vol. 1,* both available from Intercultural Press, and Gannon's (2000) *Working Across Cultures: Applications and Exercises.*

Simulations include *BaFa BaFa* (explores the impact of culture on perception, behavior, and attributions), available from Simulation Training Systems; *Barnga* (a simulation game on cultural clashes and cultural shock), available from Intercultural Press; *Ecotonos* (a multicultural problem-solving simulation), available from Intercultural Press; and *Cocktail Party Simulation* (a multicultural simulation) described by Jameson (1993).

Reference Books

Numerous reference books related to cultural differences are available. Books related to intercultural business communication include books by Axtell, Bosrock, Sabath, and Turkington. Roger Axtell's books—*Do's and Taboos Around the World* (1993); *Gestures: Do's and Taboos of Body Language Around the World* (1998); and *Do's and Taboos of International Trade* (1994)—include country-specific information presented in a concise format. The series of books by Mary M. Bosrock – *Put Your Best Foot Forward* covers Asia (1994), Canada/Mexico (1995), Europe (1995), and South America (1997); the books present general rules applying to all countries (body language, dining, dress, and punctuality) and country-specific information. The three books by Ann Marie Sabath on *International Business Etiquette* that cover Asia and the Pacific Rim (1999); Europe (1999); and Latin America (2000) contain country-specific information on such topics as greetings, business cards, dress, entertaining, gestures, and gift giving, as well as information on currency, holidays, language, and religion. In addition, Carol Turkington's *The Complete Idiot's Guide to Cultural Etiquette* (1999) contains country-specific information on numerous etiquette topics, including dress, gestures, dining, punctuality, and greetings. *CultureGrams 2004* (2003) published by Axiom Press provides four-page summaries of over 175 countries and covers information about the people, their customs and courtesies, and their lifestyle, as well as background information (history, government, economy, education, etc.). Books addressing cultural differences in general include William Gudykunst's (2004) *Bridging Differences*, Philip Harris and Robert Moran's (2000) *Managing Cultural Differences*, and Stella Ting-Toomey's (1999) *Communicating Across Cultures*. Educators and trainers may wish to consult Robert Moran and David Braaten's (1996) *International Directory of Multicultural Resources* for lists of consulting and training companies, organizations, publications, learning aids, and publishers with a multicultural focus.

Web Sites

Numerous Web sites are available and may be accessed by searching on "intercultural communication" using one of the search engines. Some sites related to bridging cultural differences that may be beneficial include the following:

- SIETAR (www.sietarhouston.org) is a professional association of intercultural consultants and researchers.

- The Interchange Institute (www.interchangeinstitute.org), 11 Hawes Street, Brookline, MA 02446, produces a *Newcomer's Almanac* on a monthly basis for people who have recently moved to the U.S.; it is distributed by e-mail.

- George Simons International (www.diversophy.com) is an intercultural research, consulting, and training company; the firm also develops intercultural education tools.

- IPR (www.iprconsulting.com) is a U.S. consulting firm that works with U.S. businesspeople going abroad and foreign businesspeople coming to the United States.

- Trompenaars Hampden-Turner (www.7d-culture.com) is a consulting firm for international business travelers.

In summary, the preceding resources that include electronic media, experiential activities and simulations, reference books, and Web sites are only a few of the numerous resources teachers may use to promote cultural understanding. In addition, consultants are available in most countries; they will work with people moving to or from their country.

SUMMARY

People who are successful in international encounters first attempt to identify cultural differences, such as ethnicity, individualism/collectivism, masculinity/femininity, low- and high-context communication, truth and trust, and perceptions and attributions, and then develop strategies to minimize these differences. Strategies that have been identified that people use when adjusting to another culture include enculturation, adaptation, and acculturation. Within acculturation the four strategies that may be used are assimilation, integration, separation, and deculturation. These four strategies range from completely discarding one's native culture, to completely accepting the new culture, to not accepting either the old culture or the new culture.

Persons who are successful interculturally avoid relying on cultural stereotypes; rather, they approach people from other cultures as individuals first. Successful intercultural communication involves knowing the ethnocentrisms of persons in other cultures. Understanding the mindsets of both oneself and the person of another culture will result in more efficient communication. In addition, learning about the norms, rules, roles, and networks within the culture, as well as about subcultures and subgroups, is important to intercultural interactions. Learning what is considered public or private information will also help determine what subjects can be discussed and what subjects should be avoided during conversations.

Theories for developing intercultural communication capabilities include uncertainty reduction theory, expectancy violation theory, systems theory, and identity negotiation theory. These theories are useful to an understanding of intercultural communication development.

Visitors to other countries should always keep in mind that it is generally the responsibility of the visitor to another culture to adjust to the values and behaviors of the people in the host culture. The well-known adage, "When in Rome, do as the Romans," still applies when visiting other countries. Heeding this advice and respecting the values of persons in other cultures will go a long way toward bridging cultural differences.

REFERENCES

Alkhazraji, K. M. (1997). *Immigrants and cultural adaptation in the American workplace: A study of Muslim employees.* New York: Garland.

Axtell, R. E. (1993). *Do's and taboos around the world.* New York: John Wiley.

Axtell, R. E. (1994). *The do's and taboos of international trade.* New York: John Wiley.

Axtell, R. E. (1998). *Gestures: Do's and taboos of body language around the world.* New York: John Wiley.

Barnlund, D. C. (1989). *Public and private self in Japan and the United States.* Yarmouth, ME: Intercultural Press.

Berry, J. W. (1983). Acculturation: A comparative analysis of alternative forms. In R. J. Samuda, & S. L. Woods (Eds.), *Perspectives in immigrant and minority education* (pp. 66-77). Lanham, MD: University Press of America.

Borden, G. A. (1991). *Cultural orientation: An approach to understanding intercultural communication.* Englewood Cliffs, NJ: Prentice Hall.

Bosrock, M. M. (1994). *Put your best foot forward: Asia.* St. Paul, MN: International Education Systems.

Bosrock, M. M. (1995). *Put your best foot forward: Canada/Mexico.* St. Paul, MN: International Education Systems.

Bosrock, M. M. (1995). *Put your best foot forward: Europe.* St. Paul, MN: International Education Systems.

Bosrock, M. M. (1997). *Put your best foot forward: South America.* St. Paul, MN: International Education Systems.

Bull HN Information Systems. (1992). *Cultural diversity.* Yarmouth, ME: Intercultural Press.

Burgoon, J. (1995). Cross-cultural and intercultural applications of expectancy violations theory. In R. Wiseman (Ed.), *Intercultural communication theory* (pp. 194-214). Thousand Oaks, CA: Sage.

Chaney, L. H., & Martin, J. S. (2004). *Intercultural business communication* (3rd ed.). Upper Saddle River, NJ: Prentice Hall.

CultureGrams 2004. (2003). Lindon, UT: Axiom Press.

Doing business in Asia [video series]. (1990). Boulder, CO: Big World Media.

Doing business in Latin America [video series]. (1997). Boulder, CO: Big World Media.

Doing business in Southeast Asia [video series]. (1998). Boulder, CO: Big World Media.

Fisher, G. (1997). *Mindsets* (2nd ed.). Yarmouth, ME: Intercultural Press.

Gannon, M. J. (2000). *Working across cultures: Applications and exercises.* Thousand Oaks, CA: Sage.

Goleman, D. (1995). *Emotional intelligence.* New York: Bantam Books.

Gudykunst, W. B. (2004). *Bridging differences* (4th ed.). Thousand Oaks, CA: Sage.

Gudykunst, W. B., & Ting-Toomey, S. (1988). *Culture and interpersonal communication.* Newbury Park, CA: Sage.

Harris, P. R., & Moran, R. T. (2000). *Managing cultural differences* (5th ed.). Houston, TX: Gulf Publishing Co.

Hofstede, G. (1991). *Cultures and organizations.* London: McGraw-Hill.

Jameson, D. A. (1993). Using a simulation to teach intercultural communication business communication courses. *The Bulletin of the Association for Business Communication, 56*(1), 3-11.

Kim, Y. Y. (2001). *Communication and cross-cultural adaptation: An integrative theory.* Clevedon, UK: Multilingual Matters.

Klopf, D. W. (1997). *Intercultural encounters* (3rd ed.). Englewood, CO: Morton.

Lane, R. D. (2000). Levels of emotional awareness: Neurological, psychological, and social perspectives. In R. Bar-On & J. D.A. Parker (Eds.), *The handbook of emotional intelligence* (pp. 171-191). San Francisco: Jossey-Bass.

Luft, J. (1984). *Group processes: An introduction to group dynamics.* Palo Alto, CA: Mayfield.

Mayer, J. D., Salovey, P., & Caruso, D. (2000). Emotional intelligence. In R. J. Sternberg (Ed.), *Handbook of intelligence* (2nd ed.) (pp. 396-421). New York: Cambridge University Press.

Moran, R. T., & Braaten, D. O. (Eds.). (1996). *International directory of multicultural resources.* Houston, TX: Gulf Publishing Co.

Sabath, A. M. (1999). *International business etiquette: Asia & the Pacific Rim.* Franklin Lakes, NJ: Career Press.

Sabath, A. M. (1999). *International business etiquette: Europe.* Franklin Lakes, NJ: Career Press.

Sabath, A. M. (2000). *International business etiquette: Latin America.* Franklin Lakes, NJ: Career Press.

Samovar, L. A., & Porter, R. E. (2001). *Communication between cultures* (4th ed.). Belmont, CA: Wadsworth/Thomson Learning.

Saphiere, D. H. (1997). *Ecotonos: A multicultural problem-solving simulation* (2nd ed.). Yarmouth, ME: Intercultural Press.

Seelye, H. N. (Ed.). (1996). *Experiential activities for intercultural learning,* Vol. 1. Yarmouth, ME: Intercultural Press.

Shirts, R. G. (1974). *BaFa BaFa.* Del Mar, CA: Simulation Training Systems.

Stringer, D. M., & Cassiday, P. A. (2003). *52 activities for exploring values differences.* Yarmouth, ME: Intercultural Press.

Thiagarajan, S., & Steinwachs, B. (1990). *Barnga: A simulation game on cultural clashes.* Yarmouth, ME: Intercultural Press.

Thiederman, S. (1991). *Bridging cultural barriers for corporate success.* New York: Lexington Books.

Ting-Toomey, S. (1999). *Communicating across cultures.* New York: The Guilford Press.

Turkington, C. (1999). *The complete idiot's guide to cultural etiquette.* Indianapolis, IN: Macmillan.

Working with Japan [video series]. (1992). Boulder, CO: Big World Media.

Yinger, M. (1994). *Ethnicity.* Albany, NY: State University of New York Press.

Culture Shock and Reverse Culture Shock: Developing Coping Skills

Roberta H. Krapels
University of Mississippi
Oxford, Mississippi

Barbara D. Davis
University of Memphis
Memphis, Tennessee

Today's global society challenges individuals as they confront the differences in another country's social and work environment as an expatriate employee, a student, or a short-term traveler. Discrepancies between how one gets along "at home" and how one interacts in the new country result in culture shock, a dissonance between what one is accustomed to and what one confronts in the new culture (Kim, 2001; Marx, 2001; Ward, Bochner, & Furnham, 2001). The lack of social reality as one has previously known it creates circumstances for which no behavioral norms exist mentally. Aspects of culture shock addressed in this chapter will include examining the constructs in cross-cultural interactions, identifying personal characteristics associated with the impact of cultural shock, and discussing external factors affecting adaptation within the new environment. Several resources for teachers to help students understand culture shock will be provided. Classroom activities simulating culture shock can assist teachers in making students more conscious of their own culture and of differences between their culture and others.

EXAMINING CROSS-CULTURAL ORIENTATION

Through normal growth and development, members of a culture experience a natural process of indoctrination or *enculturation*. By comprising of a set of values, norms, rules, and assumptions, culture establishes a comfort zone for individual attitudes and behavior. People essentially know who they are, what is expected of them, and where and how they belong. A sense of equilibrium exists in interpreting and handling the social and psychological precepts present in their environment (Black, Gregersen, &

Mendenhall, 1992; Kim, 2001; Ward, et al., 2001). However, their comfort zone often becomes decidedly uncomfortable if they venture beyond those cultural parameters to interact and function in another culture having different societal markers. Most cultural phenomena are obvious—day-to-day activities that are observable; however, inferred principles that are understood by members of that culture generally organize the accepted behaviors within a society (Kim, 2001; Ward, et al., 2001). Outsiders lack this basic knowledge and often view the foreign culture's actions as odd or "bad," a perception resulting from ethnocentric (my way is the best way) attitudes.

Phenomena of Initial Cross-Cultural Experiences

Since the characterization of culture involves many intangible factors, individuals initially experience dissonance during the transition from one culture to another. The strength of that dissonance is often related to the degree of difference between the home and host country cultures (Ward, et al., 2001). This situation could be viewed as a type of mental disconnect that occurs when individuals try to maintain their sense of equilibrium as they explain away the contrasts and try to force-fit situations into their personal cultural inventory. However, tangible factors (dress, behavior, language, food, etc.) serve as catalysts that prompt individuals to acknowledge the need for some level of change (Black et al., 1992).

While culture shock does happen with domestic adjustments among and between cocultures (Pedersen, 1995), it takes on more complex, problematic dimensions when experienced as a result of living in a new culture and examined from a global perspective. In developing a theory of adaptation, Kim (2001) discusses the commonalities faced by every person who goes to a foreign country to live or to work. Differences lie in the " . . . recognition of verbal and nonverbal codes and interpretation of the hidden assumptions underlying them . . ." (p. 5). For example, a gesture may have a new meaning resulting in embarrassment or discomfort. These differences create a major life event that results in stress (Marx, 2001; Ward et al., 2001). Then, as Black et al. (1992) state, adjusting to the new culture requires "developing new mental road maps and behaviors" (p. 115). As one adapts, the accepted behaviors within the new cultural environment become his or her understood behavioral norms—lowering the stress levels.

Culture Shock

Interacting and functioning in one's own culture is effortless in comparison to performing the same actions in a different culture. This cross-cultural initiation called *culture shock* is seldom described in neutral or positive terms, but rather in negative terms such as uncertainty, unfamiliarity, disorientation, confusion, frustration, chaos, anxiety, and pain. Although the phenomenon has been defined as any emotionally disorienting situation that results from an individual being placed in an unfamiliar situation (Carey, 1999; Black et al., 1992), both Adler (2002) and Pedersen (1995) assert that positive aspects of culture shock do exist—those associated with learning, growing, and developing. One must, however, progress through the negative aspects (e.g., discomfort, pain, etc.) to reap the benefits. Adler (2002) further discusses a perception that the most ineffective sojourners experience the least adverse effects to a new environment. Thus, some sojourners to foreign countries may manifest little evidence of culture shock, either due to an unwillingness to become involved in the new environment or a lack of interest in adapting and getting to know host country nationals. Because culture shock is very subjective in relation to impact, duration, and symptoms (Carey, 1999; Pedersen, 1995), researchers report that it typically takes a period of three to nine months to progress through the stages of the phenomena (Adler, 2002; Carey, 1999). Most authors divide the transforming periods within culture shock into four or five segments.

The first stage is often termed *honeymoon* because of the initial excitement of discovery while becoming oriented to a new environment. Individuals could have unreasonable expectations, be tremendously naïve, and try to absorb too much during this phase, which often is short-lived, typically only a few weeks. In the second stage anxiety is evident. Carey (1999) calls this stage *trepidation*, while some authors like Marx (2001) refer to it more seriously as the period of crisis and change. During this stage individuals take note of the specific nuances of the host culture, encountering varying degrees of difficulty trying to function successfully in their interactions. A gambit of behaviors from homesickness, irritation, anger, confusion, resentment, helplessness, and depression, to feelings of superiority or inferiority, may surface during this period. The typical so-journer experiences several weeks to several months of these psychological, emotional, and physical changes. The critical point for many individuals occurs between stages two and three, since stage three is characterized as the *adjustment* phase. At this point failure most often occurs for those unable to handle the transition to the new culture (Andreason, 2003; Carey, 1999). Individuals capable of successfully maneuvering through this period become more understanding and accepting within the host culture. They become more involved with and interested in forming personal alliances with host country individuals and families. Depending on the length of the cross-cultural assign-ment period, the adjustment (stage three), could last from one to three months. The last stage, *acclimation*, continues through the end of the sojourner's assignment, with cultural nuances or novelties being assessed in daily interactions. After progressing to this stage, a sense of balance occurs. Sojourners, as Black et al. (1992) imply, have reengineered, restructured, and redefined themselves, which consequently leads to new, expanded parameters of their comfort zones. Stress is reduced, and behaviors begin to feel natural in the new culture.

Culture shock begins at the point of contact with a new culture and can be graphically represented by a U-shaped curve, which indicates the positive (initial excitement as well as ending functionality) and negative aspects (period of greatest confusion during adapta-tion). When individuals are immersed in the culture at the base of the curve, the transi-tion period is usually the most traumatic; then the person becomes less stressed as new behaviors and attitudes become more natural (Adler, 2002; Pedersen, 1995).

Reverse Culture Shock

Generally, the learning curve for transitioning into another culture progresses through several stages before the transition is complete. Continuing debates on the reentry phase of culture transition focus on whether the previously theorized U-shaped curve, thought to graphically represent culture shock, should not be extended to a W-shaped curve to include the transition back to the home culture (Pedersen, 1995; Ward et al., 2001). Recognizing that cultural transitions involve adjustment swings similar to life transitions with marriage, divorce, births, and deaths provides justification to challenge the accuracy of both the U- and W-shaped theories' linear directions depicting smooth transition progressions (Kim, 2001). Within both of these transitions, sojourners experience erratic fluctuations as they cope with the effects of adapting. However, some authors list a fifth stage for the culture shock experience and refer to it as the re-entry or re-assimilation period (Carey, 1999). Other researchers consider this same occurrence as a totally new phenomenon termed *reverse culture shock* (Marx, 2001).

Individuals are often surprised when the same emotional, psychological, and physical reactions reoccur in transitioning back to their home culture. When they return to their homeland after living in a foreign country, sojourners often have difficulty readapting to their own culture. Business people find their new homeland position provides little opportunity to capitalize on the skills gained in their foreign experience, while students sometimes see themselves perceived as outsiders due to behavioral changes made abroad (Ward et al., 2001). After studying expatriate expectations upon repatriation, Stroh, Gregersen, and Black (2000) conclude that the repatriation commitment to the company depends upon the new U.S. job demands meeting the expectations of the returnee. Therefore, expatriates need realistic job previews of home country returning positions. Adler (2002) emphasizes how lax employers have been in preparing for this serious transition problem, which, during repatriation, could exactly mirror the high/low mood progressions and duration of culture shock. Some researchers feel the re-entry shock may be even more traumatic to the returning person because it involves feeling alienated and isolated from what is supposed to be the most familiar environment—the home country (Feldman & Tompson, 1993; Stroh, Gregersen, & Black, 1998).

Factors considered in selecting and preparing employees for overseas assignments (for example, predeparture training about cultural attitudes or organizational standards) are overlooked for sojourners returning to their home culture. The learning required for adjustment in a foreign culture should parallel the cultural learning required for sojourners to readjust to their home culture (Feldman & Tompson, 1993; Ward et al., 2001). This consideration is especially important when sojourners have developed a 'halo effect' about their home culture, glorifying all aspects and not acknowledging undesirable factors present in society or changes that might have occurred in their absence. Sojourners who changed during the international adaptation face friends and family who remember a different person, adding complications in what Hurn (1999) describes as " ... denial that important personal changes have taken place ... " (p. 225). After returning from lengthy assignments overseas, these individuals face personal as well as professional cultural challenges. Sojourners who successfully adapt to their host culture extend their cultural boundaries, which can alter relationships with family and friends who still function according to norms accepted prior to the international experience (Stroh et al., 2000; Ward et al., 2001). Additionally, changes in personnel, company policies and procedures, performance evaluation methods, benefits and compensation, and job responsibilities cause cultural dissonance for the returnee (O'Sullivan, 2002). Repatriation often results in the returning manager feeling unappreciated as well as underused.

The dissonance resulting from a move to a foreign country affects individuals differently, and personal stages of adaptation progress at variable rates. Culture shock is most often associated with individuals involved in global assignments for significant periods of time. However, in identifying the similar phenomenon of reverse culture shock, researchers describe the same transition process when individuals return to their home culture. For example, managers and students who have successfully coped abroad return home to find their bicultural identity unacknowledged or even resented by associates, family, and friends. Both situations involve major life changes for the individual and result in the need to identify ways to adjust successfully.

ABANDONING SELF AND DEVELOPING COPING STRATEGIES

Numerous theories attempt to explain how sojourners emerge successfully from this transforming process. The basic explanation includes the premise that sojourners sustain and endure both a conscious and unconscious loss. The loss, literally, is personal. During the most critical stages of culture shock, individuals report a sense of imbalance, lowered self-image, reduced self-confidence, separation, helplessness, and inability to adequately interpret behaviors and occurrences in their new environment. Sojourners feel analogous to being abandoned, and their feelings tend to worsen with the perception that the abandonment was self-imposed (Black et al., 1992; Pedersen, 1995; Sanchez, Spector, & Cooper, 2000).

The natural tendency to regain that which was familiar undergirds the "fight or flight" (adjust or leave) position Carey (1999) discusses. While aggressive action directed outward to some person or thing might occur, the personal, inward struggle for the sojourner is of pivotal importance. Employing appropriate coping strategies to manage the apprehension, while being receptive to new opportunities without perceiving those actions as self-betrayal, is crucial for success (Pedersen, 1995; Selmer, 1999). Meditating, exercising, writing in a journal, taking short trips home, and engaging in home-country activities in the new country are examples of ways sojourners can manage the stress while transitioning to another culture (Adler, 2002). However, Sanchez, Spector, and Cooper (2000) state that identifying the most effective behavioral methods hinges on determining if the stress associated with the cultural adjustment is symptom-focused or problem-focused. Symptom-focused and problem-focused behaviors, the two most common categories of coping strategies, seek to remedy the situation from an internal (individual or personal) or external (environment or problem) perspective, respectively (Sanchez, Spector, & Cooper, 2000; Selmer, 1999). Individuals, explains Selmer (1999), perceive an impact on an emotional level when symptom-focused strategies are employed, whereas they perceive an impact on a situational level when problem-focused strategies are used. For example, getting a fellow student to empathize after an upsetting interaction with a host country national is a symptom-focused, emotional solution, while going to the campus writing center for grammar assistance with a paper is a problem-focused solution.

Personal Traits and Abilities

Individuals react to a new culture in different ways. Katz and Seifer (1996) cite the degree of adaptability required for comfort within the particular country plus the sojourner's personal traits as major factors in the degree of discomfort with culture shock. One perspective notes that " ... as one's *experience of cultural difference* becomes more complex and sophisticated, one's potential competence in intercultural relations increases" (Hammer, Bennett, & Wiseman, 2003, p. 423). The paradox between what one has learned at home and what one experiences abroad can differ greatly. While perceptions of behavior are generally based upon prior experience, moving to a foreign country most often confounds one's idea of how and why, contradicting those preconceived ideas.

Although some individuals will fight change, others will quickly try to become more like their host country associates. The reactions of sojourners to the stress resulting from interacting with the new behaviors and expectations are greatly influenced by many factors that have an impact on cross-cultural adaptation, both psychological and sociocultural elements. The first is concerned with the individual's internal thoughts, doubts, feelings, etc., while the second deals with one's ability to master interpersonal situations in the new cultural environment. Ward et al. (2001) note that each individual's " ... behaviours, perceptions, feelings, beliefs, attitudes, and self-references" (p. 5) greatly affect intercultural interactions. In examining the literature, research identifies qualities such as self-efficacy, prior international experience, age, cross-cultural fluency, interpersonal skills, flexibility, cultural sensitivity, and adaptability as major considerations in cultural adjustment (Andreason, 2003; Black, Gregersen, & Mendenhall, 1992; Hammer, Hart & Rogan, 1998; Katz & Seifer, 1996; Selmer, 1999; Selmer, 2002; Solomon, 1994). The sojourner's success or failure in an international assignment is rooted in these basic attributes.

Self-efficacy. A positive or high self-orientation facilitates cross-cultural adjustments. Self-efficacy encompasses individuals' self-image and confidence in their ability to function successfully and adapt to a new environment. Studies, especially in relation to international learners, support this premise providing evidence that learners' attitudes about personal safety, security, strength, and self-sufficiency in a new environment are positively correlated with high self-efficacy (Myburgh, Niehaus, & Poggenpoel, 2002). That belief in one's own ability to succeed in a foreign culture greatly impacts cross-cultural success (Black et al., 1992). Biculturalism, when a person of one culture grows up in and performs successfully in the home country culture, which differs from the person's individual family culture, results in high self-efficacy. A study of bicultural success found that those bicultural individuals adapted in expatriate situations better than monocultural individuals (Bell & Harrison, 1996). Due to their belief in themselves as succeeding in both their own ethnic culture as well as their homeland culture, bicultural individuals meet the challenges with less stress and adapt quicker than monocultural individuals.

Global experience. Prior international experience is a major factor in one's ability to adjust to relocating to a foreign culture (Black et al., 1992). Individuals who have previously adjusted successfully in another culture find overcoming culture shock again less traumatic. The reason for relocation, the degree of commitment, and the age of the individual also have an impact upon one's ability to adjust (Black & Gregersen, 1991; Hammer et al., 1998; Kim, 2001). For example, students who greatly desire a graduate degree from a U.S. university, business people who are likely to have made a decision to work abroad based upon career expectations, or older more experienced sojourners generally have some preparation, resulting in greater knowledge prior to arrival in the unknown culture. However, a refugee forced to move involuntarily faces almost instant psychological and personal loss without prior preparation. Each will learn from experiences in the new environment, becoming more comfortable as the nuances of the host country culture are integrated into normal behaviors (Ward et al., 2001). Most individuals who have previously lived and worked in a foreign country report a greater awareness of their own individuality and other cultures' behavioral expectations, as reported by military personnel and their families who had experienced extensive tours of duty overseas (Kim, 2001). However, Ward et al. (2001) note that second or subsequent assignments to countries similar to previously known cultures result in greater ease of adjustment.

Adaptive Dimensions

Many researchers discuss multiple elements within cross-cultural adaptation. Ward et al. (2001) present an ABC model (affective, behavior, and cognition) to differentiate the components of culture shock. Marx (2001) also includes a model incorporating three areas to determine one's ability to overcome culture shock and become a successfully functioning individual within the new country. These elements include emotions (motivation, ability to deal with stress, and self-reliance), social skills and identity (communication, relationship skills, and people orientation), and thinking (expectations, sensitivity to different cultures, and adaptability). To cope, sojourners' behaviors that result in successfully overcoming culture shock tend to be directed toward two perspectives, emotional and situational. Comparatively, the coping strategies previously referred to by Selmer (1999) as symptom-focused or problem-focused often include three approaches to dealing with the stress of adjusting to the unfamiliar: anticipatory, psychological, and sociocultural.

Anticipatory adjustments. Greater congruence between expected differences and similarities of the two cultures and what is actually experienced upon arrival tends to improve one's ability to adjust. When the overlap occurs between what is expected and what actually happens, psychological uncertainty is reduced (Selmer, 1999), and an individual's sense of well-being is confirmed. Black, Mendenhall, and Oddou (1991) propose that both individual and organizational factors determine the importance of predeparture knowledge upon expatriates' adjustment in foreign countries. Black et al. (1992) further assert that making considerable allowances for cognitive dissonance, selectively directing any adjustments to appropriate aspects of the new culture, and reevaluating preliminary adjustments to ensure they are correctly aligned within the new culture are fundamental to "in-country adjustment" (p. 123). Avoiding continued eye contact with the elderly in Japan, for example, could be an anticipatory adjustment. If individuals are aware of this protocol before arriving in the new environment, they can make mental notes to divert eye contact with this group and accurately adjust those mental notes as well as their behavior in beginning interactions with older persons. Although cross-cultural training and previous international experience are the basis for forming accurate anticipatory expectations, the effectiveness of these factors can be compromised from both individual and organizational perspectives. Challenges such as time constraints, communication overload, significant gaps of time between previous international experiences, or dissimilar previous experiences from the current assignment can reduce the advantage for sojourners prior to the departure (Black et al., 1992). However, when one anticipates new behavioral customs based upon predeparture knowledge, the adaptation goes more smoothly.

Psychological adjustments. Individuals undergo psychological adaptation when overcoming culture shock, and the changes can include " . . . rather easily accomplished behavioral changes (e.g., ways of speaking, dressing, eating, and in one's cultural identity), or they can be more problematic, producing acculturative stress (e.g., uncertainty, anxiety, depression . . .)" (Berry, Poortinga, Segall, & Dasen, 2002, p. 352). Taking time to get to know host country individuals on a social basis can also aid the adjustment process, thereby easing the stress of culture shock, while thinking about the way things were at home tends to slow or totally disrupt the adjustment process (Selmer, 1999). Adequate assessment of behaviors when interacting with the host nationals in work situations (conditions and intensity), and nonwork environments (social and daily life experiences) generally reduces psychological uncertainty and helps individuals maintain a sense of well-being. Research supports that personality characteristics positively or negatively influence the degree of psychological adjustment. Feldman and Tompson (1993) found that " . . . psychological reappraisal (e.g., looking on the positive side of the experience . . . can positively facilitate adjustment . . .)" (p. 521). Ethnocentrism, authoritarianism, and inflexibility impede overcoming culture shock, whereas adaptability, courage, risk-taking, perceptual acuity, and extraversion facilitate it (Andreason, 2003; Sanchez, et. al., 2000; Ward, et. al., 2001). Adequate assessment of psychological adjustment is admittedly complicated because levels of satisfaction and well-being, as well as affective behavioral dimensions, are subjective; individuals will perceive situations differently (Selmer, 2002). Effective psychological adjustment is accomplished once "uncertainty reduction and adaptation produce a fit between the expatriate and the environment" (Selmer, 1999, p. 42). Being aware of the psychological effects of culture shock prepares one to address the differences in a more positive way.

Sociocultural adjustments. The attitudes of people within the host country environment affect the adaptation of newcomers. Whether the situation involves a local employee viewing the expatriate as detrimental to his or her career progress, or a student whom others in the class perceive to be receiving less critical grammatical assessment in written assignments, hostility from local people has a negative impact on sojourner adjustment (Ward, et. al, 2001). This premise supports the information by Black et al. (1992) and Adler (2002) that training should be reciprocal. Training for inpatriates, host country national employees who will interact with sojourners, as well as expatriates is needed. Additionally, Black et al. (1992) posit that expatriates should receive their most concentrated cross-cultural training shortly *after* arriving in the new environment in order to relate sociocultural differences more clearly to what is experienced. Research shows that adapting in three specific sociocultural areas is necessary for overcoming culture shock and developing successful coping strategies: adjusting to a) work or school demands, b) interpersonal situations between themselves and host country nationals, and c) differences in the everyday life activities and environment (Black et al., 1991). Each of these situations involves daily occurrences for sojourners. Due to limited transference of sociocultural skills, Selmer (2002) found a need for cross-cultural training with each expatriate posting. Expatriates who demonstrate adaptability in one culture and later accept a position in another country have reported that new cultural differences necessitate another predeparture preparation for greater adaptability (Black et al., 1991).

Support Factors

Sojourners adapt more easily with others' assistance. In a review of international student literature, Ward et al. (2001) found that educational practices such as accepted classroom behavior often create problems for foreign students. For example, in the U.S., informal conversations in learning situations are initially considered disrespectful by foreign students. However, with encouragement from host country students and from educators to challenge ideas and offer opinions, enthusiasm for the " ... active learning environment and ability to express themselves ..." (p. 157) results.

Adler (2002) notes that many expatriates who are not effective in foreign countries blame others (the company, host country associates or employees, or family members) for their lack of success. Those individuals who are successful are prepared to recognize environmental and social differences and use critical thinking and problem solving in their need to understand the differences. The ability to recognize differences and evaluate behaviors in cross-cultural situations improves, to some degree, following predeparture preparation prior to foreign assignments (Black et al., 1992). However, preparatory training is only the beginning of the organizational support needed for success abroad. Overcoming culture shock, both in the initial foreign assignment and in the return to the United States, depends greatly upon family and coworker support as well.

Organizational support. Most sources advocate predeparture preparation for cross-cultural success (Adler, 2002; Black et al., 1992; Katz & Seifer, 1996; Krapels & Chaney, 1994; O'Sullivan, 2002). Home sponsoring organizations also need to provide highly qualified individuals on the jobsite abroad, as well as the supplies and equipment needed for doing the job. For example, cell phones and laptops bought in the U.S. often need modification or replacement. Findings by Shaffer, Harrison, and Gilley (1999) indicate coworker support and logistical support have significant impact upon expatriate adjustment to the new culture. If others in the organizational environment provide mentoring (Harvey, Buckley, Novicevic, & Wiese, 1999) and supporting relationships (Andreason, 2003), the adjustment process is facilitated. Harvey et al. (1999) suggest expatriate mentoring, noting that the information exchange process develops a relationship that can be particularly important during the adjustment phase when culture shock is most evident. This mentoring relationship can provide " ... assistance in order to make sense of the culture, unfamiliar behaviors, and demands which are present in the new host environment" (p. 812). Due to the career effect on a "trailing spouse," Harvey et al. (1999) also suggest mentoring to overcome career rivalry with couples and to provide supportive, complementary behaviors at home. Organizations that introduce the traveler to other expatriates or to other foreign students in the host country assist the newcomer in learning about day-to-day living experiences such as buying food. Although such basic support is seldom necessary in the return home, O'Sullivan (2002) suggests a proactive approach is necessary. Not only must firms provide new home country positions that utilize the knowledge, skill, and abilities gained in the foreign experience, but also they must provide training and re-introduction to changes that might have occurred in the organizational structure and in the culture at home since departure. Adler (2002) notes that continuous, extensive communication either via e-mail or in meetings with the returnee prior to departure from the host country position is critical. Organizations also need to prepare home country employees to avoid allowing their " ... fear and rejection of things foreign ... " (p. 276), known as xenophobic responses, to hamper organizational benefits of the returning employees' knowledge, skills, and abilities (Adler, 2002).

Family and social support. In developing a model for female expatriate cross-cultural adaptation, Caligiuri and Lazarova (2002) posit that support in numerous relationships (colleagues at work, mentors, and host nationals both at work and in daily living situations) provides the emotional, informational, and environmental support needed for success. Shaffer and Harrison (1998) report that spousal support has great impact upon withdrawal from an expatriate experience. Black et al. (1992) note, after examining multiple studies, "The relationship is most likely reciprocal ..." (p. 128). Therefore, if the spouse experiences high levels of dissatisfaction, negative outcomes result with expatriate adjustment. According to Solomon (1994), few expatriates fail in international situations due to technical demands—most failures result from family or personal factors. Most importantly, Marx (2001) reports that managers who took advantage of support from colleagues, friends, and family reported shorter periods of culture shock than those who persevered and attempted to develop solutions on their own. Foreign students and other sojourners who have lived in cultures quite different from their home culture often find themselves on the outside upon return (Ward et al., 2001). Support and understanding from friends and family members helps ease the re-entry adjustment process.

Both individual and cultural factors have an impact on a sojourner's ability to adapt in a new cultural environment. Awareness of personal traits, willingness to try to understand others' reasons for being, prior international experience, plus knowledge of the various levels affected by cross-cultural adaptation improves one's ability to overcome culture shock. With organizational support as well as family and host country national support, the adjustments necessary for adapting in a foreign country as well as in the home country upon return become less traumatic over time.

RECLAIMING SELF AND DISSOLVING CULTURE SHOCK

The process of overcoming cultural shock equates well with the change process, according to Selmer (2002), with unfreezing, changing, and refreezing of behaviors. In change theory, to initiate behavioral change the individual needs to perceive a reason for modifying actions. Unfreezing occurs as individuals gain information through observance and in interaction with others in the new culture. As the desire to "fit in" increases, so also does the motivation to change behavior, resulting in a new way of responding to situations. When the new behavior becomes more familiar and more natural, refreezing takes place (Selmer, 2002). Refreezing here refers to the use of the new culturally accepted behavior as a normal action or response. As cultural sensemaking occurs, the individual undergoes a metamorphosis, becoming bicultural in the cross-cultural adaptation process.

Cultural Sensemaking

In their attempt to explain cultural sensemaking in executives, Osland and Bird (2000) suggest that learning the basis for cultural behavior can aid understanding. Noting that "managers can acquire attributional knowledge from personal experience, vicariously from others' experience, and from cultural mentoring" (p. 73), they state that understanding the reason behind behaviors facilitates acculturation.

Marx (2001) notes that as managers become more confident of their own abilities to respond or react within cultural expectations in the new environment, their anxiety decreases and they begin to feel more in control. She explains that individuals who ask themselves questions about their emotions (feelings in certain situations), their thinking (value of their ideas in the new culture's expectations), and social skills and identity (can I get along well?) adjust in their host country more effectively. As sojourners mentally respond to the question, they sense the need for behavioral change.

In situations with the greatest differences between home country and host country cultures, expatriates have facilitated sensemaking through mentoring (Black et al., 1992; Harvey et al., 1999). Dual career couples require a shared sensemaking, since both meet personal as well as professional challenges (Harvey et al., 1999). As individuals gain knowledge about the culture, awareness of behavioral cues increases. "A true understanding of the logic of another culture includes comprehending the interrelationships among values, or how values relate to one another in a given context" (Osland & Bird, 2000, p. 70). Pedersen (1995) incorporates the growth model theory into sensemaking, noting that sojourners learn from the cross-cultural experience. Gaining an understanding of behavior within different situational contexts provides sense to norms of the new culture thus increasing their intercultural competence.

Identity Metamorphosis

Individual identity develops through experiences in family, social, academic, and career contexts. In the move to another country and subsequent adaptation to that culture, uncertainty about one's identity develops. Behaviors that worked in prior U.S. experiences add stress in the host country situation where they are no longer appropriate (Sanchez, Spector, & Cooper, 2000). In a discussion of social identity theory as it relates to cross-cultural adaptation, Ward et al. (2001) note that individuals see themselves as members of a group. This group allegiance becomes distorted as personal changes occur throughout the adaptation process to overcome culture shock. Sojourners know that their behaviors are changing and are not sure of their true identity.

As one adapts to his or her role in the host country environment, a new bicultural identity results. Bell and Harrison (1996) note "Bicultural self-efficacy will provide the confidence necessary for an individual to build an effective repertoire of behaviors appropriate to a second culture" (p. 61). This new "self" evolves from the learning experience. Persons who have adapted to more than one culture gain a multicultural identity, comfortable in more than simply their home culture. The new behaviors become so ingrained that the sojourner buys into the host culture norms, feeling entitled to the rights, privileges, and benefits of that culture, eliminating ethnocentrism (Pedersen, 1995).

Marx (2001) reported that managers who had successfully adapted in a foreign country identified improvements in their social skills such as improved listening, greater tolerance, heightened sensitivity, better understanding of others, and increased flexibility. However, often these individuals find themselves returning to the previous foreign environment for another job, because their biculturalism has become a natural self-identity, which remains unrecognized in their homeland.

EDUCATING STUDENTS ABOUT CULTURE SHOCK

Before discussing culture shock, one must first help students become more knowledgeable about their own culturally accepted cues or behaviors, beliefs, historical roots, and social complexities. Osland and Bird (2000) note that a sensemaking approach to learning is more holistic in its approach. Providing a thorough understanding of their own culture helps " ... give students cultural dimensions and values as well as sophisticated stereotypes as basic tools" (p. 74). These authors encourage teaching students to become more flexible in their thinking about others rather than categorizing people based on assumptions.

They also suggest developing observational skills through the use of cases, which could provide contrasts of different dimensions or values.

Classroom Activities

To learn about themselves, students can take the Cross-Cultural Adaptability Inventory (CCAI), which " ... helps you assess your ability to adapt to living in another culture and to interact effectively with people of other cultures" (Kelley & Meyers, 1995).

Using a six-point scale ranging from definitely true to definitely not true, students mark their behavior in response to 50 statements. Although time-consuming, the assessment includes a planning guide, which provides the user with ideas for improving skills in specific areas after determining his or her profile.

An assignment that encourages more in-depth cultural understanding might be to require either a report or presentation about a specific country and its culture. Asking students to present the information as if they were providing other employees with guidelines for success in a future business venture with individuals in that country offers a more realistic scenario at the university level. Students can also approach the cross-cultural communication challenge as though they were going to the country as an exchange student. Questions at the end of the presentation should challenge the students' perceptions—such as, "How do we need to change our way of asking for information?" Getting a student to think about his or her changing perception of people within a culture can be helped by giving short quizzes regarding people from that particular country at the beginning and end of each student presentation. Students can more easily "see" how their viewpoint has changed with this new knowledge. Similarly, students can be required to attend a function or activity observed by another culture and asked to write a reaction paper. Some general guidelines and preparation such as class discussions on appropriate behavior or dress might be reviewed before students attend the function with discussions of student reactions (perceptions of food, dances, or other activities that took place) after the event. Students also generally enjoy conducting personal interviews of people from other cultures, which culminate in an oral presentation of the communication differences discussed. Viewing culturally specific films and listening to guest speakers from other cultures provide more passive learning tools, but ones that can prompt much classroom discussion.

Many teachers use different versions of Diversity Bingo with classes, sometimes incorporating the game as a get-acquainted activity during the early stages (Davis, 1999; Diversity Bingo, 1991). Squares on the card contain previously obtained descriptions of students in the class such as "someone who initially attended school in ___ "(a particular country). The game requires that students find the persons associated with the various clues on the bingo card and have that person sign their card. The first student to present a "bingo" (or fully signed card if class is small) wins (candy always works!). Games and simulations help students understand the perspective of someone in culture shock in a nonthreatening way.

Resources for Culture Shock Material
Resources are available for learning more about intercultural behaviors and overcoming differences in accepted customs, practices, ethics, and values. The list below includes a few publications that do not appear in the reference list:

- Black, J. S., & Gregerson, H. B. (1999). *So you're coming home.* San Diego, CA: Global Business Publisher.

- Bolt, M. (1998). Classroom exercise/student project: Cross-cultural dialogues. In M. Bolt (Ed.) *Instructor's resources to accompany David G. Myers' PSYCHOLOGY* (5th ed., chapter 1, p. 21). New York: Worth.

- Brislin, R. W., Cushner, K., Cherrie, C., & Yong, M. (1986). *Intercultural interactions: A practical guide.* Beverly Hills, CA: Sage.

- Cushner, K., & Brislin, R. W. (Eds.). (1997). *Improving intercultural interactions: Modules for cross-cultural training programs* (Vol. 2). Newbury Park, CA: Sage.

- Seelye, H. N. (Ed.). (1996). *Experiential activities for intercultural learning.* Yarmouth, ME: Intercultural Press.

- Sorti, C. (1994). *Cross-cultural dialogues.* Yarmouth, ME: Intercultural Press.

For teachers in metropolitan areas with embassies, information about cross-cultural adaptation from that culture's perspective might be available. Many professional organizations and training companies also provide products easily adapted for classroom use. A few Web sites that are beneficial include

- www.hrpress-diversity.com - includes many training activities and publications for cost

- http://www.faoa.org/journal/cshckfao.html - article by U.S. Army major about culture shock

- http://www.interculturalpress.com/shop/ - Intercultural Press homepage with many products

- www.culturegrams.com homepage - full access requires fee

- http://www.diversophy.com/products/index.htm - company with games and videos

Most universities with study abroad programs also have culture shock pages online. Check a nearby academic institution's home page as a possible source of information.

SUMMARY

As Pedersen (1995) points out, culture shock cannot be totally prevented, because newcomers face situations that sometimes cannot be anticipated or simulated in predeparture preparation. Although some inherent personality traits, such as flexibility, interpersonal skills, and self-efficacy contribute to successful cross-cultural adaptation, factors such as prior international experiences and predeparture training greatly determine a sojourner's ability to handle the nuances of a global assignment. The more sojourners increase their cultural inventory prior to a global assignment, the higher the probability that their anticipatory, psychological, and sociocultural adjustment will be successful. Additionally, organizational support through training, mentoring, and continuous communication throughout the assignment, and recognition of sojourners' contributions while abroad help to complement coping strategies. The support from family, coworkers, and host nationals is important as well. As sojourners truly immerse themselves in the host culture, employ effective coping strategies to facilitate that process, and create new mental frameworks to function in the new environment, they emerge as more culturally developed individuals, having achieved highly significant cultural competence.

The line of demarcation of cultures is becoming increasingly blurred as people from different cultures live together. Bicultural and multicultural employees will soon become a standard rather than a preference for employers. Therefore, learning designed to help students who are prospective employees achieve cultural fluency will significantly affect the adverse effects of culture shock and reverse culture shock, thereby facilitating their adjustment as they transition in and out of different environments in the future. Increasing students' cultural awareness, inventories, and experiences will create the cultural metamorphosis that will eventually elevate them from adapting to a multicultural society to becoming multicultural individuals.

REFERENCES

Adler, N. J. (2002). *International dimensions of organizational behavior* (4th ed.). Cincinnati, OH: South-Western/Thomson Learning.

Andreason, A. W. (2003). Expatriate adjustment to foreign assignments. *International Journal of Commerce and Management, 13*(1), 42-60.

Bell, M. P., & Harrison, D. A. (1996). Using intra-national diversity for international assignments: A model of bicultural competence and expatriate adjustment. *Human Resource Management, 6*(1), 47-75.

Berry, J. W., Poortinga, Y. H., Segall, M. H., & Dasen, P. R. (2002). *Cross-cultural psychology: Research and applications* (2nd ed.). Cambridge: Cambridge University Press.

Black, J. S., & Gregersen, H. B. (1991). When Yankee comes home: Factors related to expatriate and spouse repatriation adjustment. *Journal of International Business Studies, 22*(4), 671-694.

Black, J. S., Gregersen, H. B., & Mendenhall, M. (1992). *Global assignments: Successfully expatriating and repatriating international managers.* San Francisco, CA: Jossey-Bass.

Black, J. S., Mendenhall, M., & Oddou, G. (1991). Toward a comprehensive model of international adjustment: An integration of multiple theoretical perspectives. *Academy of Management Review, 16*(2), 291-318.

Caligiuri, P., & Lazarova, M. (2002). A model for the influence of social interaction and social support on female expatriates' cross-cultural adjustment. *International Journal of Human Resource Management, 13*(5), 761-772.

Carey, C. E. (1999). International HPT: Rx for culture shock. *Performance Improvement, 38*(5), 49-54.

Davis, B. D. (1999). Encouraging commuter student connectivity. *Business Communication Quarterly, 62*(2), 74-78.

Diversity Bingo. (1991). Bloomington, IN: Advancement Strategy.

Feldman, D. C., & Tompson, H. B. (1993). Expatriation, repatriation, and domestic geographical relocation: An empirical investigation. *Journal of International Business Studies, 24*(3), 507-530.

Hammer, M. R., Hart, W., & Rogan, R. (1998). Can you go home again? An analysis of the repatriation of corporate managers and spouses. *Management International Review, 38*(1), 67-86.

Hammer, M. R., Bennett, M. J., & Wiseman, R. (2003). Measuring intercultural sensitivity: The intercultural development inventory. *International Journal of Intercultural Relations, 27*, 421-443.

Harvey, M., Buckley, M. R., Novicevic, M. M., & Wiese, D. (1999). Mentoring dual-career expatriates: A sense-making and sense-giving social support process. *International Journal of Human Resource Management, 10*(5), 808-827.

Hurn, B. J. (1999). Repatriation—the toughest assignment of all. *Industrial and Commercial Training, 31*(6), 224-228.

Katz, J. P., & Seifer, D. M. (1996). It's a different world out there: Planning for expatriate success through selection, pre-departure training and on-site socialization. *Human Resource Planning, 19*(2), 32-48.

Kelley, C., & Meyers, J. (1995). *Cross-cultural adaptability inventory: Self assessment.* Minneapolis, MN: National Computer Systems.

Kim, Y. Y. (2001). *Becoming intercultural.* Thousand Oaks, CA: Sage.

Krapels, R. H., & Chaney, L. H. (1995). Intercultural business communication training methods perceived effective for predeparture preparation of U.S. international businesspeople. *Journal of the Academy of Business Administration, 1*(1), 24-33.

Marx, E. (2001). *Breaking through culture shock: What you need to succeed in international business.* London: Nicholas Brealey Intercultural.

Myburgh, C. P. H., Niehaus, L., & Poggenpoel, M. (2002). International learners' experiences and coping mechanisms within a culturally diverse context. *Education, 123*(1), 107-129.

Osland, J. S., & Bird, A. (2000). Beyond sophisticated stereotyping: Cultural sensemaking in context. *Academy of Management Executive, 14*(1), 65-80.

O'Sullivan, S. L. (2002). The protean approach to managing repatriation transitions. *International Journal of Manpower, 23*(7), 597-616.

Pedersen, P. (1995). *The five stages of culture shock: Critical incidents around the world.* Westport, CT: Greenwood Press.

Sanchez, J. I., Spector, P. E., & Cooper, C. L. (2000). Adapting to a boundaryless world: A developmental expatriate model. *Academy of Management Executive, 14*(2), 96-106.

Selmer, J. (1999). Effects of coping strategies on sociocultural and psychological adjustment of western expatriate managers in the PRC. *Journal of World Business, 34*(1), 41-51.

Selmer, J. (2002). Practice makes perfect? International experience and expatriate adjustment. *Management International Review, 42*(1), 71-87.

Shaffer, M. A., & Harrison, D. A. (1998). Expatriates' psychological withdrawal from international assignments: Work, nonwork, and family. *Personnel Psychology, 51*(1), 87-118.

Shaffer, M. A., Harrison, D. A., & Gilley, K. M. (1999). Dimensions, determinants, and differences in the expatriate adjustment process. *Journal of International Business Studies, 30*(3), 557-581.

Solomon, M. (1994). Success abroad depends on more than job skills. *Personnel Journal, 73*(4), 51-58.

Stroh, L. K., Gregersen, H. B., & Black, J. S. (1998). Closing the gap: Expectations versus reality among repatriates. *Journal of World Business, 33*(2), 111-124.

Stroh, L. K., Gregersen, H. B., & Black, J. S. (2000). Triumphs and tragedies: Expectations and commitments upon repatriation. *The International Journal of Human Resource Management, 11*(4), 681-697.

Ward, C., Bochner, S., & Furnham, A. (2001). *Psychology of culture shock.* Philadelphia: Taylor & Francis.

English: A Global Language

James Calvert Scott
Utah State University
Logan, Utah

Why did English, the native language of only 5% of the world's population (Crystal, 2003), meteorically rise in prominence and become a global language? Why does English have a special role to play in a global society? What other languages are threatening the worldwide dominance of English? How will English fare in the years ahead? How should business educators respond regarding English and other languages? This chapter answers these questions by discussing the prominence of the English language, its special role as a lingua franca, challenges to English by other languages, the future of English, and suggestions for business educators regarding English and other languages.

PROMINENCE OF ENGLISH

Why is English such a globally prominent language? Crystal (2003) succinctly identi-fied six major reasons why the English language has risen in global prominence. None of these reasons have to do with the inherent superiority of the English language (Crystal, 2003).

Language of Economically and Politically Dominant Countries

First, English is the language of economically and politically dominant countries. As the native language of the economically successful and politically influential countries of the nineteenth and twentieth centuries, the United Kingdom of Great Britain and Northern Ireland and the United States of America, respectively, the English language has risen in worldwide prominence. Through their imperialistic policies, these countries have transferred to their colonies—spread around the world—their societal institutions such as educational systems, economic systems, and governmental systems, all of which are dominated and regulated by the English language (Crystal, 2003).

Language for Bridging Linguistic Differences

Second, English is a language for bridging linguistic differences. In many instances the English language has been used effectively to bridge linguistic differences among existing languages. For example, in India where there are many competing languages, English serves as a common language that helps to unite the citizens of the world's largest democracy (Crystal, 2003).

Language of World's Dominant Superpower

Third, English is the language of the world's dominant business superpower, the United State of America. As its status has increased over time, other countries and their citizens interested in advancing economically have emulated its example, including using its language for business and other purposes (Crystal, 2003). As Pakir (1997) observed, "English is money" (p. 171).

Language of International Activities

Fourth, English is the language of international activities. English is considered the de facto or de jure language of many international activities that involve people from countries around the world. Just as English serves as the international language of aviation, it likewise serves as the international language of academia, business, tourism, technology, sailing, law enforcement, and emergency services, to name but a few examples. In fact, English is unrivaled as a language with special worldwide practical uses (Crystal, 2003).

Language of Influential Global Academic, Scientific, and Technological Communities

Fifth, English is widely considered to be the primary language of the influential global academic, scientific, and technological communities. These important guardians of intellectual knowledge primarily create and/or disseminate in English. In other words, most important academic, scientific, and technological work is accomplished in English and/or shared with others directly or indirectly through translation and interpretation via the English language (Crystal, 2003). About 90% of all of the world's information that is stored electronically is recorded in the English language (Language Link, 2000-2001). Further, 93% of Web site pages are recorded in the English language (Kasim, 2002). Such facts make a strong case that English is the essential language for various types of intellectual pursuits.

Language of Popular Global Culture

Sixth, English is the language of popular global culture. No language dominates popular global culture like English does. Among the diverse forms of popular culture affected are music, movies, television, advertising, computing, gaming, and other entertainment forms to name but a few (Crystal, 2003). Impressionable youth around the world seem to have an insatiable appetite for English-language popular culture.

Thus, a number of compelling reasons exist why the English language has disproportionate influence around the world and has come to tower over all other languages for global influence. But what is the role of English around the world?

ENGLISH AS A LINGUA FRANCA

Today "English is the most influential language the world has ever known" (Dovring, 1997, p. 22). It has risen to such prominence that it functions as a lingua franca, a common language shared by many people who are dispersed around the world, but who wish to communicate together. In many senses, English today functions like Latin did for more than a thousand years among Western civilizations (Crystal, 2003). This family of English speakers includes many different groups and continues to grow.

Family of English Speakers

In a seminal work Kachru (1985) visualized three concentric rings of English speakers that represent the family of English speakers. The inner circle represents where English is the primary language and has between 320 and 380 million English speakers. The inner circle can be represented by such countries as the United States of America and the United Kingdom of Great Britain and Northern Ireland. The outer circle represents where English was first spread and where it has become such an important part of societal life that it functions as a critical lingua franca among different linguistic groups and has between 150 and 300 million English speakers. The outer circle can be represented by such countries as India and Singapore. The expanding circle represents where English does not have any special status, but where it is acknowledged to be an important international language and has between 100 million and 1 billion English speakers. The expanding circle can be represented by such countries as Japan and the People's Republic of China (Kachru, 1985).

When the number of native and nonnative English speakers from the three circles is totaled, it at least equals and likely exceeds the number of Mandarin Chinese speakers, the closest competitor in terms of total number of language speakers (Crystal, 2003; Fox, 2000). All of this means that in terms of total number of speakers, English is likely the most common language worldwide, which gives it considerable power and influence as a means of global communication, and which motivates others to learn to speak it, further enhancing its status as a lingua franca.

English as the Dominant Business Language

Without a doubt, English is widely regarded as the dominant language of global business (Colback & Maconochie, 1989; Gilsdorf, 2002; Victor, 1992). When communicating domestically, businesspersons around the world typically use the locally predominant language while engaging in business. Even so, English is oftentimes used to transact business, since it is an important commercial language in a number of countries with large business sectors. When communicating internationally, businesspersons around the world typically use English because it is the language that they share in common as a first, second, or third language. It is this ability of English to serve as a workable, albeit imperfect link among native speakers of various languages that makes English so valuable as the lingua franca of business, the tool that facilitates the accomplishment of global business transactions.

Native speakers of English possess some possible advantages over nonnative English speakers. The primary advantage is that their native language, the one in which they have the most fluency, is the dominant language of worldwide business. As such, they are relatively skilled in its usage and are at least somewhat aware of its subtleties and nuances. This gives them self-confidence and a possible competitive advantage as they interact with other less fluent speakers for whom English is a second or a third language (Colback & Maconochie, 1989).

Native speakers of English also possess some possible disadvantages. The primary disadvantage is that because they are already fluent for business purposes in the dominant business language, many are overconfident and unwilling to bother learning one or more additional languages for business purposes (Graddol, 1997). While English is the most important global business language, it is certainly not the only language for conducting global business, with bilingual and multilingual businesspersons having a competitive advantage over those who only speak English. Given the prevalence of English speakers worldwide, being a native speaker of English is no longer a major advantage; speaking multiple languages is rapidly becoming a major advantage (Graddol, 2001). Since many native speakers of English have not seriously studied another language, they lack empathy and understanding for those who do not speak English relatively well. They may be "blind to linguistic and cultural interference that may underlie a foreigner's ostensible facility in English" (Gilsdorf, 2002, p. 368).

Value of Other Languages for Business Purposes

While speaking the important commercial language of English is highly desirable, this does not detract from the fact that any language can potentially be used for business purposes. Even predominantly ecclesiastical languages such as Hebrew can be used to conduct business, in spite of the fact that their vocabularies are better suited for religious purposes. All that is required are two or more speakers of a language who wish to engage in commerce with serious intentions as potential buyers and sellers. Nevertheless, of the approximate 3,000 languages—not counting their 7,000 to 8,000 dialects—currently being spoken somewhere in the world, most languages are spoken by so few people that their practical usefulness for international business communication purposes is negligible, although never absent (Victor, 1992).

More than twenty years ago in a notable book, Berlitz (1982) reported that most people worldwide either speak or are familiar with one of 14 languages—Chinese, English, Hindustani, Russian, Spanish, Japanese, German, Indonesian, Portuguese, French, Arabic, Bengali, Malay, or Italian—or with one of three additional languages— Dutch, Greek, or Swahili—or with a language from the Scandinavian, Turkish, or Slavic families. By speaking these 20 languages, it would be possible to communicate with most of the world's inhabitants. However, most people have not the inclination, the aptitude, and the time to develop fluency in that many languages—or even more than two or three languages. As a practical result, most people look for languages besides their native tongues with practical utility, and the English language often fills that bill.

Englishes as Lingua Francas

In some areas that are not primarily English speaking, the English language is a common language choice. Consider the case of Western Europe. There, "47% of the total population, 65% of young adults, 77% of college students, and 69% of managers speak English" (Scott, 2002, p. 6). About 89% of all pupils study English in non-English-speaking European Union countries (European Commission, 2004). With so many first-, second-, and third-language English speakers throughout Western Europe, the English language thrives as a lingua franca that transcends national and cultural boundaries.

As Dennett (1992) observed, "English may be the language of the global village, but the villagers are far from agreement on what is good use of the language" (p. 13). Further, "the price a world language must be prepared to pay is submission to many different kinds of use" (Achebe, 1975, p. 100). Even two businesspersons enculturated in the same country do not have reservoirs of language understanding that always provide identical meaning matches between the sender and the receiver (Scott, 1999). As Gilsdorf (2002) noted, "only approximate commonality of meaning" (p. 364) exists. When the businesspersons are from different cultures, each of which has created its own peculiar version of the English language, and even if they are thoroughly acculturated in the other form of English, which rarely occurs, communication via English between the businesspersons will be less than perfect because of ongoing message meaning mis-matches (Scott, 1999). Having the ability to use the English language provides no guarantee whatsoever of commonality of meaning among businesspersons because of the multiplicity of Englishes, variant forms of the English language, around the world (Gilsdorf, 2002). In other words, the notion of English as a lingua franca for business and other purposes works much better in theory than in practice, where it is fraught with errors. Nevertheless, many businesspersons around the world work diligently to overcome the shortcomings of their Englishes as lingua francas, strive diligently toward shared meaning and understanding, and manage to accomplish commercial transactions with global partners in spite of the challenges. This meeting of the minds occurs only if the core vocabulary of users remains intelligible to English speakers worldwide (Gilsdorf, 2002).

Thus, for many people worldwide the English language serves as a lingua franca for business and other purposes, even though the development of multiple Englishes makes it less than a flawless tool. But what are the potential challenges to English?

CHALLENGES TO ENGLISH

The English language is well entrenched globally. It "is used by more people than any other language on Earth" although "its mother-tongue speakers make up only a quarter or a fifth of the total" (Strevens, 1992, p. 28). The fact that the English language has some type of special status in more than 70 countries spread around the world illustrates its place on the world stage. English has more status than any other language in spite of the fact that French, German, Spanish, Russian, and Arabic also have notable official use around the world (Crystal, 1997).

Position of English Versus Other Languages

It is doubtful that any language will replace the English language as a global lingua franca within the next fifty years. In the future it is likely that a small number of languages will create a linguistic oligopoly in which those languages predominate, and each will have its spheres of influences and regional bases. Languages that serve regional communities, such as Spanish in Latin America, are apt to rise in importance in the years ahead (Graddol, 2001).

Graddol (2001) created an index that reflects the relative global influence of major world languages circa 1995. English topped the index, with a score of 100. The next five languages and their scores follow: German, 42; French, 33; Japanese, 32; Spanish, 31; and Chinese, 22. The order of the second- through sixth-place languages is likely to change in the years ahead, with those languages closest to English—German, French, and Japanese—likely to grow more slowly in importance and Spanish and perhaps Chinese likely to grow more rapidly in importance. Nevertheless, English is likely to retain the first-place position into the foreseeable future (Graddol, 2001).

By 2050 Graddol (2001) anticipates that a new global language hierarchy will evolve. At the top of the hierarchy will be the big languages, Chinese, Hindi/Urdu, English, Spanish, and Arabic. Below the big languages will be the regional languages that serve major trading blocs, Arabic, Malay, Chinese, English, Russian, and Spanish. Beneath the regional languages will be the national languages, about 90 in number that serve about 220 countries. Beneath the national languages will be the local languages, about 1,000 or fewer languages with varying degrees of official recognition. The evolution from today's linguistic monopoly to tomorrow's linguistic oligopoly brings not only pluralism but also loss of language diversity (Graddol, 2001).

Threats from Electronic Challengers

Interestingly, the challenges to English are appearing primarily in electronic form. The Internet is rapidly becoming today's Tower of Babel with many competing languages (Scott, 2003). When the Internet was first devised, its only language was that of its creators, English. However, as that technology has diffused around the world and become widely accessible, speakers of other languages wanted Internet access, and they preferred to use their own native languages if possible. Of the total worldwide online population, 60% is from non-English-speaking zones, and 40% is from English-speaking zones. The 338.5 million non-English speakers outnumber the 228 million English speakers by nearly 50% (Nua, 2001). By 2003 non-English language material was estimated to account for more than half of all Web site content (Nua, 1999a). Further, by 2005 it is estimated that 57% of Internet users will not be English speakers (Nua, 1999b). All of this means that the dominance of the English language electronically is diminishing.

Where do the electronic challengers to English come from? In descending order by number of user-speakers, the following are eroding the domination of English on the Internet: Chinese, 55.5 million user-speakers; Japanese, 52.1 million user-speakers; Spanish, 40.8 million user-speakers; German, 38.6 million user-speakers; Korean, 25.2 million user-speakers; French, 22 million user-speakers; and Italian, 20.2 million user-speakers (Nua, 2002). Portuguese and Scandinavian languages have seen large percentage increases in numbers of Internet users but not in total numbers of speakers (Nua, 1998). It is plausible that a number of native speakers of other languages also use English as a second or third language. Many of these people would likely be at least somewhat comfortable using English on the Internet, although they might prefer to use their native language whenever possible.

Threats from Automatic or Machine Translation and Interpretation

One plausible threat to the English language in the future is automatic or machine translation and interpretation, which eliminates the need for a worldwide language or a lingua franca such as English. If as much progress is made in the next several decades as has been made in the past decade, then it is possible that people will be able to communicate effectively in writing in their native languages with the aid of automatic or machine translation programs. While some programs for doing so already exist at the basic translation level, the available software is very limited in its ability to process idiomatic, stylistic, and other linguistic features. Currently available software can speed up the cumbersome translation process, but it cannot replace the professional judgment that a highly competent translator brings to the task. Existing speech-to-speech automatic interpretation programs, while making great strides in recent years, are still relatively primitive. Even though these technologies will improve greatly over coming decades, it will take much longer for them to be widely available around the world, allowing the English language to remain entrenched as a global language (Crystal, 1997).

Thus, although the English language is well placed when compared to other major world languages, over time its importance is apt to diminish somewhat, especially as electronic communication and automatic or machine translation and interpretation grow in popularity. What, then, is the future of English?

FUTURE OF ENGLISH

While predicting the future of any language involves risk, the English language "seems set to play an ever more important role in world communications, international business, and social and cultural affairs" (Graddol, 2001, p. 26). Increasing use of English will tend to put pressure in the direction of global uniformity and raise concerns about such things as declining standards and linguistic diversity. But as the number of second-language speakers of English increases, so does the number of local varieties of English (Graddol, 2001).

Drives of Intelligibility and Identity

At play are two competing drives, one focusing around intelligibility and one focusing around identity. The drive for intelligibility emphasizes common English-language standards that ensure accurate message comprehension among all English speakers. The drive for identity emphasizes the development of diverse local varieties of English that reflect unique national cultural identities. Tension exists between these opposing drives, and when one drive becomes too influential, power is exerted in the opposite direction. For example, after attending an international meeting and being unable to understand an Indian delegate speaking in English, Indira Gandhi complained to the Ministry of Education about the declining English standards in India (Crystal, 1997). Such noteworthy events represent the power struggle for control over the direction of the English language.

Factors with Influence on the Future of English

Crystal (1997) discusses five factors that bear on the future of global English in *English as a Global Language*. These include (a) English rejection; (b) the United States' situation; (c) new Englishes; (d) English fragmentation; and (e) unique events.

English rejection. The English language is sometimes rejected by people who feel antagonistic or ambivalent about it. These individuals and their countries consciously choose not to give the English language any special status. It is not surprising that after years of colonialism, some would prefer to reject the language that was imposed on them by the colonial power in favor of indigenous languages. Nevertheless, most former colonies of what is now the United Kingdom of Great Britain and Northern Ireland and those of the United States have chosen to retain English as an official language. Interestingly, even the former French colony of Algeria chose to replace French with English as its primary foreign language, which partially counters the English-rejection idea.

Countries that envision themselves operating more on a regional basis than on a global basis might reject English in favor of a more local lingua franca. For example, Spanish-speaking countries of the Western Hemisphere might gravitate toward Spanish, much like the countries of northern Africa gravitate toward Arabic. Any decision to reject English bears on the identity of the country and reverberates around the English-speaking world. To date there have been only a few outright rejections of the English language by countries, and the involved countries have had negligible influence on the status of English overall (Crystal, 1997).

United States' situation. The situation in the United States has considerable influence over the future of English since it was largely responsible for the growth of English during the twentieth century. With the largest number of native speakers of English by far, the United States exerts more influence on the development of English worldwide than any other single country. Should the economic or military power of the United States falter significantly, which seems a remote possibility, the global status of English would be affected (Crystal, 1997).

The longstanding battle between the drives for intelligibility and identity in the United States has manifested itself in the English-as-the-official-language movements at the state and federal levels. Some are expressing concern that recent immigrants are retaining too many of their original cultural values—including their native languages—at the expense of adopting mainstream American cultural values—including the English language. This polarizing problem, accompanied by strong emotions, makes resolution challenging (Crystal, 1997).

New Englishes. New Englishes influence the future of global English. Even the powerful and influential United States has only about 20% of the worldwide English-speaking population, and it cannot claim sole ownership rights to the English language. The fact that no country can claim ownership rights for the English language supports the argument that English is truly a global language. Given the rapidly changing demographics of English speakers worldwide, inner circle English speakers are increasingly the smaller minority, and outer circle and expanding circle English speakers are increasingly the larger majority. This strengthens the argument that ownership of English is truly globally based (Crystal, 1997).

As English has spread around the world, new varieties have emerged, each somewhat different from the others. Just as American English is different from British English for a variety of reasons, so, too, are Indian English and Japanese English. Such international varieties of English express their speakers' national identities and are compromises between intelligibility and identity. They allow speakers from different countries to use somewhat different Englishes, thus retaining identity, and still remain bound by a common written language, thus retaining intelligibility (Crystal, 1997).

English fragmentation. With the emergence of new Englishes comes the possibility of the fragmentation of the English language into a series of mutually unintelligible tongues. While new varieties of English abound, to date the family of Englishes remains mutually intelligible. Although there may occasionally be comprehension difficulties among English speakers, especially between inner circle speakers of English and outer circle and expanding circle speakers of English, those problems can usually be resolved. Such factors as standard written English, which varies little from English-speaking country to country, and international television programs help to expose English speakers worldwide to a variety of existing norms (Crystal, 1997).

People who were once colonized under the English language appear content to remake English in their own fashion, feeling relaxed about how they use English. Even if their new Englishes become increasingly different, the result wouldn't necessarily be catastrophic. People would simply adapt by speaking more than one dialect of the English language. World Standard Spoken English, a form of spoken English with a common core of words whose meanings are uniform, regionally neutral, and prestigious around the world, would likely emerge, supplementing the national dialects. People would continue to speak their dialects with people from their own countries, thus preserving identity, and World Standard Spoken English with people from other countries, thus preserving intelligibility (Crystal, 1997). For example, one Briton might tell another Briton that he is "knackered," but would tell an American that he is really tired.

Unique event. That English is so widely dispersed around the world and spoken by so many people is an unparalleled event that is unique in the annals of time. With no precedents of a language with global status to rely upon, predictions about the future of English are speculative at best. The delicate balance between intelligibility and identity could be affected by such social changes as modifications in immigration policy, political alliances, or population shifts. English may already have a critical mass of speakers around the world that makes it difficult for one group or alliance to limit its growth or influence its future direction. Even major change in the United States will have diminishing influence on the English language over time as the number of English speakers elsewhere grows. Provided a critical mass of English speakers exists, is the evolution of the English language into a global language a unique event? Perhaps English in one form or another will serve the global community forever (Crystal, 1997).

Thus, besides the competing drives of intelligibility and identity, such factors as English rejection, the United States' situation, new Englishes, English fragmentation, and the unique event will influence the future of English. But how should business educators respond?

SUGGESTIONS FOR BUSINESS EDUCATORS

Where information about English and other languages is relevant in their curriculum, business educators should present to their students appropriate factual information similar to that found in the preceding sections of this chapter and suitable application activities. Business educators should also promote mastery of English and other languages for business purposes, offering a range of domestic and international business communication units and courses and working cooperatively with foreign-language educators whenever appropriate. In addition, business educators should serve as effective role models for their students through their demonstrated skill in using English and other languages for various communication purposes.

The breadth and depth of the information provided by business educators to students will be influenced by such factors as the nature of the course in which the content is relevant, the amount of available instructional time, the maturity level of the students, the appeal of the information to students, and the like. When it is possible, instructors should actively rather than passively engage students in learning, especially at the middle school and high school levels. A few teaching ideas are offered to suggest the range of opportunities creative business educators have to incorporate information about English and other languages into their courses.

Suggestions for Business Communication Courses

Since language is the primary tool of business communication, business educators have opportunities to incorporate information about English and other languages into courses that focus on both domestic and international business communication. For example, business educators might discuss the spread of the English language around the world and then present Kachru's (1985) conceptualization of the inner, outer, and expanding circles of English speakers. As a follow-up activity, instructors could have individual students or groups of students construct collages, artistic compositions made by affixing various items to a poster board or scrapbook-page surface, depicting the three concentric rings of English speakers. Students could affix such things as outline maps of representative countries, pictures of typical English speakers, and typical words of each group of English speakers. Instructors wanting to learn more about this useful conceptualization of English speakers can consult Kachru's (1985) article or page 107 of Crystal's (2003) *Cambridge Encyclopedia of the English Language.*

Business educators can ask students individually or in groups to investigate using print and electronic resources variant forms of the English language, since most students are familiar only with the variety of English that they speak and do not realize the degree of diversity within the family of Englishes. Students might search for the primary characteristics of one form of English and then share their findings with others in written or oral form. Some possible varieties of English to explore include Black English, Canadian English, British English, Estuary English, Irish English, Australian English, New Zealand English, Caribbean English, South African English, Indian English, and Japanese English to name but a few. Potentially useful print sources for this activity include McArthur's (1996) *The Oxford Companion to the English Language* and Crystal's (2003) *Cambridge Encyclopedia of the English Language.*

After having students research the English-as-the-official-language movement in their home state, territory, province, or country using electronic sources, business educators can have students write persuasive letters as representatives of the business community to an identified governmental official, building the case for why that official should or should not support the movement. As an alternative assignment after the research has been completed, instructors could divide the class into two teams, assign one team to argue for and the other against English as the official language, and debate the issue.

Suggestions for Information Technology Courses

Since students enrolled in information technology courses usually are interested in how technology can help with various tasks, business educators can divide the class in half, asking (a) one group to search the Internet for information about automatic or machine translation from one written language to another and (b) the other group to search the Internet for information about automatic or machine interpretation from one spoken language to another. Instructors can have students print their most useful documents and create a written or an oral report of a specified length. If printing the retrieved documents is not feasible, then students can take detailed notes that are used to prepare the report. If desired, teachers can also require students to prepare a related PowerPoint presentation with specified features to augment the report.

Business educators might ask students to (a) go the Web site for International Business Machines, www.ibm.org; (b) click on "Select country/region"; (c) click on the triangle at the end of the "Home page by country/region and language" box; and (d) scroll down the list of countries/regions and note all of the different languages available.

At this point instructors can ask students why an American-based global corporation such as IBM would have Web sites in so many different languages. Teachers might follow up by asking students to speculate what they think the major challenges would be with having Web sites for so many different countries, regions, and languages. Instructors could ask students why combining foreign language study with information technology study could potentially increase employment options in the future. Business educators can then ask students to (a) click on one of the countries with a home page in a foreign language, (b) click on "Go," and (c) spend a minute or two scanning that home page and sample related pages. Teachers might then ask students why they find English words in foreign-language Web sites and what this suggests about the influence of the English language for global business purposes.

While teaching about the features of Dragon Naturally Speaking using version 7, business educators can explain the process of selecting from these five Englishes for input and playback purposes: U.S. (American), U.K. (British), Australian, Indian, and Southeast Asian. By creating five users and by having the same text played back in each variety of English, instructors are able not only to demonstrate this software capability, but also to expose students to a variety of English-language accents.

Thus, as the general guidance and the business communication and information technology teaching ideas suggest, business educators have varied opportunities to promote English and other languages in their curriculum.

SUMMARY

In summary, the English language has major worldwide influence for a number of compelling reasons. Many people around the world use English as a lingua franca, an imperfect communication tool because of the development of multiple Englishes. Over time the importance of English as a global language is likely to diminish somewhat, especially with the anticipated growth in electronic communication and automatic or machine translation and interpretation. The future of the English language will be influenced by such factors as the competing drives of intelligibility and identity; the rejection of the English language; the situation of the United States; the evolution of new Englishes; the possible fragmentation of the English language; and the unique event where one language, English, is so widely dispersed and spoken around the world. Consequently, creative business educators will find opportunities to promote English and other languages where relevant, using ideas similar to those presented. The history of the English language has been characterized by ongoing change; so will its future.

REFERENCES

Achebe, C. (1975). *Morning yet on creation day: Essays.* Garden City, NY: Anchor Press.

Berlitz, C. (1982). *Native tongues.* New York: Perigee Books.

Colback, S., & Maconochie, M. (1989, October 29). . . . And the rise of the executive nomad. *The [London] Times Magazine,* 22-23, 25.

Crystal, D. (2003). *The Cambridge encyclopedia of the English language.* (2nd ed.). Cambridge, United Kingdom: Cambridge University Press.

Crystal, D. (1997). *English as a global language.* Cambridge, United Kingdom: Cambridge University Press.

Dennett, J. T. (1992). World language does not ensure world class usage. *IEEE Transactions of Professional Communication, 35*(1), 13.

Dovring, K. (1997). *English as lingua franca: Double talk in global persuasion.* Westport, CT: Praeger.

European Commission. (2004). *Languages in Europe.* Retrieved February 3, 2004, from http://europa.eu.int/comm/education/policies/lang/languages/1.../european languages_en.htm

Fox, J. (2000). The triumph of English. *Fortune, 142*(6), 209-210, 212.

Gilsdorf, J. (2002). Standard Englishes and World Englishes: Living with a polymorph business language. *The Journal of Business Communication, 39*(3), 364-378.

Graddol, D. (1997). *The future of English?* London: British Council.

Graddol, D. (2001). English in the future. In A. Burns & C. Coffin (Eds.), *Analysing English in a global context* (pp. 26-37). London: Routledge.

Kachru, B. B. (1985). Standards, codification and sociolinguistic realism: The English language in the outer circle. In R. Quirk and H. G. Widdowson (Eds.), *English in the world* (pp. 11-30). Cambridge, United Kingdom: Cambridge University Press.

Kasim, S. (2002, August 29). English and the digital divide. *New Straits Times [Kuala Lumpur, Malaysia]*, p. 2. Retrieved September 10, 2003, from the ABI/INFORM database.

Language Link. (2000-2001). *English language courses.* Retrieved January 8, 2003, from http:www.languagelink.ru/e/english/

McArthur, T. (1996). *The Oxford companion to the English language* (abridged ed.). Oxford, United Kingdom: Oxford University Press.

Nua.[1] (1998, June 30). *Emarketer: Non-English speakers catch up.* Retrieved June 21, 2003, from http://www.nua.com/surveys

Nua. (1999a, March 29). *Techserver: Internationalisation of the Web.* Retrieved June 21, 2003, from http://www.nua.com/surveys

Nua. (1999b, June 10). *Computer economics: Majority of users will be non-English speakers.* Retrieved June 21, 2003, from http://www.nua.com/surveys

Nua. (2001, May 17). *Ipsos-Reid: U.S. no longer dominates the Net.* Retrieved June 21, 2003, from http://www.nua.com/surveys

Nua. (2002, May 24). *Global reach: English is not the Net's only language.* Retrieved June 21, 2003, from http://www.nua.com/surveys

Pakir, A. (1997). Standards and codification for World Englishes. In L. E. Smith & M. L. Forman (Eds.), *World Englishes 2000: Selected essays* (pp. 169-181). Honolulu, HI: University of Hawaii and the East-West Center.

Scott, J. C. (1999). Developing cultural fluency: The goal of international business-communication instruction in the 21st century. *Journal of Education for Business, 74*(3), 140-143.

Scott, J. C. (2002). A diminishing role for the English language online. *International Society for Business Education Network, 33*(1), 5-6.

Scott, J. C. (2003). English and the Internet: Implications for global business educators. *Journal for Global Business Education, 3,* 17-31.

Strevens, P. (1992). English as an international language: Directions in the 1990s. In B. B. Kachru (Ed.), *The other tongue: English across cultures* (2nd ed.) (pp. 27-47). Urbana, IL: University of Illinois Press.

Victor, D. A. (1992). *International business communication.* New York: HarperCollins Publishers, Inc.

[1] Nua is an online Internet survey portal for market research, statistics, demographics, metrics, and Web trends.

Nonverbal Communication: The Silent but Important Language

Marsha L. Bayless
Stephen F. Austin State University
Nacogdoches, Texas

Nonverbal communication in an intercultural or international setting can be quite complex. A gesture in one culture does not always carry the same meaning or value as the same gesture in another culture. In addition, cultural norms vary for nonverbal messages. Nonverbal communication "includes all messages other than words that people exchange in interactive contexts. To qualify as a message, a behavior typically must be sent with intent and/or it must typically be interpreted by others" (Hecht, DeVito, & Guerrero, 1999, p. 5). Nonverbal communication includes eye contact, touching, tone of voice, dress, posture, and distance (Miller, 2000). It is a silent language that communicates in conjunction with the verbal or may stand by itself.

This chapter will discuss active elements of nonverbal communication, passive elements of nonverbal communications, and teaching ideas and resources.

ACTIVE ELEMENTS OF NONVERBAL COMMUNICATION

Active elements of nonverbal communication include appearance, body movements (or *kinesics*), touching behaviors (or *haptics*), eye behaviors (or *oculesics*), space utilization (or *proxemics*), and paralanguage. Nonverbal communication's active elements are usually defined as nonverbal behavior that the communicator can recognize and control (Victor, 1992).

Appearance

How the communicator looks is an important factor in communication. In fact, how the speaker looks in a presentation can weigh more with the audience than what is said

(Leech, 2004). Does the appearance present a polished, professional look, or does the communicator look sloppy with poorly chosen clothes? Dressing too casually in the work setting can reduce one's personal power, can defeat competence and abilities, can attack one's confidence and self-esteem, can create communication barriers, and can jeopardize one's trustworthiness and credibility (Maysonave, 1999).

In a study of London hospital patients, doctors were trying to make patients feel more comfortable by dressing informally. However, the results of the study indicated that a greater number of patients responded positively when doctors assumed a more professional dress of suit or white coat. Patients thought the doctor's authority and status should be easy to identify by the appearance of the doctor (Sigman, 2002).

C. Q. Vicary in *Cross-Cultural Perspectives in Nonverbal Communication* (Poyatos, 1988) further discusses how clothing communicates about the wearer. Clothing can be subdivided into garments, ornaments, cosmetics, devices, treatments, equipment, and tools. All of these elements can be combined to speak nonverbally for the wearer. The person who appears with tattoos, multiple piercings, pink hair, and black clothing presents an image that says that he or she is the antithesis of the conventional businessperson.

Appropriate international dress varies. In Japan clothing can communicate the wearer's background, wealth, or social status. The style of clothing is conservative and formal. Bold designs and bright colors that might make one stand out from a crowd are rarely worn, as the Japanese do not seek to stand out. Women do not wear slacks, sleeveless tops, or revealing styles and men usually wear dark two-piece suits with white shirts and conservative ties (A beginner's..., 2001). When Arabs do business in Arab countries, they often wear traditional dress of white robes and headdresses (Varner & Beamer, 2005). In Saudi Arabia conservative dress is required for both men and women. Women wear loose-fitting and concealing clothing with long skirts, modest necklines, and elbow-length sleeves. Another custom related to dress is that the sole of the foot should not be pointed at anyone as this action is considered rude (Business..., 2003).

Body Movements (Kinesics)

Kinesics are motions that are often used to accompany verbal communication. For example, a person who gives directions to a motorist may make hand gestures to emphasize which way the motorist should travel. Sometimes the use of kinesics appears instinctive rather than planned or thought out. For this reason, many viewers of such motions believe the motion, if there is a conflict between what is spoken and the motion. For example, if a person says he or she is very interested in what you have to say, but the listener doesn't maintain eye contact and continually looks at the clock, it will be difficult to believe words over actions (Wainwright, 2003).

Nonverbal communication through kinesics must support rather than undermine the executive's plan of action. For example, if an executive has encouraged subordinates to submit innovative ideas, the executive's reaction when the ideas are presented is critical. If the executive sighs, shakes the head, frowns, or uses other negative kinesics, the innovator will feel like the poor idea was a waste of the executive's time. Soon the executive will be wondering why no employees are coming up with innovative ideas. A better plan would be to be noncommittal or nod encouragingly during the explanations, even if the executive knows the idea has flaws. If employees know that their ideas will be well received, they will bring forth more ideas that may be the effective ones the executive is seeking (Robbins, 2001).

For a speaker in the United States to develop a credible first impression, he or she should appear relaxed by speaking in a slower, lower style. Body language should be subtle with fewer gestures, as people associate self-confidence with a more controlled body style. A person who is too full of energy, talks too fast, and uses sharp and energetic gestures may think he or she made a good impression. In fact, the interpretation might be that the person tried too hard to impress or had too much caffeine (Zielinski, 2001).

Gestures are considered a key communication element around the world. However, a gesture in one country does not always mean the same in another country. Using your hand to make an OK sign means that everything is good to someone from the United States. The same OK sign in Japan stands for money—more specifically, coins. Using that sign in Japan may mean that coins are desired. In France, the OK sign stands for something that is worthless. If a businessperson gave the OK sign to the agent who was assigning a rental car to signify approval of the car, the agent would think that the car was unsatisfactory. If a person giving a V for victory sign in England made the sign with the palm facing inward, the meaning is not victory but rather a rude insult. The same gesture in Madeira stands for two of something (Axtell, 1998).

Posture can also send a nonverbal message. Standing tall indicates confidence in the Western culture. In some cultures the manager stands erect when talking to subordinates while the subordinates may drop their shoulders when listening to the manager (Varner & Beamer, 2005). Posture, especially when sitting, has become more casual in the Western culture. When communicating with others from other cultures, Americans should recognize the more formal posture of other countries. A slouching American can appear rude and unprofessional simply by posture.

Touching Behaviors (Haptics)
When describing touching behavior, the term used is haptics. To clarify, "touching" behaviors occur when someone deliberately touches another while "bodily contact" refers to accidental, unconscious touching (Wainwright, 1993). Touching is more likely in certain situations such as when giving information or advice, when trying to persuade, when listening to another's problems, and when communicating in social occasions (Wainwright, 2003).

The most common touching behavior in business in the United States is a handshake. The handshake should not be too limp (dead fish) or too strong (bone crusher) or too tentative (timidity) (Griffin, 1998; Miller, 2000). However, an American-style handshake is not always the most appropriate way to greet in an international environment (Varner & Beamer, 2005). Germans may pump the hand only once, while some Africans may snap their fingers after a handshake (Perry, 2001). In Russia, good friends start with a strong, firm handshake followed by a bear hug. However, the Finns who border Russia reject the idea of a hug in greeting (Axtell, 1998). The Swiss and Germans prefer to shake hands frequently and may do so more often than those in the United States. Women in Europe often shake hands. Shaking hands for women in the United States is often generational with younger women extending handshakes to both men and women in business (Robinson, 2003). The French shake hands on greeting and departing and in social and business contexts, winning them acknowledgment as one of the cultures that shakes hands most frequently. If you are a businessman traveling to Islamic countries, you should not offer to shake hands with women, as unrelated men are forbidden to touch women (Axtell, 1998).

Some cultures prefer a hugging embrace, while others use bows for greeting. For instance, in southern Europe and Central and South America, the handshake may be longer with the left hand used to touch a person's forearm or elbow. In Latin American countries a hug upon greeting is accepted procedure. The Japanese have perfected the bow on greeting to reflect varying levels of respect. While those from the United States may not be expected to bow in Japan, an acknowledgment of the culture through bowing is appreciated (Axtell, 1998). Because of sexual harassment issues (many people associate touching with a sexual motive), businesses in the United States discourage excessive touching. In an educational environment, sensitivity to the issue of child abuse is an additional consideration when using touching behaviors (Muse, 1996).

In their day-to-day interactions, most business people in the United States use business cards. Sometimes they barely glance at the cards, and sometimes they immediately flip cards over to write notes or additional phone numbers. In other cultures such as in Japan, card information should be written in English on one side of the card and in Japanese on the other side. The card is presented with both hands and a bow of the appropriate depth for the situation. The person receiving the card immediately reads it. The job title is important because that will signal to the person who receives the card the depth of the bow he or she must return. With this degree of formality, it can be easy to understand how the Japanese businessperson could be insulted by the American who immediately stuffs the business card in his or her pocket without even examining it. In contrast, the Japanese businessperson treats the business card with respect and takes the time to read it in the presence of the person who presented the card (A beginner's..., 2001).

Eye Behaviors (Oculesics)

In the culture of American business, direct eye contact is interpreted favorably, as someone who can look you in the eye and speak with you. Direct eye contact is seen as a sign of honesty and trust. If a person looks away or down and doesn't meet the eyes, the person is considered shifty or dishonest. Too much eye contact can communicate as superiority, lack of respect, a threat or threatening attitude, and a wish to insult. On the other hand, too little eye contact can also be interpreted as being impolite, being insincere, showing dishonesty, or being shy (Sphar, 1998; Wainwright, 2003). In some cultures, averting one's eyes is considered a sign of respect. While direct eye contact is important to Americans, it is even more important in Arab cultures. The belief in those cultures is that the eye doesn't lie, and Arabs frequently move closer to the speaker to see the eye better. For communicators from Japan, direct eye contact is usually avoided and would make the communicator feel uncomfortable (Varner & Beamer, 2005).

Communication in social settings is important in the business world, because business people prefer to do business with people that they know and respect. Eye contact is important in such a setting. If eye contact is made with someone within ten feet of you, recognize that person with a smile or a nod. Once the person is within five feet of you, offer a verbal greeting (How to be a confident..., 2003).

Many Americans rely on their mastery of English—the global language of business—to assist them in negotiations and often disregard or simply fail to recognize important nonverbal cues from those of other cultures (Briggs, 1998).

Space Utilization
Space is of importance in nonverbal communication. Individuals in different cultures learn to use space differently. While there are many levels of space, communicating with a range of eighteen inches to three feet is usually comfortable for most parties. A person may have, in effect, a space bubble surrounding him or her which is a range the individual prefers that others don't infringe. If someone invades the space bubble, the owner of the bubble may feel uncomfortable and may try to gain more space by moving away (Muse, 1996; Varner & Beamer, 2005).

While North Americans usually prefer to be in environments with a large amount of space around them, those from the Middle East are used to less space. In a conversation between people of the two cultures, the Middle Eastern representative may move closer to the North American representative than feels comfortable to the North American, who responds by stepping away from the speaker (Varner & Beamer, 2005).

In crowded situations with fixed seating such as in movie theatres or on airplanes, communicators tolerate having less space. In a gender variance, although both men and women desire the same amount of space, women are comfortable with less space (Yogarajah, 2001).

Paralanguage
Paralanguage includes the nonverbal voice qualities such as tone, timbre, resonance, volume, tempo, accents, laughing, crying, and shouting (Poyatos, 1988). Tone is an

important paralanguage element. Listeners may rely on "how" something was said rather than the actual composition of the language. For example, an inquiry of "are you busy?" might result in an answer of "I am so busy." The tone could agree with the words revealing that the speaker is very busy. Or, the tone could place emphasis on the word "so," implying that the speaker was not busy at all.

Accents have been examined to determine if they make a difference in communication. Research results indicate that in a particular country the most preferred accent is the one that is the dominant English-language accent of that country (Scott, Green, & Rosewarne, 2000).

When a speaker wants to be more persuasive or to emphasize a point, one idea is to increase both the rate of speech and the volume to gain the interest of the listener. This technique is used effectively in television commercials (Muse, 1996).

Active nonverbal communication includes appearance, kinesics or body movements, touching behaviors or haptics, eye behaviors or oculesics, space utilization or proxemics, and paralanguage. In addition to active nonverbal communication, passive nonverbal communication must also be considered when evaluating messages.

PASSIVE ASPECTS OF NONVERBAL COMMUNICATION

Some aspects of nonverbal communication are passive rather than active. Passive nonverbal communication is a secondary reference that is less personal. The sender of the message has less control of passive elements. Passive nonverbal elements used in business communication include numerals and counting indicators, colors, emblems or symbols, and olfactory communication (Victor, 1992).

Numerals and Counting Indicators

In different cultures the use of numerals and counting indicators may vary. For example, the use of the term "billion" is not the same across the world. In German, the term would be milliarden. Even in British English there is a variation with Britain's billion interpreted as a trillion in the United States (Varner & Beamer, 2005).

Simple confusion can arise in such things as counting on the fingers. While people in North America begin counting with the index finger, those in Europe start with the thumb. So, raising your index finger for one item at the local market in Germany might result in your getting two items instead. In Japan fingers are combined in counting, starting with the index finger as one. If two items were desired, the communicator would hold up the index finger and second finger together. The upright thumb alone stands for five (Axtell, 1998). Think of the difficulty if you intended to order one item but five were delivered.

Another counting example is that of counting floors in buildings. In the United States the ground floor of a building is called the first floor. In Europe, the first floor is the floor above the ground level or what would be considered the second floor in the United States. Many Europeans, Americans, and Australians find the number *13* unlucky. Hotels and office buildings in those countries often have floor numbering that goes from 12 to 14 and skips the unlucky *13* (Victor, 1992). The number four is pronounced "Sei" in Cantonese, which means death. Mazda had planned to name their new MPV the Mazda 4 until concerns were raised about selling the vehicle in Asian markets. Mazda is in the process of reconsidering the vehicle's name (Number 4 jinxes…, 2004).

Colors

Colors have different meanings in various cultures. In the United States and Europe black is usually the color of mourning. In contrast, in Japan and many Asian countries white is the color of mourning. Learning which colors are meaningful in a culture may help to better understand how people relate in that culture (Victor, 1992).

Colors can also be used to send a message. Yellow is a color used to indicate danger and a need for caution in the workplace in the United States. The same yellow has more positive associations in Europe (Victor, 1992). In a review of preferred colors in eight countries, blue was the overwhelmingly favorite color choice. Blue often stands for water, sky, heaven, constancy, dependability, trustworthiness, stature, and professionalism. The colors white and green followed with black and red completing the top five color choices by those in most countries (Scott, 2002).

Emblems

Emblems or symbols are used by all cultures and represent intrinsic meanings of value to the culture. Flags and figures are examples of emblems (Victor, 1992). When an American salutes the flag of the United States, the emblem of the country stands for much more than an actual cloth flag. Feelings of patriotism and pride are also called forth. Representatives of other cultures can be expected to have similar feelings about their nations' flags. A circle with a diagonal line through it is universally accepted as "no." So, such a sign with a smoking cigarette inside is understandable as a symbol to all for no smoking (Victor, 1992).

Olfactory Communication

Olfactory communication involves smells. Some cultures such as in the Americas, northern Europe, Japan, Australia, and New Zealand can be described as nonolfactory cultures. The absence of smell is very important. Participants in those cultures bathe frequently, and use deodorants and mouthwash. Perfumes and colognes are added to provide a pleasant smell and to lend confidence to the wearer (Griffin, 1998). Those from nonolfactory cultures are offended by those from olfactory cultures such as Arabic, African, and southern European cultures, where the natural odors of the body are encouraged. In fact, those from olfactory cultures may consider the lack of natural smell as an indicator that something is wrong with an individual. The difference between these two cultural approaches to smell can cause some serious communication problems, as those from nonolfactory cultures may refuse to communicate with those from olfactory cultures when they find natural smells offensive (Victor, 1992). The bias against a natural smell can be so intense in nonolfactory cultures that few will ever bring it up or actually tell a person that they have a bad mouth or body odor, although the odor may certainly be noticed.

The passive nonverbal communication includes numerals and counting indicators, colors, emblems, and olfactory communication. These nonverbal components make communicating more challenging when in an intercultural setting. Business graduates will need to learn about other cultures and develop a level of understanding for nonverbal communication in those cultures. The following ideas and resources provide a starting point for the business teacher to begin the awareness training that will be critical to future business students' success.

TEACHING IDEAS AND RESOURCES

Including information about nonverbal communication can be a highlight for any business class. The following suggestions may be incorporated in business communication classes, in general business classes, or in other broad-based business classes.

Cultural Study

Use secondary resources such as magazines, books, newspapers, and the Internet to examine a specific culture. The focus of the research should be on nonverbal communication. Ask students to examine greeting behaviors, communication, and dress, as well as any other issues referred to in this chapter that seem relevant. After students have found as much information as they can, ask them to add a primary research component by interviewing someone from that culture to verify their information and fill in any gaps they may have. Students then prepare a presentation using PowerPoint that will showcase the research results.

This project could be used as an individual project with each student assigned a different culture. However, it might be more attractive to students as a team project. Another idea is to have the class as a whole study a specific culture. Then each team could focus on a specific aspect of that culture. Alternatively, each team could study a different culture. At the end of the activity, the instructor could have an international day (or week) with students presenting their results to the rest of the class. In addition to a presentation, students could be asked to write an informational report, to write an analysis comparing the culture to their own, or to write some guidelines for interacting with those from the selected culture.

Internet Resources

The Association for Business Communication is an international association interested in promoting effective communication in business. One of their committees, the Intercultural Committee, has prepared activities and case studies that may be used by educators and are available free of charge online. Several case studies are appropriate for international nonverbal communication. Their site, www.businesscommunication.org, also includes a directory referring to country information.

Another useful organizational Web site is that of the National Business Education Association found at www.nbea.org. The online bookstore offers resources for international business including books about gestures and taboos in international business.

Delta Pi Epsilon offers information about best practices in business education, which include issues relating to international business. For details, see www.dpe.org.

Country specific information, including information relating to nonverbal customs, can also be found at U.S. government sites. For trade information, check www.export.gov, which is the U.S. government export portal. Also available through this site is information from the Trade Information Center of the U.S. Department of Commerce. Other government sites are linked here as well.

Perspective Adjustments

Ask students to change their perspective about nonverbal international communication. Rather than looking at the situation through the eyes of one living in the United States, ask them to assume they are from a culture outside of the United States. Have them write some guidelines for getting along nonverbally in the United States. The Rochester Institute of Technology has written an online handbook (International Student..., 2000) for international students that gives some suggestions. By changing their perspective, students might look at routine activities in a new light.

Nonverbal Communication in Movies

Cultures are displayed vividly through movies. Have students watch a foreign language film. Have them report on all the nonverbal language they observe. They should pay attention to gestures that are not familiar. Students should also look for use of eye contact, posture, head nods, and other body language. Watching films from a variety of countries will provide coverage of many cultures (Victor, 1992; Wainwright, 2003).

One college business communication instructor asks her students to watch the 1992 Tom Selleck movie, *Mr. Baseball*. In this comedy about a baseball player's move to Japan and attempt to adapt to his new surroundings, the character manages to alienate many. After viewing the movie, students are asked to assess the verbal and nonverbal communication of the main character in a short writing assignment. Other movies may also lend themselves to this treatment.

In-Class International Nonverbal Communication Activity

In this activity, the class is a population of a particular city (outside the United States). Select several students to be citizens of the United States who are visiting the city. The U.S. citizens are unable to communicate in the city's language. Give each of the visitors a task that they can read silently from a piece of paper. Ideas could include bargaining for something in the market, finding a hotel, getting directions to a restaurant, finding a hospital, and locating a restroom. The U.S. citizens can communicate in English (which the citizens of the city do not understand very well), but might have better luck nonverbally.

The remaining students can be divided into two groups: the citizens of the city and the observers. The citizens of the city may also be given roles such as police officer, grocer, postal service employee, shopper, etc. The city citizens should wear tags that identify their role in the society. The observers will watch the action and make notes of what they see. Assign observers to watch specific visitors. The teacher may wish to videotape the action for analysis later.

Once all of the roles are assigned, the role-playing activity can begin with the visitors (U.S. citizens) trying to find answers to their questions. At the conclusion of the activity, ask each group to analyze how the interaction worked.

The activities proposed to develop the business students' awareness of nonverbal international communication included cultural studies, Internet resources, perspective adjustments, nonverbal communication in movies, and an in-class international nonverbal communication activity. Some or all of these activities could be used through-out a business course to enhance student knowledge of nonverbal international communi-cation.

SUMMARY

Nonverbal communication is a silent language of communication. An ability to understand the meaning of intercultural/international nonverbal communication will add to communication skills of the business student. A study of the active components of nonverbal communication could include appearance, body movements, touching behaviors, eye behaviors, space utilization, and paralanguage. An examination of passive components of nonverbal communication includes numerals and counting behaviors, colors, emblems, and olfactory communication.

A series of activities focusing on nonverbal international communication is included in the chapter. These activities include suggested cultural studies, Internet resources, perspective adjustments, nonverbal communication in movies, and an in-class interna-tional nonverbal communication activity. The activities could be added to many different business courses to provide a better understanding of intercultural nonverbal communi-cation.

Communicating with those in other cultures requires some current research about the country or culture to provide a relevant understanding about the nonverbal communica-tion components and how they affect the communication process. The silent language of nonverbal communication is indeed an important component of successful communica-tion in the international realm.

REFERENCES

Axtell, R. E. (1998). *Gestures: The do's and taboos of body language around the world.* New York: John Wiley & Sons.

Briggs, W. (1998). Next for communicators: Global negotiation. *Communication World, 16*(1), 12-15.

Griffin, J. (1998). *How to say it at work: Putting yourself across with power words, phrases, body language, and communication secrets.* NY: Prentice Hall.

Hecht, M. L., DeVito, J. A., & Guerrero, L. K. (1999). Perspectives on nonverbal communication: Codes, functions, and contexts. In *The nonverbal communication reader: Classic and contemporary readings,* 2nd Ed. Prospect Heights, IL: Waveland Press, Inc.

How to be a confident business socializer. (2003). *Broker Magazine, 5*(3), 6-10.

International Student Handbook. (2000). Retrieved March 12, 2004, from Rochester Institute of Technology, Center for Student Transition and Support Web Site, http://www.rit.edu/~306www/international/handbook/nonverbalcommunication.html.

Leech, T. (2004). *How to prepare, stage, and deliver winning presentations.* New York: American Management Association.

Maysonave, S. (1999). *Casual power: How to power up your nonverbal communication and dress down for success.* Austin, TX: Bright Books.

Miller, P. W. (2000). *Nonverbal communication in the workplace.* Chicago, IL: Patrick W. Miller & Associates.

Muse, I. (1996). *Oral and nonverbal expression.* Princeton, NJ: Eye on Education.

Number 4 jinxes Mazda minivan name. (2004, June 6). *New Straits Times Press* [Malaysia], p. 6.

Perry, J. (2001). Palm power in the workplace. *American Salesman, 46*(10), 22.

Poyatos, F. (Ed.) (1988). *Cross-cultural perspectives in nonverbal communication.* Toronto, Canada: C. J. Hogrefe, Inc.

Robbins, S. (2001). Culture as communication. *Harvard Management Communication Letter, 4*(8), 1-3.

Robinson, D. (2003). *Business protocol: Contemporary American practice.* Cincinnati, OH: Atomic Dog Publishing.

Scott, J. C., Green, D. J., & Rosewarne, D. D. (2000). Perceptions of prospective and practicing United Kingdom-based businesspersons about three major indigenous English-language accents. *Delta Pi Epsilon Journal, 42*(4), 223-234.

Scott, J. C. (2002). The colorful world of international business. *Business Education Forum, 57*(1), 40-43.

Sigman, A. (2002). Body of evidence. *People Management, 8*(5), 48-50.

Sphar, E. R. (1998). The other international language. *Office Pro, 58*(9), 2-4.

Times Square Travel Centre. *A beginner's guide to Japan.* (2001). Retrieved June 28, 2004, from http://www.shinnova.com/part/99-japa/abj19-e.htm.

Trade Information Center, U. S. Department of Commerce. *Business customs: Saudi Arabia.* (2003). Retrieved June 29, 2004, from www.trade.gov/td/tic

Varner, I., & Beamer, L. (2005). *Intercultural communication in the global workplace* (3rd ed.). New York: McGraw Hill/Irwin.

Victor, D. A. (1992). *International business communication.* New York: HarperCollins Publishers.

Wainwright, G. R. (1993). *Body language.* Chicago, IL: NTC Publishing Group.

Wainwright, G. R. (2003). *Teach yourself body language.* Chicago, IL: McGraw Hill.

Yogarajah, J. (2001, February 10). Gender bias in body language. *New Straits Times-Management Times.* [Malaysia].

Zielinski, D. (2001). Presentations: What you think you know about body language may be hurting your career. *Body Language, 15*(4), 36-40.

Contexting: The Relative Directness of Intercultural Communication

Janet K. Winter
Central Missouri State University
Warrensburg, Missouri

Esther J. Winter
Central Community College
Hastings, Nebraska

Communicating across cultures is fraught with perils. Many aspects that are irrelevant or taken for granted when communicating within one's own culture need to be considered in the global marketplace: translation accuracy, religious beliefs, geographic considerations that dictate cultural tastes, and the list goes on. Current textbooks for business communication address intercultural communication and discuss its importance (Guffey, 2003; Lesikar, Pettit, & Flatley, 1999; Ober, 2003; O'Rourke, 2004; Penrose, Rasberry, & Myers, 2001).

Effective intercultural communication depends first on a clear understanding of culture. Researchers Kluckholm, Strodtbeck, Hall, Hofstede, Hampden-Turner, Trompenaars, Stewart, Bennet, and Rhinesmith have developed very useful models for describing cultures (summarized in Walker, Walker, & Schmitz, 2003). Understanding and using these models can help members of one culture learn how to interact more effectively and empathically with members of another. Through these models the researchers have identified several dimensions of human action and interaction that can be used to define cultures—the attitudes toward and views of environment, time, action, space, power, individualism, competitiveness, and structure, and the patterns of thinking and communication.

The differences all manifest themselves during communication, but communication also has its own specific subset of areas that require attention. These include whether the communication is direct or indirect, expressive or instrumental, formal or informal, and high- or low-context. This chapter focuses on the last of these issues: context.

During the course of the chapter, context is defined with reference to the research of Edward T. Hall, who is its primary theorist, and to the ideas and models put forward by later writers. How context manifests itself in various international cultures and situations is presented and discussed. The chapter proceeds to offer analogous situations in which the importance of context can be observed, even in what might initially be considered monocultural situations. Having defined and illustrated the concept of context, the chapter proceeds to discuss how the difficulties created by conflicting levels of context can be ameliorated by choosing the appropriate level of directness and following 23 clear guidelines for cross-cultural communication. Finally, the authors suggest instructional activities that can develop general cultural sensitivity and focused experience in dealing with context in communication.

UNDERSTANDING CULTURAL CONTEXT

Relative context is a barrier to successful communication when it is not understood. It causes business negotiations to fail and contracts to be disregarded. When participants do understand it, its cultural context makes communicating efficient and satisfying on many levels. Context is particularly useful in helping members of a legalistic and individualistic culture interact appropriately with members of a social or collectivistic culture.

Defining Cultural Context

Edward T. Hall, a pioneer in analysis of and accommodation for intercultural communication, defined cultural context as follows (Hall & Hall, 1990):

> Context is the information that surrounds an event; it is inextricably bound up with the meaning of that event. The elements that combine to produce a given meaning—events and context—are in different proportions depending on the culture. The cultures of the world can be compared on a scale from high to low context (p. 6).

In his 1976 book *Beyond Culture*, Hall had defined the continuum as follows:

> A high-context (HC) communication or message is one in which *most* of the information is already in the person, while very little is in the coded, explicit, transmitted part of the message. A low context (LC) communication is just the opposite: i.e., the mass of the information is vested in the explicit code (Hall & Hall, 1990, p. 6).

Of all the dimensions of difference in intercultural communication, context probably has the greatest effect on the actual business conducted. For most other dimensions (power distance, uncertainty avoidance, individualism/collectivism, masculinity/femininity, etc.), relations may be affected or feelings may be hurt, but ignoring the cultural context may have financial and legal consequences if parties to an agreement perceive the contract's meaning differently.

According to Ober (2003), context sensitivity deals with how the cultures "emphasize the surrounding circumstances (or context), make extensive use of body language, and take the time to build relationships and establish trust" (p. 52). One of the most important distinctions for Hall (1991), is that for high-context cultures, language is art. Much of what is expressed is dictated by etiquette, tradition, a desire to appear graceful, and the high value placed on eloquence. Language serves to unify and preserve in a high-context culture, not to reflect temporary and changing conditions; meaning, therefore, has to be communicated through some means other than verbal communication.

A variety of models attempt to quantify the relationship between various cultures and to place cultures on a continuum. Copeland and Griggs (1985) offer a simple vertical list, ranking some of the more widely recognized cultures from highest- to lowest-context: Japanese, Arab, Greek, Spanish, Italian, English, French, American, Scandinavian, German, and German-Swiss. Hall proposes a "context triangle" to illustrate how the cultures derive meaning from a combination of stored and transmitted information (Victor, 1992). Rosch and Segler in "Communication with Japanese" (cited in Victor, 1992, p. 143) place Latin American countries between Arab and Italian cultures and identify "American" as "North American." Central and Eastern Europeans are considered to be high-context, but their communication may be direct or indirect, depending upon the specific country and the situation (Walker, Walker, & Schmitz, 2003).

While this attempt at a ranking does provide a useful introduction to the subject, it does not address the complexity of the issue. No culture is consistent across all its members, and even in quite homogeneous cultures such as the Japanese, the population will exhibit a range of degrees of high-context behaviors. In the above listing, note the placement of the "American" culture, but then consider what is meant by "American" culture. Even in a business context, many variations of North American exist. Doing business in Dallas and Fargo are not the same at all, as their eponymous television series and movie demonstrate; and Toronto's downtown district and its Chinatown are culturally worlds apart.

Sometimes the context changes for a culture, even regarding the workings of the law. Hall, in his 1959 *The Silent Language,* describes such a situation in the case of police officer Sancho of Spanish origins. He was notorious for ticketing Spanish and American motorists alike for doing even one mile over the 15-mph limit. The high-context Spanish culprits accepted the tickets, while the American miscreants complained, ran the officer off the road at 60 miles per hour, broke his legs, and beat him severely on more than one occasion. Once in court, however, the Americans paid the fines as directed, while most of the Spanish drivers avoided fines by virtue of relationships with the court officials.

Sometimes even the researchers have difficulty identifying the prevailing context—the Copeland and Griggs (1985) vertical continuum labels the French a low-context culture between the English and the Americans; but Hall (1990) describes the French as a high-context culture. As Samovar and Porter (1991) point out, "Context is a form of cultural adaptation to a particular setting or environment" (p. 233) and is, therefore, in a continual state of flux. Each corporation also has its unique culture dictating what must be directly communicated and what is understood.

Identifying the context can be a first step in describing a culture and establishing guidelines for interacting, but simply pigeonholing a particular culture is not enough. It is important to understand that huge differences may exist, to be alert to the signals given out by other parties, and to know the ways that high- or low-context cultures manifest themselves as such.

Examining Manifestations of Context

Victor (1992) describes five aspects of context that affect communication across cultures: emphasis on personal relationships; belief in explicit communication, the law, and contracts; reliance on verbal communication; uncertainty avoidance variations; and face-saving. After identifying the relative degree of context employed by a culture, one must consider these specific aspects. The following examples illustrate how context manifests itself in a variety of cultures.

The high-context Japanese emphasize personal relationships and must agree on general terms before they will even consider specific details of business dealings. For them, the people involved in the negotiation are more important than the words of the contract (Victor, 1992). High-context cultures prefer to spend time developing relationships, and discussion of business will occur after the partners know enough about each other to have established a trusting relationship. In many cases, even though the papers have been signed, if the original signers of the contract leave the firm or the project, the high-context partners may consider the agreement void and stop fulfilling their part of it (Victor, 1992).

The Germans, in contrast, focus on the words spoken and written—the explicit communication—tending to discount nonverbal contradictions and paying little attention to personal relationships. Low-context cultures dislike silences in discussions and focus on making sure that the spoken and written words are clear and leave no room for variation. Low-context cultures are committed to the letter of the contract, regardless of the individuals administering it.

Low-context cultures follow the law to the letter; but for high-context cultures such as the Turkish, an American's stopping for a stop sign in the middle of a deserted desert is ludicrous (Victor, 1992). People of high-context cultures consider the law to be a guide, rather than an absolute—it can be bent to suit the circumstances.

American courts are an example of the absolute power of words—frequently the examiner will demand that the witness answer only "Yes" or "No," totally disregarding any context. Still, not all low-context cultures are consistent. An example of this comes out of England, generally identified as being low-context. It is well documented in the literature set against the backdrop of the Regency Period (the works of Georgette Heyer, for example), that although duels were illegal, it was privately accepted that certain actions required a formal challenge and duel for honor to be upheld. In this case, not the low-context public letter of the law, but the high-context personal cultural mores, dictated appropriate action.

In high-context Korea, signing a contract is simply an indication of the opening of the negotiations (Victor, 1992). The Japanese even distinguish between a public truth and a real truth—the letter of the law versus the spirit of the law applied in context. Low-context cultures such as the Swiss and German are most likely to determine points of law based on the written law, disregarding precedents, while high-context cultures are more likely to use general principles interpreted individually by an administrator in each unique situation (Victor, 1992).

The two types of cultures vary in their reliance on verbal communication and view words differently. Where low-context cultures may use words to argue and to accomplish tasks, high-context cultures are more focused on understanding the heart of the person, avoiding conflict, and seeking compromise. They are inclined to use rhetoric more formally and stylistically, simply because of the beauty of language, and perhaps also because facility with the language denotes intelligence and status. The French and Italian even use letter salutations and closings to provide hints of the relationship of sender and receiver. According to Victor (1992), the Arabs practice "over-expression," using poetic and exaggerated verbiage, sometimes muddying the water to the point of confusion for the low-context participant who "must separate the central information from the peripheral—while keeping in mind that, as background for context, all peripheral information can, in time, come to the fore as central information" (p. 156).

This emphasis carries over into the area of questioning. In most North American classrooms, which are fairly low-context, teachers encourage student questions by asserting, "There is no such thing as a stupid question." On the other hand, the high-context Navajo culture considers that learning should come not from asking, but from forming and testing hypotheses (Beck & Walter, 1977).

The difference in framing ideas is illustrated by Victor (1992) in the following sign board printed in three languages: the German "Walking on the grass is forbidden" (p. 156) is a clear statement of fact, barely escaping being an order; the English "Please do not walk on the grass" (p. 156) uses courtesy to hint that there may be some choice; while the French "Those who respect the environment will avoid walking on the grass" (p. 157) makes it an option, depending on the reader's attitude to the environment.

High-context cultures prefer to avoid uncertainty by communicating only within their known culture, wishing to already know as much as they can about their partners and contract terms. According to Victor (1992), they tend to stick close to the established rules and emphasize job stability; and they experience high anxiety, job stress, and worries about the future as a result of changes in the environment/context. Low-context cultures, however, can work with more uncertainty as long as the salient points are clear. People from these cultures take pride in being flexible in matters not dictated by contracts or policies. Walker, Walker, and Schmitz (2003) describe such tolerance for ambiguity clearly as

> the degree to which uncertainty is perceived as a threat, leading to anxiety about the future and the protection of society through technology, rules, and rituals. In places with high uncertainty avoidance (such as Japan, France, Russia, and Latin America), there is a need for comprehensive rules and regulations, a belief in the power of experts, and a search for absolute truths and values, whereas in places with low uncertainty avoidance (such as the United States, Indonesia, China, and northern Europe), there is less emphasis on rules and procedures, a greater reliance on relativism and empiricism, and more of a belief in generalists and common sense. (p. 47)

In high-context cultures, face-saving is extremely important. Such cultures prefer indirect communication and avoid accusing anyone for a problem to the point that the Japanese may apologize for even mentioning a problem, usually saying, "Yes," even if the answer is "No." Low-context cultures, although perceiving personal pride and dignity as important, focus on the fairness and are more likely to be confrontational, seeing indirectness as unclear and deceitful. Members of high-context cultures tend to feel shame, while those of low-context cultures tend to feel guilt (Victor, 1992) or just embarrassment. In high-context cultures, the damage is to the reputation of the whole group. In low-context cultures, making reparation usually solves the problem. Although private reprimands are universally more acceptable than public ones, a high-context culture attaches much greater stigma to a public reprimand.

The different approaches of high-context and low-context cultures to information tend to affect their attitudes towards each other. According to Hall and Hall (1990), "High-context people are apt to become impatient and irritated when low-context people insist on giving them information they don't need. Conversely, low-context people are at a loss when high-context people do not provide *enough* information" (p. 9). They further suggest that those from high-context cultures may feel insulted when given too much information. Samovar and Porter (1991) generalize that high-context cultures tend to see people from low-context cultures as neither credible nor authoritative because of their dependence on the spoken or written word, while low-context cultures find it irresponsible of high-context cultures to disregard the exchanged words. They note that what one culture may interpret as mediating, the other sees as meddling; what one sees as honorable compromise, the other views as surrender (p. 240). Obviously finding a common meeting ground is crucial and may be achieved by understanding the relevant cultures.

Using Analogies to Help Understand Context

As students work to understand the concept of cultures as being high-context or low-context, the following analogies can help them relate and empathize. They may also serve to illustrate the fundamental truth that there is no single right or wrong way of doing things.

An example of a high-context culture is a small, rural high school where the population remains constant and the faculty has little turnover. Syllabi and assignment descriptions are almost superfluous: everyone already knows what the teacher expects. If a student was not paying attention in class, an older sibling can usually explain how the teacher wants papers prepared and what is likely to affect a grade. In this case, the context—consisting of teacher, school, and course—carries all the required information. A teacher in this system knows the board, parents, and superintendent, has taught older siblings of current class members, and has probably encountered the current students before. There is little need to communicate formally with the parents or the board. The policies may be written down, but there is no real need to refer to them; knowing the individuals involved takes precedence over conforming to the policies.

On the opposite end of the scale is the college or university, a very low-context culture. Relationships between people hardly matter as student and instructor may have very limited contact with each other—everything is transacted on paper. The assignment description details a wealth of minutiae—print size, margins, length, and the appropriate style sheet that dictates number of spaces, use of capitals, and whether a comma is needed between author and page number—and following the guidelines to the letter matters. The syllabus specifies when the instructor can be accessed, how many minutes constitute an absence, and whether the student will be excused to attend a funeral. Then there are department policies, the student handbook, the college catalog. The experienced college student understands that no matter how good a relationship exists with the instructor, success depends on meeting the published obligations.

A "culture clash" occurs when a recent college graduate assumes a position in the high-context culture of the rural school. If the interaction is to be successful, the cultures must meet in the middle. An older teacher may serve as mentor to "translate" the culture, and supervisors will probably make available manuals and policies and explain which ones are actually adhered to. The new teacher has to learn to read the new culture, understanding its defining values (it may be inappropriate to take attendance the first day of deer-hunting season) and establishing the relationships that allow participation in the high-context culture.

Personal relationships also contain elements of high and low context. Generally, the longer the relationship has existed, the less it depends on words for communication. Early in a relationship, would-be partners spend a lot of time explaining themselves to each other and seeking clarification of underlying intentions. High school relationships are classic examples of this phenomenon, where half of the energy invested in the early stages of a relationship goes into seeking explanations from friends of what particular actions or utterances really mean. Information has to be put into words and conveyed by a trusted intermediary before it can be processed and believed. Long-term couples, in contrast, read the context, which might include body language, shared history, knowledge of each other's values, and sometimes even private codes, so words are not needed. The disjunction between high- and low-context communication is felt quite keenly by someone who has recently left a long-term relationship and is embarking on a new one. Where things once were simply understood, they now need to be carefully verbalized and clarified.

Families and established teams usually represent high-context versions of what might be a generally lower-context culture. While it may take the community many letters to the editor and an election to convey its displeasure with a particular city council member, a parent can communicate the same thing to a child with a raised eyebrow, a heavy pause, or a significant cough. When a community or organization wants to honor one of its members, it requires written recommendations, public speeches, even a plaque with the words engraved upon it—just to make sure the low-context culture gets the point. Within the same culture, however, one player can recognize the achievements of another with a simple slap on the back.

Because people tend to be ethnocentric, determining whether a culture is high- or low-context, analyzing the five aspects of cultural difference, and using analogies like these can be a means of coming to terms with differences. Recognizing the differences that one has come to know and accept in one's own culture can be the first step in learning to accept the larger differences between cultures.

MINIMIZING PROBLEMS CREATED BY CONTEXT

The next step for an intercultural communicator is to learn strategies to adapt for the differences. People from outside a culture need more information (usually in words) about the procedures and norms for the culture. When Americans try to establish business relationships in areas where procedures are known through long-standing traditions and relationships, they must be patient, tolerant, and attuned to existing communication conventions of the specific context.

Selecting the Appropriate Level of Directness

Because each culture is different, there are no hard-and-fast rules about when to be direct and when to be indirect. For example, while the Chinese take a long time to develop relationships before they begin talking business, they are relatively abrupt when ending a telephone call. Still, some general characteristics can be established.

For high-context cultures, one should usually be indirect and formal, show concern for the individual (not just the business deal), give multiple options (avoid simple Yes/No answers), follow the lines of authority, and be flexible or vague about deadlines. It is best to conduct business through personal meetings, especially at the start of a relationship.

For low-context cultures, effective communicators will be reasonably direct and utilize a variety of levels of formality, provide and adhere to schedules, follow orderly sequences, provide logical proof, focus on one topic at a time, provide information early, be prompt and prepared, and give clear information and details verbally. Whenever possible, they will utilize print media that can constitute a permanent record (i.e., letters, faxes, e-mail). When communication is oral, recordings can constitute a permanent record if both parties agree to their use.

When in doubt, a good rule of thumb is to be extremely courteous and focus on the other party's best interests, no matter what the message and degree of directness. The best practice is to identify the level of contexting required and then consider each specific culture and situation. It is even useful to know how one's own culture is described for others. The body of information describing individual cultures is rapidly expanding, but here are two of the most reliable resources. Intercultural Press Inc. (www.interculturalpress.com) publishes a variety of general and specific culture guide-books, along with a wide selection of useful teaching texts. *CultureGrams* (www.culturegrams.com) through Brigham Young University include a comprehensive list of culture profiles that are regularly updated.

Identifying Guidelines for Communicating

In 1991, Harris and Moran found that difficulties in dealing with other cultures accounted for 33% of the failures among Americans doing business abroad. What follows is a compendium gleaned from the authors cited throughout this chapter, offering guidelines for North Americans doing business interculturally. There are 23 guidelines; the first 13 are general principles for use in all crosscultural communication situations, even when the other party belongs to a similarly low-context culture, such as the English, French, Scandinavians and Germans, who are all ranked adjacent to North Americans in most models.

1. Know the specific culture and adjust for its unique characteristics.

2. Follow the pecking order (someone losing face may resort to sabotage or even revenge).

3. Know the kind, direction, and frequency of information flow to avoid offending anyone.

4. Watch for nonverbal cues and translate them appropriately for the specific culture.

5. Understand and adapt to the personal distance expectations of the other culture.

6. Be wary of assisting others with job duties or making suggestions—such help may be implying that the worker is inept.

7. If appropriate, be passionate and enthusiastic (e.g., Middle East), or silent and restrained (e.g., Japan), but maintain an attitude of courtesy and respect.

8. Be sensitive to historical issues and avoid political discussions.

9. Follow the conventions of greetings, terms of address, gift giving, and entertaining.

10. Abide by the conventions for formal and informal speech. The Japanese, for example, have both types of speech. Many languages (e.g., German) have special pronouns to be used in formal situations and other pronouns for discussions with friends.

11. Avoid mixing humor with business and other formal situations.

12. Allow for silences in face-to-face meetings. Follow the Chinese proverb, "He who speaks has no knowledge, and he who has knowledge does not speak."

13. Balance the desire to preserve harmony with the competitive spirit—beware of giving out information that may be used against you.

Guidelines 14-23 are additional techniques that must be employed when low-context North Americans are interacting with any higher-context culture and should be considered in all situations.

14. Ask multiple-choice questions, rather than Yes/No questions, to save face. Ask for advice rather than answers. Never say, "No"; instead, provide conditions and results.

15. Use the indirect approach.

16. Keep in mind the situational nature of rules, but provide clear guidelines and procedures.

17. Expect to take a long time to get to business; plan several preliminary social meetings.

18. Be patient and go with the flow, even if the main topic seems to be getting lost or being avoided. Mention positive aspects of the weather, etc., as well as positive aspects of the business dealings—be friendly without losing the formality required of the situation and the participants.

19. Do not expect others to follow the letter of the contract; consider the conditions and look for mutually profitable solutions. Share information freely to maintain control.

20. Avoid admiring a personal possession; the owner may feel obliged to make a gift of it.

21. Be careful of mentioning deadlines or time constraints, thereby suggesting a lack of trust.

22. Limit messages to one topic, but perhaps provide many separate reports to adapt to the limited reliance on communication but the real need for information.

23. After receiving a "Yes" answer from someone, follow up with a question addressing the opposite condition. If another "Yes" answer is forthcoming, try a multiple-choice question.

These 23 guidelines can be useful as a standard for communicating across cultures. The most important one, though, is the first. Each culture is different, and any cultural model is just a stereotype of the most common condition.

DEVELOPING CULTURAL SENSITIVITY IN THE CLASSROOM

The following activities can be useful in the classroom. They can help students understand how the concept of high and low context affects intercultural communication.

Exploring with Games, Movies, and Simulations

The game *Barnga* (Thiagarajan & Steinwachs, 1990), available from Intercultural Press, provides an excellent classroom simulation exercise. Participants form groups to play cards and establish their culture based on a given, printed set of rules for the game, with a different set for each group. As play progresses, groups are in a constant state of flux as original members leave and new members need to be assimilated, but participants may not communicate in speech or writing. Conflicts arise and must be resolved as students go from culture to culture, and as the group in general goes from being an assortment of consistently low-context cultures abiding by common written rules to a heterogeneous mix of insiders and outsiders, forced by the absence of typical communication channels to become high-context cultures.

Foreign movies create mini-immersion experiences, especially if not dubbed. Observing the pace and manner of interaction and comparing that with how people from another culture would interact develops an attitude of attentiveness to cultural context. It also provides specific knowledge of other cultures. *The Gods Must Be Crazy* (1980, directed by Jamie Uys) set in Botswana and *The Road Home* (2000, directed by Yimou Zhang) from China are generally available at video rental places and provide insight into other cultures. A dubbed movie also has value because it forces students to read the words, which sometimes means they miss out on the nonverbal cues; and this is what happens to the low-context participant in a high-context situation.

Students might identify the various cultures of which they have knowledge (perhaps wrestling, hunting, sculpting, or body piercing) and discuss the levels of context in that culture. They could determine how one moves from being an outsider to an insider within the culture.

Another activity that may be useful in the business classroom is presented by Jameson (1993) in the *Bulletin of the Association for Business Communication*. The article describes a simulation that models a realistic business situation, using three fictional cultures.

Analyzing Adages as Reflections of Culture
Cultural values are commonly expressed in the sayings used to explain and shape behavior. Students might discuss whether an adage, such as those given below (sources unknown), originates from a high- or low-context culture, based on the attitudes expressed.

1. One does not make the wind blow, but is blown by it. (Asian)

2. The nail that stands out gets hammered down. (Asian)

3. The first man to raise his voice loses the argument. (Chinese)

4. Order is half of life. (German)

5. A friend to everybody is a friend to nobody. (German)

6. Life is a dance, not a race. (Irish)

7. How blessed is a man who finds wisdom. (Jewish)

8. No need to know the person, only the family. (Chinese)

9. A zebra does not despise its stripes. (Maasai)

10. Empty cans clatter the loudest. (Indonesian)

Using and/or Establishing the Value-Orientation Continuum
To become involved with the various cultural nuances, students could research a particular culture and then prepare reports, such as the following, discussing the differences:

Level 1: Report on the cultures and customs in an essay.

Level 2: Report the modifications needed to interact in a setting such as a dinner meeting.

Level 3: Hold a meeting to discuss and set up a conference or other meeting where several different cultures must be accommodated. Students must discuss timing, decorations, greetings, announcements, gifts, meals (timing, customs, menu), translators (or other devices such as printed handouts), and religious customs that may affect the meeting situation.

Experimenting through Business Communication Activities

To help students understand how writing directly and indirectly is appropriate for different cultures, the following exercises using business letters may also be useful:

Level 1: Provide students with a letter from a Japanese counterpart using high-context openings, prevarications, and apologies. Have them revise it using more direct low-context style.

Level 2: Provide students with a letter in a low-context style. Have them revise it using more high-context openings, prevarications, and apologies.

Level 3: Provide students with a letter in a high-context style and have them respond in kind.

Young people are often led by the media and their own insularity to believe that the global village is becoming more homogeneous. Some might suggest that as civilization approaches a world culture, the ends of the continuum will be squeezed together, but many of the commonalities used as evidence of this world culture (ubiquity of McDonald's, similarities in fashion and pop music, increasing use of English), are quite superficial. Just because a person speaks English, it does not mean that he or she thinks, feels, and processes in an American, Canadian, British, Australian (or any other culture that uses English as its main language) way. This is a point worth reiterating when it comes to international business, where interpreters are frequently used. A person's culture goes much deeper than education, language, or appearance. A Korean interpreter, speaking Boston-accented English, wearing an Armani suit, is just as likely to be guided by his Korean belief in *nunchi* (where real communication happens through the eyes) as by his Harvard MBA class in business law. Engaging students in actual business tasks as well as experiential and analytical exercises can help them to understand the differences in contexting manifest in the customs of specific cultures. In addition, the activities can help them to develop awareness as well as practical skills appropriate for the global marketplace.

SUMMARY

Attention to the nuances of context levels in culture will help the intercultural communicator avoid the perils of global interaction. Defining the culture and describing some of its characteristics are the first steps in interacting appropriately with those of another culture. Analogies that illustrate how their own culture includes both high- and low-context communications can help American students, many of whom have little experience beyond their own communities, to understand how culture drives action and perceptions. Identifying the relative levels of context and selecting the appropriate level of directness to minimize difference is one way to reduce the problems created as a result of differing contexts. The effective communicator will also focus on building relationships, being extremely accurate and detailed, and constantly seeking feedback.

Despite the shrinking of the global village, the differences between appearance and practice can still cause the ruin of a business enterprise. The executive who can effectively interact within the global partner's culture will experience the most success.

REFERENCES

Beck, P. V., & Walter, A. L. (1977). *The sacred: Ways of knowledge, sources of life.* Tsaile, AZ: Navajo Community College Press.

Copeland, L., & Griggs, L. (1985). *Going international: How to make friends and deal effectively in the global marketplace.* New York: Random House.

Guffey, M. E. (2003). *Business communication: Process and product* (4th Ed.). Mason, OH: South-Western/Thomson Learning.

Hall, E. T. (1959). *The silent language.* Garden City, NY: Doubleday & Company, Inc.

Hall, E. T., & Hall, M. R. (1990). *Understanding cultural differences.* Yarmouth, ME: Intercultural Press, Inc.

Hall, E. (1991). Context and meaning. In L.A. Samovar & R.E. Porter (Eds.), *Intercultural communication: A reader* (pp. 46-55). Belmont, CA: Wadsworth Publishing Company.

Harris, P. R., & Moran, R. T. (1991). *Managing cultural differences* (3rd Ed.). Houston: Gulf Publishing Company.

Jameson, D. A. (1993). Using a simulation to teach intercultural communication in business communication courses. *Bulletin of the Association for Business Communication, 56*(1), 3-11.

Lesikar, R.V., Pettit, J. D., Jr., & Flatley, M. E. (1999). *Lesikar's basic business communication* (8th Ed.). Boston: McGraw-Hill Companies, Inc.

Ober, S. D. (2003). *Contemporary business communication* (5th Ed.). Boston: Houghton Mifflin Company.

O'Rourke, J. S., IV (2004). *Management communication: A case analysis approach* (2nd Ed.). Upper Saddle River, NJ: Pearson Prentice Hall.

Penrose, J. M., Rasberry, R. W., & Myers, R. J. (2001). *Advanced business communication* (4th Ed.). Cincinnati, OH: South-Western College Publishing.

Samovar, L. A., & Porter, R. E. (1991). *Communication between cultures.* Belmont, CA: Wadsworth Publishing.

Thiagarajan, S., & Steinwachs, B. (1990). *Barnga.* Yarmouth, ME: Intercultural Press, Inc.

Victor, D. A. (1992). *International business communication.* New York: HarperCollins Publishers, Inc.

Walker, D. M., Walker, T., & Schmitz, J. (2003). *Doing business internationally: The guide to cross-cultural success* (2nd Ed.). New York: McGraw-Hill.

Face: Western and Eastern Perspectives

Peter W. Cardon
Utah State University
Logan, Utah

Fundamental to international business relationships is respect and trust among businesspersons. Closely related to notions of respect and trust is *face*, a metaphor that approximates notions of prestige, dignity, pride, honor, and sense of identity. This rich metaphor originated in the Chinese language and has since become a part of Far Eastern languages as well as many Western languages. The notion of face plays an important role in business because it relates to how people believe they can demonstrate respect to others and how they expect to be treated by others. This chapter contrasts Western and Eastern perspectives of face and related communication patterns, with the United States and China discussed respectively as representative cultures of the West and the East. This chapter includes four major sections: (a) perspectives of face in American and Chinese business cultures; (b) face-related communication patterns in American and Chinese business cultures; (c) perspectives of face in other Western and Eastern cultures; and (d) suggestions for teaching about face.

PERSPECTIVES OF FACE IN AMERICAN AND CHINESE BUSINESS CULTURES

American and Chinese businesspersons conceptualize face quite differently, primarily because of the different nature of business relationships in American and Chinese society. Everyday language about face reveals additional aspects of how face operates in business relationships. Together, the nature of business relationships and the everyday language about face reveal a basic logic of face. This section describes differing perspectives of face by contrasting (a) business relationships in American and Chinese culture, (b) the language about face in American and Chinese culture, and (c) the logic of face in American and Chinese culture.

Business Relationships in the American and Chinese Cultures

The nature of American and Chinese business relationships form the foundation for how face is conceptualized differently. Americans tend to be individualists, whereas the Chinese tend to be collectivists. As a result, members of each culture hold different views and attitudes about how business relationships should be formed. This section includes a brief description of the American individualist view of relationships and the Chinese collectivist view of relationships, as well as implications for the logic of face in each culture.

American individualism is grounded in Western liberalism. As individualists, Americans tend to value individual over group goals. Primary values in interpersonal relationships include autonomy, independence, and equality. American business relationships are comparatively short-term, loose, and tied together by mutual interest. A person's identity is largely dependent on personal achievement and is distinctly separate from other closely tied businesspersons. Affiliation with others, including those within the same company, is a secondary aspect of identity. As a result, the American perspective of face primarily involves a person's record of individual achievement and success (Hofestede, 2001; Morisaki & Gudykunst, 1994).

Chinese collectivism is grounded in Confucianism, which is a moral philosophy about the ideals of interpersonal relationships. As collectivists, Chinese tend to value group goals over individual goals. Primary values in interpersonal relationships include harmony, loyalty, obligation, and hierarchy. Chinese business relationships tend to be comparatively rigid and long-term. A person's identity is highly dependent on one's social connections. In fact, individual identity is an obscure notion since identity is so meshed with others in one's social group. Personal achievement, while important in many situations, is a secondary aspect of identity. As a result, the Chinese perception of face largely involves a person's record of maintaining effective and ongoing relationships and is a measure of social rank (Chang & Holt, 1994; Hofestede, 2001; Wong & Leung, 2001).

Language about Face in the American and Chinese Cultures

Everyday language about face reveals certain characteristics about the logic of face in interpersonal relationships. The use of face in English demonstrates a comparatively simple perspective of face and the reactive nature of related behavior in American society. Also, face is primarily a matter of individual identity and only loosely related to social ties. The use of face in Chinese, on the other hand, demonstrates an extremely complex perspective of face and the primarily proactive nature of related behavior in Chinese society. Furthermore, face is mostly a matter of social identity and cannot be separated from the context of social networks (Chang & Holt, 1994; Wong & Leung, 2001).

Language about Face in English

Americans use limited English-language terms related to face. Most Americans are only familiar with phrases such as "saving face" and "losing face." These phrases are generally reserved for rare events and focus on what could potentially make a person look bad in the eyes of others. The notion of gaining or enhancing face is not part of everyday language (Jia, 2001; Li, 1996).

Of course, Americans are concerned about issues of respect and reputation within interpersonal relationships but usually express such ideas differently. Phrases about respect demonstrate that various related attitudes, actions, and goals are possible: to show respect, to command respect, to demand respect, to lose respect, and so on. Phrases about impressions and reputations demonstrate related attitudes, actions, and goals: to make a good impression, to make a bad impression, to maintain a good reputation, to lose a reputation, to gain a reputation, to rely on a reputation, and so on. Much theory about business communication focuses on issues about how to treat or respect others as well as how to gain respect and trust from others (e.g., you-attitude, you-emphasis, politeness theory, and impression management) (Bell & Smith, 1999; Rodman, 2001). These theories and practices are deeply rooted in values of American individualism such as autonomy, equality, individual identity, and individual performance.

Language about Face in Chinese
The language about face in the Chinese language, compared to the English language, is incredibly complex and sophisticated. Hundreds of phrases describe face and related behaviors in the Chinese language. The notion of face itself has at least three major variants, each of which include Chinese-language characters that literally mean face and also contain metaphorical meanings of dignity, pride, or honor. Each variant word, while generally overlapping in meaning, subtly varies in terms of context and emphasis, such as moral dignity versus social reputation (Jia, 2001; Zhai, 1995).

Several idioms in Chinese reveal the critical need for having face. There is a Chinese phrase that states that a person without face is like a tree without bark. This indicates that survival itself depends on having face. Face must be protected in order to function in a social network. One idiom states that a person is willing to make his face bigger by hitting it so much it swells up like a fat person. This idiom, applied to individuals overly concerned about face, is an exaggeration and often used in a negative sense, but it reveals what drastic behavior some Chinese will take to obtain face (Jia, 2001; Zhai, 1995).

Dozens of Chinese verbs take face as the object. For example, the Chinese talk about losing face, saving face, giving face, loving face, paying attention to face, struggling for face, needing face, protecting face, buying face, borrowing face, sweeping face away, and rewarding face. The Chinese talk about how much face a person has: a person may have a lot of face, not much face, no face, or more face than others. Face, however, extends much further than just the individual's face. For example, the Chinese say that when a person loses face, his or her whole family loses face, implying that face is interconnected with members of one's social network. Face can even be applied to entire groups; for instance, the Chinese can talk about the face of a company or the face of the entire nation. These phrases and many others demonstrate the sophisticated behavior and characteristics relating to face in Chinese society. In particular, they demonstrate that face is a valuable and shared resource that acts as a social currency that facilitates social exchanges. Face can be expended for immediate needs, invested when seeking a stream of dividends, and saved and accumulated for future returns. Yet, although face serves instrumental and practical needs, sincere emotion and devotion generally coincide and more often than not serve as the foundation for what often appears on the surface, to foreigners at least, to be merely exchanges of mutual interest (Hu, 1944; Jia, 2001; Zhai, 1995).

In interpersonal business relations, the most important Chinese concepts of face are to save face and to give face. To save face is primarily a reactive tactic—oftentimes a form of damage prevention or control. On the other hand, to give face is proactive. Giving face means to actively seek to increase the face of others, which in turn obligates others to return face when requested. This proactive tactic is the most common face-related behavior among Chinese businesspersons (Cardon & Scott, 2003).

Logic of Face in the American and Chinese Cultures

The differing nature of business relationships and the use of face in everyday language reveal contrasting logics of face between Americans and Chinese. Americans tend to use an individualist or personal logic of face, whereas the Chinese tend to use a collectivist or group logic of face. These contrasting logics of face differ in terms of importance and function.

Importance of Face

In terms of importance, face is preferred but not necessary in the American business culture. An American businessperson can operate effectively without having face or honoring the face of others. Concern with profits and other corporate benefits typically precede concern with the dignity of individuals involved in business interactions. However, with few exceptions, Americans prefer maintaining a feeling of respect between businesspersons. In terms of negative consequences, even if an American businessperson loses face or causes others to lose, he or she can often repair the damage within a short period of time. If necessary, he or she has many alternatives to move to a new work environment based on personal achievement and competence, to build new relationships, and to make a fresh start. Knowledge of face-losing behavior is generally confined only to the individuals involved in an interaction and spreads slowly (Beamer & Varner, 2001; Hall, 1977).

In Chinese business culture, by contrast, face plays a defining and indispensable role in business relationships. An individual without face cannot operate effectively in the Chinese business environment because status within social networks is the primary source of success and influence. In terms of negative consequences, losing face essentially ruptures relationships or, at a minimum, lowers social position within social networks. Once an individual loses face, gaining it back is much more difficult. Furthermore, the knowledge of the face-losing behavior quickly spreads through the entire social network, since in a collectivist society, the behavior affects the face of the entire social network (Hall, 1977; Wong & Leung, 2001).

Function of Face

In terms of function, face serves as a way of respecting individual autonomy and identity in American business culture. Face is primarily an individual matter. It is earned through achievement and relates little to social networks. In interpersonal relations, to save face for others and to show respect to others is based on values of autonomy, individual identity, and equality (Ting-Toomey & Kurogi, 1998).

In Chinese business culture, on the other hand, the function of face is to maintain harmony in social networks, which amounts to affirming membership and rank within networks. While face can be gained through achievement, a more significant factor in gaining face is adeptness at face-giving and face-saving, which implies trust. Moreover, face implies obligation between and among individuals and serves to initiate business interactions. Face-saving and face-giving are based on values of hierarchy, obligation, and loyalty (Chang & Holt, 1994).

Thus, perspectives about face differ between Americans and Chinese largely based on the differing nature of business relationships. These business relationships can be described in terms of American individualism and Chinese collectivism. The language about face in American English and Chinese reveals additional characteristics about the logic of face in each business culture. The American perspective of face follows the individualist logic of face. In the individualist logic of face, face is preferred but not necessary and functions to show respect for individual autonomy and to uphold equality. The Chinese perspective of face follows the collectivist logic of face. In the collectivist logic of face, face is essential in business and functions to respect social rank within social networks and to maintain harmony.

FACE-RELATED COMMUNICATION PATTERNS IN AMERICAN AND CHINESE BUSINESS CULTURES

American and Chinese businesspersons differ in communication patterns as a result of differing perspectives of face. To this point, the logic of face has been contrasted between the American and Chinese cultures and provides a framework for understanding differing communication practices. In addition, contexting aids in the understanding of differing communication patterns. The first part of this section briefly discusses contexting. The second section contrasts several face-related communication patterns.

Contexting in Communication

Face-related communication patterns of the West and the East differ significantly based on level of contexting, which is the extent to which meaning is contained in the words versus the context. Americans, as members of a low-context culture, send and receive messages with the assumption that the majority of meaning is within words. In contrast, the Chinese send and receive messages with the assumption that the words are but a small part of the meaning. Moreover, low-context cultures such as the American culture tend to view communication purely as a tool, whereas high-context cultures such as the Chinese culture tend to view communication as art that is prized for its aesthetic value (Beamer & Varner, 2001; Hall, 1977).

Many aspects of context affect Chinese face-related communication patterns. Most importantly, rank and position within social networks affect communication patterns. Also, distinctions between public or private environments and roles between individuals, such as host and guest, provide a unique context for interpersonal relations. Particularly influential in Chinese interactions is whether or not individuals are considered insiders or outsiders. Also, the role of Chinese traditions and history are a prominent feature of public discourse. Each of these aspects of context creates unique situations that alter communication patterns. Furthermore, each of these aspects of context is most often understood and communicated without the use of words (Blackman, 1997; Hall, 1977).

Types of Face-Related Communication Patterns

Several types of communication patterns help illustrate how Americans and Chinese communicate differently based on their differing logics of face. The communication patterns that will be contrasted in this section are (a) favors and gifts, (b) politeness and protocol, and (c) ambiguity and directness.

Favors and gifts. Favors and gifts are often given as symbols of goodwill and friendship. As such, they are important aspects of face-related communication. However, American and Chinese businesspersons give and receive favors and gifts based on different perspectives of face (Chan, Denton, & Tsang, 2003; Fu & Yukl, 2000).

In American business culture, favors and gifts play small and secondary roles in demonstrating respect to others. In fact, the idea of favors is oftentimes perceived negatively, implying special treatment that is undeserved. The notion that business transactions are heavily influenced by personal warmth and friendship between and among businesspersons is generally frowned upon. More often than not, personal friendship between businesspersons is desired but not considered relevant to business. Generally speaking, gifts are given without an expectation of return and are based on the individualist logic of avoiding obligation. If American businesspersons feel they should reciprocate with gifts, their goal is generally to pay back the kindness so that there is no feeling of owing that person anything. Moreover, gifts are generally selected with little thought about tradition and focus more on the personality of giver and recipient (Beamer & Varner, 2001; Fu & Yukl, 2000).

For Chinese, the giving and accepting of favors and gifts, perhaps more than any other type of communication, cements and strengthens relationships. To give and accept favors is to give face. To decline and fail to grant favors is to not give face, which essentially severs the relationship. Giving and accepting favors and gifts are intended to inject personal emotion, sincerity, trust, and mutual indebtedness into the business relationship. Without these, there is discomfort and lack of trust (Chan, Denton, & Tsang, 2003; Hwang, 1987).

Favors and gifts operate on the principles of reciprocity and obligation for Chinese. In other words, by granting a favor, one can expect favors to be returned in the future. By accepting a favor, one expects to pay back favors in the future. However, favors are not paid back with comparable favors. Each returned favor surpasses the previous favor in value, ensuring that indebtedness and obligation remain between individuals. It is these longstanding open accounts between individuals that demonstrate friendship and respect. Mutual indebtedness is psychologically comforting to many Chinese but not to most Americans (Hwang, 1987).

In a business context, favors come in many forms. A major type of business favor comes in the form of recommendations. Chinese businesspersons constantly use the strength of their face to introduce and recommend unacquainted individuals to one another for business purposes. The unacquainted individuals will cooperate out of respect for the mutually known person's face. In longstanding buyer-supplier relationships, buyers will sometimes pay slightly higher prices to suppliers in order to give face, even though they may be able to obtain better prices elsewhere. In negotiations, both sides should appear to be winners in business deals. Discounts and concessions are often made simply as a way of saving face and allowing negotiators to appear competent, even if the discount is essentially immaterial and the deal is less than favorable. If longstanding associates ask for help finding a job for a friend or relative, the other partner is obligated to help find a position. Businesspersons frequently treat one another to lavish banquets and feasts, imbued in tradition, to give one another face (Hwang, 1987).

Gifts are also a common way of giving face that is highly symbolic and oftentimes connected with Chinese history. Gift giving symbolizes the nature of the relationship and is intended to demonstrate social rank. For example, popular Chinese New Year gifts are red envelopes containing money to symbolize good fortune and prosperity for the coming year. However, these envelopes are usually given by superiors to subordinates. Wine and candies are given from subordinates to superiors. Such gifts are often not opened in public to protect the face of the giver in the case the gift is deemed inadequate (Chan, Denton, & Tsang, 2003).

Where favors and gifts are concerned, the Chinese distinguish themselves from their American counterparts in several ways. First, Chinese are often comfortable allowing the emotion of interpersonal relationships to enter the logic and dialogue of business dealings and do so more often than not without words but through favors and gifts. To take out the emotional aspect of relationships can be construed as not giving face. Second, the giving and receiving of favors and gifts is intended to create mutual indebtedness. Without indebtedness, there is no face. Third, and perhaps most importantly, the giving of favors and gifts identifies social position within a social network (Chan, Denton, & Tsang, 2003; Fu & Yukl, 2000; Hwang, 1987).

Politeness and protocol. Politeness and protocol are often employed to show respect for the face of others. While Americans and Chinese both value and employ politeness, they apply different communication patterns based on differing perspectives of face. American politeness is based on the individualist logic of face, whereas Chinese politeness is based on the collectivist logic of face (Chang & Holt, 1994; Ting-Toomey & Kurogi, 1998).

American businesspersons use a variety of politeness devices, which are intended to show respect for the autonomy of others and to emphasize equality. Words like please and thank you recognize others' autonomy and implicitly treat requests as impositions on others. Americans tend to prefer casual forms of address that emphasize equality. First names are often used when businesspersons address one another to de-emphasize status. When titles are used in direct address, they seldom have many levels of distinction and hierarchy. Americans often view protocol and formality as inefficient use of time. This view of inefficient use of time partially stems from American individualism, in which unnecessary work time impinges on an individual's personal life and may be perceived as rude and/or inconsiderate (Bell & Smith, 1999; Brown & Levinson, 1987; Hall & Hall, 1990).

Chinese politeness and protocol, on the other hand, are often employed to recognize status and role within relationships and emphasize obligation. Politeness is generally reserved to recognize the social rank of others and is employed most often from subordinates to superiors and between peers in public settings. As a result, the use of correct titles is very important because it helps individuals identify social rank relative to one another (Cardon & Scott, 2003; Chang & Holt, 1994; Jia, 2001; Zhai, 1995).

De-emphasizing obligation and emphasizing personal choice may be considered impolite, even face-losing. This is particularly evident in host-guest relationships, in which Americans frequently find themselves while working in Asia. In Chinese society the host and guest act out rituals in which the host really makes the decisions for the guest, and the guest shows politeness by always refusing the favors several times before accepting the favors. In a similar fashion, requests made between individuals often do not recognize the right of the other person to choose. Individuals are obligated to help one another. To treat others as if they have a choice in the matter can be perceived as a statement about the weakness of the relationship, perhaps even creating the perception that it is an insider-outsider relationship and, as a result, causes loss of face. The vast majority of this communication lies outside of words (Chen, 1991).

Protocol, especially for formal events, is very important to the Chinese. The level of protocol and formality at public events is often specifically intended to honor the face of the participants, particularly high-level leaders. At business meetings it is very important that businesspersons enter the room in the proper order and sit in the proper seats to indicate their relative status. Looking at the seating arrangement in a Chinese business meeting can literally reveal who is ranked number one, number two, number three, and so on (Beamer & Varner, 2001; De Mente, 1989).

Ambiguity and directness. Ambiguity and directness in speech are frequently employed to protect and enhance face. Americans tend to prefer directness in business communication, whereas the Chinese tend to be less direct, especially with words. Chinese generally prefer ambiguity. However, great variation in the use of ambiguity and directness among the Chinese is common, and in certain cases Chinese are much more direct than Americans (Ting-Toomey & Kurogi, 1998).

American businesspersons tend to trust the use of words to convey messages. From a managerial perspective, directness lends itself to accomplishing tasks more easily. From an ethical perspective, being direct fits in with the American sense of honesty and fair play and is oftentimes viewed as being respectful to others. In fact, there is a general belief that openly discussing differences of opinion is productive. Of course, Americans use indirectness in some situations, such as when implying bad news in communications (Bell & Smith, 1999; Hall & Hall, 1990).

From a Chinese perspective, ambiguity and directness are both employed, depending on the situation. In most situations Chinese prefer ambiguity for a number of face-related reasons. First and most importantly, conflict is generally viewed as counterproductive and potentially face-losing. As a result, especially in public situations, Chinese avoid directly discussing conflict and prefer not to reject openly the ideas, positions, and offers of others. Secondly, ambiguity also leaves a way out so that face can be protected if unforeseen circumstances emerge. Finally, the use of ambiguity often appeals to the Chinese sense of artistic communication. Allowing the subtle meanings to exist outside of the words demonstrates the sophistication and manners of an individual (Cardon & Scott, 2003; Hall, 1977; Jia, 2001).

Because conflict is often avoided when possible, the use of intermediaries is very important in China. Potential conflict between high-level business leaders creates the possibility of extensive loss of face. Subordinates are often used to feel out the true feelings and ideas of counterparts and often negotiate acceptable solutions in conflict situations. When open conflict has occurred, an intermediary with a lot of face who is known to both parties will often step in to restore the relationship (Jia, 2001).

However, there are a number of occasions in which Chinese are quite direct, even more so than Americans. For example, the discussion of business details during negotiation is frequently quite direct and frank. Chinese are known for being very effective and, at times, fierce negotiators. Most Chinese businesspersons accept the haggling and warlike aspects of negotiation. In fact, winning in the negotiation room affects how much face a negotiator has, and Chinese negotiators will often employ tactics that seem rude and confrontational to Americans. Moreover, superiors are generally extremely direct with subordinates, often issuing requests that sound like orders and commands to the American observer. These orders may violate the American's individualist logic of face that so highly values equality. Because Chinese often have a desire to know the social rank of others, they will directly ask about matters that Americans consider quite intrusive, such as salary level and age (Blackman, 1997).

Thus, this section has identified how face-related communication patterns differ between Americans and Chinese. The use of favors and gifts, politeness and protocol, and directness and ambiguity all differ based on the different logics of face and different levels of contexting.

WESTERN AND EASTERN PERSPECTIVES OF FACE

The discussion about face so far has focused on the United States as a representative culture of the West and China as a representative culture of the East. The purpose of this section is to briefly compare and contrast face within several Western cultures and several Eastern cultures and make some generalizations about Western and Eastern perspectives of face and related communication patterns.

Face in Other Western Cultures

Western cultures, generally speaking, have very similar perspectives of face and related communication patterns to those of the United States. Nevertheless, there is certainly variation among Western cultures, although these variations are small when compared to the difference between the West and the East. Two cultures that provide some interesting comparisons and contrasts with the American culture are the German and French cultures, both of which have adopted notions of face into their languages.

Germans are known for being quite direct compared to Americans and French, and Americans and French often perceive Germans as too blunt. Yet, despite a preference for directness, Germans are more concerned with formalities and protocol than Americans. In fact, many German managers are known for spending an average of 20 minutes per day shaking hands with colleagues. Furthermore, Germans are more status-conscious than Americans, with an insistence on using titles. They are also known for being very private and speaking less about personal matters during business. As a result, they like to get immediately to issues at hand, not feeling as much need as Americans do for small talk (Hall & Hall, 1990; Oetzel et al., 2001).

The French are less direct than both Americans and Germans. They enjoy discussion, even of nonbusiness issues, and enjoy the linguistic arts of wit and nuance. As such, they prefer a higher level of contexting. Although not to the extent of Eastern cultures, the French want to have close business relationships that involve social outings, such as meals. It is interesting to note that the average business lunch in America is approximately 67 minutes compared to 124 minutes in France. Like the Germans, the French are much more formal than Americans. Informality can cause a loss of respect and, in fact, be intrusive. Tact and courtesy are highly valued in French professional relationships (Hall & Hall, 1990).

Differences in face-related communication patterns among Western cultures, however, are not difficult for members of these cultures to ascertain because of similarities in the individualist logic of face. So, even though the French may prefer politeness in speech more so than the Germans and Americans, Germans and Americans can understand French politeness quite easily, since it is aimed at respecting autonomy.

Face in Other Eastern Countries

Eastern cultures tend to have very similar perceptions of face and related communication patterns as those of the Chinese. For example, other Confucian societies, such as the Japanese and Korean societies, also have similar ideas of face and have adopted highly sophisticated language about face similar to that found in the Chinese language. However, there are quite a few contrasts within these cultures. In this section a few differences will be mentioned involving the Chinese, Japanese, and Korean cultures (Choi & Lee, 2002; Sueda, 1998; Ting-Toomey & Kurogi, 1998).

Japanese, compared to Chinese, are much more likely to establish relationships in which face plays an important role within large and interrelated organizational and company structures. Chinese, by contrast, form social networks that are less bound by organizational structures. Also, ritual, often distinctly organizational, tends to play a more important role in face-related communication in Japan. For example, ritualistic apology is used more often to satisfy the need of maintaining social ranks of members in a network. Moreover, the Japanese tend to use more linguistic politeness than the Chinese. In fact, the Japanese have much more elaborate systems of addressing superiors and inferiors. Verbs and adjectives are conjugated on many distinct levels to demonstrate that one is talking to someone of higher or lower status. Bowing is also used to demonstrate social rank. Further, the Japanese tend to be less direct than the Chinese in conflict situations (Hall & Hall, 1987; Morisaki & Gudykunst, 1994; Sueda, 1995, 1998; Ting-Toomey et al., 1991).

In Korean culture the role of face more closely resembles that of the Japanese than it does that of the Chinese. Like the Japanese, the Koreans are less direct than the Chinese. The Koreans are extremely sensitive to criticism and avoid bearing bad news at all costs. Less so than the Japanese but more so than the Chinese, Koreans use extremely respectful language to address superiors. Koreans also tend to emphasize not only social rank but also social class as an element of face (Choi & Lee, 2002; De Mente, 1988; Ting-Toomey et al., 1991).

Although there are contrasts in face-related communication patterns among Eastern cultures, members of these cultures can easily understand these differences because of similarities in the collectivist logic of face. For example, even though the Japanese use more linguistic politeness than the Chinese, the Chinese can easily understand that Japanese politeness is intended to recognize social rank in highly interrelated social networks.

Thus, this section has compared and contrasted perspectives of face and related communication patterns in several additional Western and Eastern cultures. Although there are contrasts within Western and Eastern cultures, Western cultures primarily use the individualist logic of face, and Eastern cultures primarily use the collectivist logic of face. Furthermore, Western cultures generally employ a low level of contexting, whereas the Eastern cultures employ a high level of contexting in communication.

SUGGESTIONS FOR TEACHING ABOUT FACE

Students can enhance their understanding of how Western and Eastern businesspersons conceptualize and practice face differently by participating in the learning exercises described in this section. This section provides ideas for teaching about face to students who have not had much exposure to this concept, as well as references to more advanced learning materials for students with a rudimentary understanding of face.

Ideas for Teaching about Face

Teachers may use the ideas for teaching about face in conjunction with one another or independently. These teaching ideas include (a) contrasting perceptions of face in the West and the East and (b) contrasting face-related communication patterns between the West and the East.

Contrasting face-related concepts. This learning activity includes three steps: (a) analyzing face-related concepts in the American (or other Western) culture; (b) teaching about face in Eastern cultures; and (c) contrasting face between the West and the East.

Because many students will be unfamiliar with the term face, the first activity they should undertake is identifying face-related concepts in American culture. Take several face-related concepts in American culture, such as respect and reputation, and ask students to identify the role of these concepts in the professional world. For example, the teacher will ask the students to address such questions such as these: How important is respect in the business world? How do you think businesspersons show respect to each other? When businesspersons show respect for one another, to what values are they paying attention? The teacher can ask these same questions about other face-related concepts such as reputation or a good image.

Once the students have considered the role of face-related concepts in their own culture, they are prepared to learn about face in Eastern cultures. The teacher may begin by describing the various Chinese-language phrases about face as identified in Language about Face, in the Chinese section of this article. Then the teacher can probe to find out if students can identify values that might be different from those in the West. For example, the teacher might ask students about the following Chinese-language adage: "When a person loses face, his or her whole family loses face." Students might be able to identify the value of the group over the individual.

Once the teacher has introduced the students to the Eastern concept of face, students are prepared to make direct contrasts between the West and the East. The teacher can ask students to contrast the Western and Eastern views of face in terms of importance and function, much like they are discussed in the Logic of Face section of this chapter.

Contrasting face-related communication patterns. Once students have an introduction to the differing logics of face between Westerners and members of Eastern cultures, they are prepared to understand different communication patterns. The teacher can list a number of scenarios and ask the students to describe how the Westerners and the Easterners would feel or behave. For example, the teacher might describe the following scenario: An old classmate of a successful business executive asks the business executive to help his son get a job. Students would speculate about how members of each culture would respond. Appropriate answers might include the following: The member of the Eastern culture feels obligated to help his old friend. If he or she does not help the friend, the executive will lose face and the relationship will suffer. If he or she does help the friend, the friend will become indebted and obligated to give even a greater favor in the future. The business executive in the Western culture does not feel obligated to help, although he or she may be willing to help. However, it is even possible that the executive will feel offended that a friend would ask for a personal favor and inject a personal matter into professional life. The teacher can choose from a number of scenarios that are described in the Types of Face-Related Communication Patterns section of this article.

Other Learning Materials about Face

For students who have a rudimentary understanding of face, there are a number of learning resources that address the issue of face in Asian cultures. For example, Cardon and Scott (2003) created several learning exercises about face and compiled a list of learning exercises about face from other publications. These various learning exercises include case studies, research projects, and role plays.

SUMMARY

Understanding differing perspectives of face plays a significant role in the ability to show respect across cultures. American business relationships, which are usually flexible and short-term, tend to be based on individualist values such as autonomy and equality. Everyday language about face in English suggests that the notion of face is fairly simple and reactive. Although face is preferred, it is not the top priority in business interactions. Face recognizes individual autonomy and operates under the principle of equality. By contrast, Chinese business relationships, which are usually rigid and long-term, tend to be based on collectivist values such as hierarchy and harmony. Everyday language about face in Chinese suggests that face is extremely complex and proactive. Face is essential to business success and operates as a foundation to facilitate business interactions. Face recognizes social rank within interrelated social networks. Its value is maintaining harmony in hierarchical relationships. Under the American individualist logic of face, communication patterns are employed with autonomy and equality as objectives. These communication patterns depend little on context, with the majority of meanings contained in words. By contrast, under the Chinese collectivist logic of face, communication patterns are employed with harmony and hierarchy as objectives. These communication patterns are highly contexted, with most meaning contained outside of words. Face-related communication includes the exchange of favors and gifts, use of politeness and protocol, and timing and preference for ambiguity and directness. Other Western cultures tend to use the individualist logic of face and corresponding communication patterns just as other Eastern cultures tend to use the collectivist logic of face and corresponding communication patterns. By using ideas presented in this chapter and elsewhere, a teacher can effectively teach about face in Western and Eastern cultures.

REFERENCES

Beamer, L., & Varner, I. (2001). *Intercultural communication in the global workplace* (2nd ed.). New York: McGraw-Hill/Irwin.

Bell, A. H., & Smith, D. M. (1999). *Management communication.* New York: John Wiley & Sons.

Blackman, C. (1997). *Negotiating China: Case studies and strategies.* Crows Nest, Australia: Allen & Unwin.

Brown, P., & Levinson, S. C. (1987). *Politeness: Some universals in language usage.* New York: Cambridge University Press.

Cardon, P. W., & Scott, J. C. (2003). Chinese business face: Communication behaviors and teaching approaches. *Business Communication Quarterly, 66*(4), 9-22.

Chan, A. K. K., Denton, L. T., & Tsang, A. S. L. (2003). The art of gift giving in China. *Business Horizons, 46*(4), 47-52.

Chang, H.-C., & Holt, G. R. (1994). A Chinese perspective on face as inter-relational concern. In S. Ting-Toomey (Ed.), *The challenge of facework: Cross-cultural and interpersonal issues* (pp. 95-132). Albany, NY: State University Press.

Chen, V. (1991). Mien tze at the Chinese dinner table: A study of the interactional accomplishment of face. *Research on Language and Social Interaction, 24,* 109-140.

Choi, S.-C., & Lee, S.-J. (2002). Two-component model of chemyon-oriented behaviors in Korea. *Journal of Cross-Cultural Psychology, 33*(3), 332-345.

De Mente, B. (1988). *Korean etiquette and ethics in business.* Lincolnwood, IL: NTC Business Books.

De Mente, B. (1989). *Chinese etiquette and ethics in business.* Lincolnwood, IL: NTC Publishing Group.

Fu, P. P., & Yukl, G. (2000). Perceived effectiveness of influence tactics in the United States and China. *Leadership Quarterly, 11*(2), 251-266.

Hall, E. T. (1977). *Beyond culture.* Garden City, NY: Anchor Books.

Hall, E. T., & Hall, M. R. (1987). *Hidden differences: Doing business with the Japanese.* New York: Anchor Books.

Hall, E. T., & Hall, M. R. (1990). *Understanding cultural differences: Germans, French, and Americans.* Yarmouth, ME: Intercultural Press.

Hofstede, G. (2001). *Culture's consequences: Comparing values, behaviors, institutions, and organizations across nations* (2nd ed.). Thousand Oaks, CA: Sage.

Hu, H. C. (1944). The Chinese concepts of 'face.' *American Anthropologist, 46,* 45-64.

Hwang, K. (1987). Face and favor: The Chinese power game. *American Journal of Sociology, 92,* 944-974.

Jia, W. (2001). *The remaking of the Chinese character and identity in the 21st century: The Chinese face practices.* Wesport, CT: Ablex Publishing.

Li, F. (1996). The cultural meanings and social functions of 'face' in Sino-U.S. business negotiations. *Dissertations Abstracts International, 57*(09), 4028. (UMI No. 9705054).

Morisaki, S., & Gudykunst, W. B. (1994). Face in Japan and the United States. In S. Ting-Toomey (Ed.), *The challenge of facework: Cross-cultural and interpersonal issues* (pp. 47-94). Albany, NY: State University Press.

Oetzel, J., Ting-Toomey, S., Masumoto, T., Yokochi, Y., Pan, X., Takai, J., & Wilcox, R. (2001). Face and facework in conflict: A cross-cultural comparison of China, Germany, Japan, and the United States. *Communication Monographs, 68*(3), 235-258.

Rodman, L. (2001). You-attitude: A linguistic perspective. *Business Communication Quarterly 64*(4), 9-25.

Sueda, K. (1995). Differences in the perception of face: Chinese mien-tzu and Japanese mentsu. *World Communication, 24*(1), 23-31.

Sueda, K. (1998). A quantitative analysis of differing perceptions of mien-tzu/mentsu between Chinese and Japanese students: A case study. [In Japanese]. *Japanese Journal of Social Psychology, 13*(2), 103-111.

Ting-Toomey, S., Gao, G., Trubisky, P., Yang, Z., Kim, H. S., Lin, S.-L., & Nishida, T. (1991). Culture, face maintenance, and styles of handling interpersonal conflict: A study of five cultures. *The International Journal of Conflict Management, 2*(4), 275-296.

Ting-Toomey, S., & Kurogi, A. (1998). Facework competence in intercultural conflict: An updated face-negotiation theory. *International Journal of Intercultural Relations, 22*(2), 187-225.

Wong, Y. H., & Leung, T. K. P. (2001). *Guanxi: Relationship marketing in a Chinese context*. New York: International Business Press.

Zhai, X. (1995). The Chinese perspectives on face: A study of social psychology in the Chinese context. [In Chinese]. Taibei, Taiwan: Guiguan Publishing Company.

Group Dynamics: Working Effectively in a Multicultural Setting

Sherri Lee Arosteguy
Fruita Monument High School
Fruita, Colorado

The need for understanding and accepting human differences and for fostering harmony among groups of people—in schools, workplaces, communities, nations, and throughout the world—is paramount to the continued development and existence of the global society of the 21st century (Ramler, 2002). In terms of teaching about group dynamics, students must learn about the complexities of multicultural and international organizations and develop communication and interpersonal skills for working with people with varied life experiences, behavioral norms, and perspectives (Czarra, 2002-2003; McCain, 1996). This chapter provides an overview of the interpersonal dynamics of groups in international and multicultural settings. Environmental conditions and leadership styles that enhance and/or limit the effectiveness of multicultural groups are discussed, and limitations and strengths of multicultural group settings are identified. The chapter concludes with a discussion about teaching multicultural and global group dynamics in the business education curriculum.

CULTURAL PATTERNS OF INDIVIDUALS AND GROUPS

Experts define culture as the assumptions, values, behavioral norms, and artifacts that are patterned by members of a group (Schein, 1992). Cross-cultural and multicultural research provides a framework for understanding how these patterns vary across groups and among individuals. Each person occupies a variety of subject positions—socially, economically, politically, geographically, and the like. A person may in one situation identify himself or herself by gender, in another by nationality, in another by occupation, and in another by religion. Depending on the circumstance, the individual may benefit from or be hindered by the identification. Multiculturalism, then, insofar as it groups individuals into categories, may overlook the practical reality that no one is one-dimensional (Ford, 2004). Even so, recognizing one's own cultural patterns fosters a better understanding and appreciation for the complexities of others and may serve as a compass for navigating interpersonal relations with others.

National cultural patterns are considered to be particularly persuasive in defining who people are, and their effects on individuals are thought to be exceptionally resistant to change. When faced with other types of differences such as gender, age, or job status, multicultural group members often choose national culture as the primary form of identity (Erez & Earley, 1993). For the purposes of this chapter, national culture will be the primary cultural characteristic considered. To better understand the similarities and differences that are associated with national culture, researchers (most notably Hofstede, 2003; see also Robbins, 1993; Triandis & Gelfand, 1998) use cultural dimensions to explain how different cultures respond to various stimuli. Some of these constructs, including collectivism-individualism, power distance, communication context, nature orientation, time perception, and risk tolerance will be discussed and referenced throughout the chapter.

The study of cultural patterns lays a foundation for understanding the complexities of individuals and groups. By learning about national cultural constructs, students can begin to understand how their own cultural patterns and the cultural patterns of others influence their interactions in various life situations.

TYPES OF MULTICULTURAL WORK GROUPS

Even if employees never leave their home country, the opportunities for multicultural and global interactions continue to increase. Businesses buy and sell to clients from other countries. Domestic companies are being purchased by international conglomerates. International project teams may be formed for specific purposes. Advances in telecommunications enable business associates from around the world to dialogue using e-mail, telephones, faxes, and videoconferences. Migration of workers and refugees to domestic lands and outsourcing of jobs to foreign lands have also increased the mobility and cultural differences of the global workforce (Grosse, 2002; Laroche, 2001; Milliman, Taylor, & Czaplewski, 2002).

The influence that cultural variation has on relationships within organizations changes with the types of organizations and the functions they perform. A domestic multicultural nonprofit may have no interactions with foreign groups, yet have a diverse workforce or customer base, or both. In contrast, a domestic corporation may export products to many different foreign clients, yet have a relatively homogenous workforce. A multinational agency would likely have both a multicultural workforce and a customer base. The most complex patterns of multiculturalism occur in global organizations that have multiple sites in various countries and serve markets throughout the world (Adler, 1991).

The mobility and diversity of the global workforce call for today's workers to have an understanding of how organizations are structured and how cultural patterns are predisposed by organizational structure and function. Conditions under which multicultural groups are most effective will be explored in the section that follows.

CONDITIONS OF MULTICULTURAL WORK GROUP EFFECTIVENESS

Researchers agree that compared to homogenous teams, multicultural teams have the potential to be more creative, generate better and more varied approaches to problems, and create better and more comprehensive criteria for evaluating alternatives (Boyacigiller & Adler, 1991). However, in practice, global teams often fail to meet such high expectations. Some studies have shown that multicultural teams actually tend to perform worse than homogenous ones (DiStefano & Maznevski, 2000).

The circumstances under which the group is formed, the environment in which it functions and the choice of communication technologies used, the tasks to be completed, and the stage of operation in which the group is functioning are primary conditions that influence the productivity and comfort experienced by multicultural and international work groups (Adler, 1991).

Formation, Selection, and Composition

Whether the multicultural group is formed naturally—a result of the local work-force composition, or created intentionally—a response to international client needs may have a significant impact on the dynamics and interactions of the group. A group might be homogenous except for a token ethnic member. Other group members may rely on their memories of an ethnic stereotype and ascribe traits of that stereotype to the individual group member, or they may highly value the token member's diverse knowledge and rely on the individual to speak for and represent the ethnic group at large. In either case, a tremendous burden has been placed on the individual member, and the information exchanged may not be accurate (Adler, 1991).

Bicultural and multicultural groups may be formed as a result of business partnerships, international committees, or special projects. Ideally, the work group will recognize and integrate cultural perspectives of all members of the group. However, membership ratio, group location, skill level, available technologies, technical skill of members, and perceived power differences may cause one or more cultures to be more valued and dominant over the others (Adler, 1991).

The more homogenous the group, the more likely members are to view, value, and evaluate the world more similarly than do members of heterogeneous groups. A homogenous group tends to speak the same language—they use the same expressions and rely on the same verbal and nonverbal cues. They often have a common history, economically, socially, and politically. In contrast, heterogeneous group members are likely to differ on several cultural dimensions. While they may all speak English as their first language, they might have different dialects. Hence, the same expressions mean different things. For some members English may be a second language. Thus, they might have a fundamental knowledge of the language but lack the understanding of common idioms used by other members (Miller, Fields, Kumar, & Ortiz, 2000).

When heterogeneous members are selected because of their task-related abilities, they might differ in many respects, but they often will have an inherent common bond by virtue of their occupation or interest. For example, an international association of environmentalists may hold different world perspectives but share a familiar language and enthusiasm for their common discipline (Miller, Fields, Kumar, & Ortiz, 2000).

Environment and Technology
The environment in which the multicultural group works will also influence the effectiveness of the group. A domestic multicultural group is likely to conduct much of its business face to face. Likewise, it is probable that a multinational organization will employ multiple technologies including e-mail, telephones, faxes, videoconferences, and face-to-face meetings in various geographic locations. In low-context cultures, in which communication is explicit and direct and little attention is given to external stimuli (e.g., facial expressions, tone of voice, and eye contact), such as those of the United States and Germany, short and direct communication channels are preferred. Telephone queries, faxes, and e-mail messages are used frequently and require a high level of commitment from both the sender and receiver. In contrast, high-context cultures, in which communication is more implicit and indirect and a great deal of meaning is attached to external stimuli, such as that of China, highly value personal contact as a means for building relationships. Electronic media is rarely used as the primary communication vehicle (Beu, Honold, & Yuan, 2000; Pan Fan & Zhang Zigang, 2004).

Task Assignment
Multiculturalism becomes most valuable when the need for agreement remains low relative to the need for invention or creativity. When a task requires participants to perform highly specialized tasks in new and inventive ways, multiculturalism is advantageous. International consulting and design teams generally work most effectively when they include a variety of specialists such as accountants, marketers, and design and production engineers. Each member brings a specific technical knowledge as well as a unique cultural knowledge to the team, thus providing for maximum creativity and alternative approaches to problem solving. On the other hand, when everyone must do similar tasks, it is easier if members think and behave similarly. Assembly line teams generally perform better when all members have the same level of skill and coordination (Adler, 1991).

Operational Phases
Adler (1991) describes the life cycle of the work group as occurring in four basic phases: orientation, problem development, decision making, and implementation. Formation of positive relationships among group members tends to be best developed during the orientation phase of group work. Unfortunately, on first meeting, group

members generally are drawn to people who are most like them. Individuals tend to stay within their own subgroups and not mingle with members of other subgroups; hence the more varied the group, the more difficult the integration process. Additionally, individuals from high-context/polychronic cultures, in which communication is more implicit and time allocation is lenient and spontaneous, such as those found in Latin America and the Middle East, highly value time devoted to relationship building. In contrast, low-context/monochronic cultures, in which communication is more explicit and time allocation and prioritization of tasks is highly valued, such as those found in the United States and Germany, prefer to address the business issues at hand and may become impatient with their counterparts' attempts to engage in casual conversation (Hofstede, 2003; Milliman et al., 2002).

In the second phase of the process, the team begins defining the problem, analyzing information, and developing alternative solutions. Divergent perspectives foster creative solutions; thus, the more varied the group's thinking patterns, the more likely new and different ideas will emerge. The third and fourth phases again call for group cohesiveness so that a decision can be made and all participants can support and act on the decision (Adler, 1991).

Having an understanding of how factors such as group formation, environmental conditions, communication technologies, task assignment, and operational phases influence the productivity and effectiveness of group activity better prepares today's workers for the multicultural work environment. Those who have these skills will be well-suited for opportunities of advancement into management and leadership in the ever-expanding global market.

MANAGEMENT AND LEADERSHIP OF MULTICULTURAL WORK GROUPS

Leadership styles of people in authority can vary from autocratic to democratic, socialistic, or consultative. While each of these styles may be highly effective in working within a particular culture, the most effective style for the global executive might be a flexible one that can be adapted to match the dominant style of the group culture. Research by Berger (1998) into characteristics of international managers identified well-developed cultural, linguistic, and information technology skills as highly desirable. Hurn (1999) suggested that international managers should have the ability to function in complex, uncertain environments; access and interpret information through multicultural filters; and understand differences in career motivations of other cultures. They should have technical knowledge of international, national, and local laws and regulations. Furthermore, Odenwald (1996) suggested that global leaders should be persuasive yet patient and be able to gain consensus among group members. Most importantly, they should have an orientation toward change.

Largely defining the culture of the organization are the style and means of communication; the types of training models used; the degree of structure within the organization;

and the style, purpose, and frequency of meetings. How the organization manages conflict, conducts evaluations, and provides feedback largely determines the climate of the organization (Berger, 1998).

Communication Styles

Differences in communication styles vary across cultures from high context to low context. In high-context cultures such as that of Taiwan, people attach a great deal of meaning to the stimuli surrounding a communication occurrence. The receiver of the message must take into account the surrounding context—eye contact and facial expressions, voice inflection, attire, and geographic location. Alternatively, in low-context cultures such as that of Switzerland, emphasis is on the accuracy and explicitness of the verbal message (Hofstede, 2003; Milliman et al., 2002). How then does one converse with a group of individuals with variable communication expectations?

Berger (1998) offered four suggestions for developing cross-cultural communication skills: (a) gauge one's level of jargon and speed of delivery to the language fluency of the listener; (b) recognize differing cultural meanings of verbal and nonverbal behavior; (c) listen and question to understand the views and opinions of others; and (d) be aware of what is expected at the initial stage of building a relationship in order to build sufficient trust to work together productively.

Effective communication in multicultural groups occurs when members hear what was intended. It requires a strong commitment among all members to listen actively, speak clearly and simply, check for understanding and provide feedback, and be sensitive to and show respect for cultural differences (Berger, 1998; Grosse, 2002).

Group Management

The degree of structure expected among group members can range from a high reliance on structures, plans, and procedures to a preference for minimal structure (Berger, 1998; Hofstede, 2003). Coming to agreement on how the group will value organizational procedures, meeting structures and times, and project deadlines enables the administrator to prepare and communicate action plans for conducting business, to prepare appropriate meeting agendas and supporting materials, and to set expectations for progress reports and project completion dates. Additionally, a clearly defined structural framework provides group members with guidelines for achieving these expectations (Berger, 1998).

The organization, purpose, and flow of communication in company meetings can be largely dependent on the cultural style of the host participants or on the style of the group administrator (Berger, 1998). Cultural differences can be particularly apparent at business meetings: Members from cultures with low tolerance for risk and high need for structure, such as the Japanese, will more likely focus on the stated agenda and on achieving a concrete result or action plan within a specified time. In contrast, members from cultures with high risk tolerance and low need for structure, such as people of Hong Kong, may wish to engage in in-depth discussions of all aspects of the problem. Their concern about time frames may be minimal, while their interest in fully analyzing the problem is significant (Laroche, 2001).

Cultural differences in approaches to time perception and structure influence how members will view the purpose of the meeting, the importance of the agenda, time constraints, and actions to be taken. Highly structured or less structured meeting styles can be appropriate and effective depending on the project phase, expected results of the meeting, and acceptance by group members of the selected style (Berger, 1998).

How can cultural variation be used as a tool to create synergy and to build an international network? Just as cultural working patterns differ, so do learning patterns. Three common learning styles include instructional, consensus building, and personal openness (Berger, 1998). Members from cultures that value *power distance*, a hierarchy of power distribution between management and employees, may be most familiar and comfortable with direct instructional approaches that are provided by a field specialist. For this type of training to work, the trainer must have the support of senior management and be recognized by the group members as an authority. Members from *collectivist cultures*, in which employee participation and equality of power between management and employees is valued, may prefer a cooperative instructional approach, in which the group is given problem-solving activities that require the group to work together as a unit and then report back their conclusions to the training facilitator. Cooperative learning models tend to take more time than direct approaches but may ultimately lead to a stronger commitment by all team members. Members from *individualistic cultures* often prefer an inductive approach in which each member develops his or her own learning approach to solve a given problem. Members then give and receive feedback from other group members and debate the strengths and weaknesses of each member's proposal (Berger, 1998.)

Regardless of learning-style preference, effective multicultural training typically occurs over a three-phase process: training for understanding each other's cultures—mapping; recognizing one another's strengths—bridging; and finding cooperative ways of working—integrating (DeStefano & Maznevski, 2002). When developing training programs for cross-cultural teams, consideration should be given to clearly defining the objectives of the training, determining an optimal degree of organizational structure, and adapting the training model to the preferred learning styles of the group members (Arai, Wanca-Thibault, & Shockley-Zalabak, 2001; Berger, 1998.

Conflict Management

Cross-cultural misunderstandings often generate emotions of conflict, frustration, and anger that lead to communication breakdown and low morale. Prolonged conflict can result in poor group performance and high turnover rates. If not addressed, similar situations are likely to occur among other groups within the organization. Yet, when properly handled, a critical incident can lead to organizational learning that can benefit the entire enterprise (Milliman et al., 2002; Trefry & Vaillant, 2002).

Hunter (2001) suggested that two positions often assumed in group conflicts are mainstream and margins. Members who regularly have their interests recognized are mainstream members. Members whose voices are not recognized by the group are marginal members. Both positions are important to the development of group cohesiveness. The mainstream members offer commonality and validation of accepted behavioral group norms (Salk & Brannen, 2000). The marginal members offer opportunities for organizational change in performance, perspective, and knowledge (Hunter, 2001).

Hunter (2001) provided these suggestions for managing group conflict: (a) listen to the concerns of the margins, (b) allow for group tension to occur, (c) encourage the mainstream to respond, and (d) deal openly with conflict. By encouraging individuals to voice their concerns, an effective leader can validate the experiences of the margins, help balance the discussion between the margins and the mainstream, curtail preliminary judgments from being voiced, and gently encourage both sides to engage in the dialogue. By openly dealing with conflict, an effective leader can develop trust among members by creating a safe environment for conflict to occur; in essence, this is an environment in which not everyone will be comfortable all of the time, but all will have an understanding and willingness to agree to disagree and be respectful of each other's differences.

Group Success and Performance

Some cultures define success by increases in efficiency, profit margins, and competitive rankings, while other cultures define success in terms of quality of life measures such as improved health care, safety practices, and environmental protection. DiStefano and Maznevski (2000) suggested that in addition to productivity and efficiency measures, a team's performance should be evaluated on (a) how satisfied participants feel with the organizational process, (b) how willing they are to work on a team again, and (c) how positively they perceive their team's performance. Teams that score high on each of these indicators tend to share three qualities: effective communication, collaborative conflict resolution, and constructive processes. Team members send and receive messages as they were intended. As such, group members understand each other because they understand each other's perspective. Team members are able to air and resolve differences without alienating one another and maintain a balance between their own goals and concern for others' goals. Team members build on one another's ideas rather than quarrel to make their own prevail. Solutions to problems are an amalgamation of several members' ideas rather than those of an individual. These three indicators for evaluating the communication process among group members can serve as a guideline for assessing team performance and planning future training programs and group processes.

Performance feedback is an important way in which administrators can focus the direction of the multinational work group and cultivate its success. However, like other cultural dimensions, significant differences exist among groups in how performance feedback is given and received. Using the cultural dimensions of (a) power distance, (b) *nature orientation*—a belief about whether events are controlled by fate and/or other factors outside of one's control, and (c) *communication context*—the amount of meaning attributed to external stimuli surrounding communication events, Milliman et al. (2002) identified four characteristics of performance feedback: achievement level, feedback approach, performance accountability, and communication style.

Achievement level. In an individualist culture, in which work, performance, and decisions are the responsibility of the individual, with low-context (explicit) communication such as that found in Austria, a manager will most likely use constructive and critical feedback. Such task-oriented feedback is viewed as an essential way to improve individual performance and self-confidence of the person being evaluated. In contrast, collectivistic cultures, in which work, performance, and decisions are a collective process with high-context (implicit) communication, such as that found in Malaysia, view harmony and loyalty among members as key to high group performance. Overt and critical individual feedback is likely to be perceived as inappropriate because it threatens the overall harmony of the group, particularly when delivered by an outsider (Tuan & Napier, 2000).

Feedback approach. Managers from cultures that value *low power distance* (a belief in equal distribution of power) such as those in Denmark tend to provide opportunities for individuals to participate in the performance evaluation and often encourage subordinates to self-evaluate their performances. In contrast, managers from cultures that value *high power distance* (a belief in unequal distribution of power) such as those in Mexico typically try to control the performance evaluation process to avoid perceptions of managerial weakness. They often discourage and/or prohibit participation of subordinates in the evaluation process (Laroche, 2001).

Performance accountability. In cultures with a *deterministic* orientation toward nature, a belief that nature and life events can be controlled, subordinates are held accountable for their own performance. Individuals are encouraged to believe that they can improve their own performance through greater individual effort. On the other hand, cultures with a fatalistic orientation toward nature, a belief that nature and life events are controlled by fate or other factors outside of one's control, consider external work factors such as relations with other employees and customers, economic conditions, political influences, and the like to be important determinants of an individual's work performance; they believe these factors should be considered as part of the evaluation process (Milliman et al., 2002).

Communication style. Low-context workers expect communication to be direct and explicit. Evaluation feedback is often given immediately and informally in verbal form and then followed up with a formal written summary. High-context workers expect communication to be less verbal and more subtle. Emphasis is placed on the surrounding context of the conversation. The manager and subordinate pay close attention to the body language of each other. In deference to the superior and for preservation of the group's face, the subordinate may be expected to interpret the unspoken message regarding the performance evaluation (Milliman et al., 2002).

Effective leadership in multicultural settings requires well-developed cultural, linguistic, and information technology skills. Successful managers are able to adapt their communication styles for working with people from low-context to high-context communication cultures. They have an understanding of the impact that power distance, nature orientation, risk tolerance, and time perception have on multicultural group dynamics and conflict management and can effectively evaluate group performance to provide constructive feedback to individuals with varied perceptions and backgrounds. Given these expectations, one might question the value and practicality of using multicultural work groups. The following section explores strengths and limitations of multicultural work groups.

STRENGTHS AND LIMITATIONS OF MULTICULTURAL WORK GROUPS

Communication between two like-minded individuals can be a complex process simply because of subtle variations in the use of verbal and nonverbal cues, idioms, vernaculars, hyperbole, and the like. The complexity grows exponentially when the communication process is woven across groups of people with differing orientations toward language, nationality, gender, age, education, and profession. When the communication process is properly managed, many favorable qualities of multicultural work groups can be capitalized. Multiculturalism enhances creativity and approaches to problem solving by expanding the range of perspectives brought to the discussion. Multiculturalism commands deliberate attention to understanding others' ideas. Multiculturalism provides for greater opportunities to interact and learn from people different from ourselves. Problems are more clearly defined. More and various alternatives are considered, resulting in better solutions and increased group productivity (DiStefano & Maznevski, 2000; Gassman, 2001).

Without adequate communication management, multicultural groups make performance difficult. As the complexity of the communication process increases, so does the chance of misperceptions, misunderstandings, and misjudgments (Adler, 1991). Multiculturalism makes group cohesiveness more difficult to build among members. Multiculturalism makes the communication process take more time and creates more stress. Multiculturalism increases ambiguity, complexity, and confusion in the communication process. Productivity declines as the group is unable to validate each other's ideas, reach consensus, or take concerted action (DiStefano & Maznevski, 2000).

Even so, essential learning can occur at both individual and organizational levels by interacting with those of different cultures. Trefry and Vaillant (2002) identified five organizational learning benefits derived from multicultural work groups: (a) awareness of limited personal perspectives through exposure to varied perspectives and beliefs held by others; (b) enhanced criteria used to understand and explore problems; (c) expanded frames of reference used to perceive and interpret problems; (c) increased flexibility and adaptability among work group members; and (d) increased opportunities for organizational effectiveness.

Organizations of the 21st century must be willing to view the use of multicultural work groups as a strategic investment for survival and prosperity in the global marketplace. Managerial infrastructures, policies, processes, and procedures must embrace multiculturalism and provide the time and mechanisms for organizational learning to take place. If business education students are to be adequately prepared for working with and managing multicultural work groups, the business education curriculum must be adapted to provide quality instruction and activities for exploring, practicing, and learning effective strategies for working with individuals from varied backgrounds. The following section provides sample activities and resources for teaching about group dynamics in multicultural settings.

APPLICATIONS FOR THE BUSINESS EDUCATION CLASSROOM

Whether at the secondary, college, or industry level, business education students need opportunities to develop and practice interpersonal skills in multicultural and global settings. Through formal instruction, job training, and on-the-job-learning, students can develop strategies for effectively working and communicating with varied groups of people (Scott & Martinez, 2003).

The remainder of this chapter presents five instructional components that should be considered when developing curricula for teaching group dynamics in multicultural and global settings. These components include introducing multiculturalism, using cooperative work group projects, adapting the environment and technology, and teaching cross-cultural leadership and communication skills.

Introducing Multiculturalism

Central to understanding group dynamics is accepting one's own cultural identity and biases toward other cultural identities. By using introductory icebreakers such as Name Stories, an exercise in which participants write and share stories about their names and nicknames, explaining what their names mean, why they were given to them, and how they relate to their names, business teachers can foster initial steps in community-building among students of varied cultural backgrounds. Introspective exercises can then be used to engage students in the reflective process of exploring their own cultural orientations and biases. One such activity, Exploring Definitions, engages students in a discussion about how they define words such as prejudice, discrimination, and racism. This type of activity provides a foundation for students to begin understanding the complexities of group dynamics. These two activities and others are fully described on the Multicultural Pavilion Web site http://www.edchange.org/multicultural. The Anti-Defamation League Web site, www.adl.org, also provides quality multicultural and anti-bias curricula for secondary schools, colleges, corporations, small businesses, government agencies, nonprofit organizations, and professional groups.

Using Cooperative Work Group Projects

When used deliberately and methodically, cooperative group projects can facilitate the learning of cooperation, tolerance, and conflict management. For example, a collaborative oral presentation, in which students role-play at being international team members who are presenting a marketing plan for a product, provides students with opportunities to experience the challenges faced when communicating and working with individuals with varied styles of communication and beliefs about time, hierarchal power, and risk. However, as observed by McCain (1996), often little thought is given to the selection process, task assignment, operational processes, performance evaluation, or feedback methods used for group assignments. Young and Henquinet (2000) suggested that group projects be designed around three elements: pedagogical purposes, evaluation criteria and process, and fit—the relationship between use of groups and what is evaluated. In the activity described previously, evaluation criteria may emphasize students' reflections about the group process and de-emphasize the quality of the end product, the presentation.

Adapting the Environment and Technology

Students need opportunities to observe how differences in environments and technology impact the interactions of people working in multicultural groups. Business educators can teach students about the strengths and limitations of e-mail, telephones, faxes, video conferences, and face-to-face encounters by adapting and simulating virtual and physical environments and using various technologies in courses such as business communication, management, and telecommunications. For example, while conducting mock interviews, students can observe differences in perceptions when an interview is conducted by telephone, videoconference, and face to face. Resources such as the Global Schoolhouse, http://www.gsn.org, and its associated links provide numerous online opportunities for students at the K-12 level to participate in and communicate with others from around the world in global projects such as the Newsday newswire, a school newspaper based on articles submitted by global student correspondents; Online Expeditions, in which students follow the journeys of real people as they travel to various international locations; and Doors to Diplomacy, a competitive Web-based project in which students learn about international affairs and diplomacy.

Teaching Cross-Cultural Leadership and Communication Skills

Regardless of career aspirations, students of the 21st century need opportunities to develop leadership skills such delegating, scheduling, planning, problem solving, decision making, and negotiating. They need practice in using interpersonal, verbal, and written skills to communicate with a multicultural population. Simulations such as those sponsored by GlobalEdge, http://globaledge.msu.edu/academy/academy.asp, provide students with opportunities to build a company from the ground up and to make decisions on all aspects of the business while negotiating via e-mail, chat rooms, and posting boards with international students at other locations to buy and sell products. GlobalEdge is a Web-portal created by the Center for International Business Education and Research at Michigan State University and is geared toward the undergraduate and graduate levels.

Strategies such as role play and simulation can be used at the secondary, college, or industry level to rehearse dialogue for diffusing conflict and building group consensus.

Case studies, Socratic inquiry, and debate engage students in issue analysis, problem solving, interpretation, and reasoned persuasion. CasePlace.org (a free service of the Aspen Institute's Business and Society Program) houses hundreds of case studies and supporting materials concerning international and multicultural issues, conflict management, negotiations, corporate citizenship, and the like. Students can practice interpersonal skills such as active listening, negotiation, and giving and receiving feedback through well-planned team activities such as classroom debates and panel discussions that are paired with self- and peer-evaluation measures.

SUMMARY

Accepting human variation and fostering harmony among groups of people is vital to the continued development of the global society of the 21st century. Students need to learn about the complexities of international organizations and how cultural variation is influenced by organizational structure and function. Students who have an understanding for how group performance is affected by formation, environmental and technical conditions, task complexity, and operational processes will be better prepared for functioning and performing in multicultural group settings. Students who develop strong cultural, linguistic, and information technology skills will be well-suited for international and multicultural organizational leadership. Those most successful will be adaptive and sensitive to differences in communication styles, power structures, risk tolerance, and time perception. They will have the skills for managing conflict, conducting effective evaluations, and providing feedback to individuals with varied perceptions and backgrounds. Business educators can provide students with opportunities to practice their interpersonal skills through well-planned group activities, incorporating different environmental conditions and technologies into the classroom, and modeling and teaching effective multicultural leadership and communication styles.

REFERENCES

Adler, N. (1991). *International dimensions of organizational behavior* (2nd ed.). Boston: PWS-Kent Publishing Company.

Arai, M., Wanca-Thibault, W., Shockley-Zalabak, P. (2001). Communication theory and training approaches for multiculturally diverse organizations: Have academics and practitioners missed the connection? *Public Personnel Management, 30*(4), 445-455.

Beu, A., Honold, P., & Yuan, X. (2000). How to build up an infrastructure for intercultural usability. *International Journal of Human-Computer Interaction, 12*(3-4), 347-359.

Berger, M. (1998). Going global: Implications for communication and leadership training. *Industrial and Commercial Training, 30*(4), 123-127.

Boyacigiller, N., & Adler, N. (1991). The parochial dinosaur: The organizational sciences in a global context. *Academy of Management Review, 16*, 1-32.

Czarra, F. (2002-2003). Global education checklist for teachers, schools, school systems, and state education agencies. *The American Forum for Global Education*, No. 173. Retrieved February 1, 2004, from http://www.globaled.org/issues/173.pdf

DiStefano, J. J., & Maznevski, M. L. (2000). Creating value with diverse teams in global management. *Organizational Dynamics, 29*(1), 45-64.

Erez, M., & Earley, P. (1993). *Culture, self-identity and work*. New York: Oxford University Press.

Ford, R. (2004). Understanding multicultural vocabulary. *Public Relations Tactics, 11*(1), 6-7.

Gassman, O. (2001). Multicultural teams: Increasing creativity and innovation by diversity. *Creativity and Innovation Management, 10*(2), 88-95.

Grosse, C. U. (2002). Managing communication within virtual intercultural teams. *Business Communication Quarterly, 65*(4), 22-38.

Hofstede, G. (2003) *Culture's consequences, comparing values, behaviors, institutions, and organizations across nations* (2nd ed.). Thousand Oaks, CA: Sage Publications.

Hunter, D. (2001). Internal dynamics: A case study of the Multicultural Alliance. Retrieved June 19, 2003, from http://www.cs.earlham.edu/~hyrax/personal/files/student_res/internalMCA.htm

Hurn, B. (1999). The new Euro-executive. *Industrial and Commercial Training, 31*(1), 19-23.

Laroche, L. (2001, April). Teaming up. *CMA Management*, 22-25.

McCain, B. (1996). Multicultural team learning: An approach toward communication competency. *Management Decision, 34*(6), 65-68.

Miller, M., Fields, R., Kumar, A., & Ortiz, R. (2000, November/December). Leadership and organizational vision in managing a multiethnic and multicultural project team. *Journal of Management in Engineering*, 18-22.

Milliman, J., Taylor, S., & Czaplewski, A. (2002). Cross-cultural performance feedback in multinational enterprises: Opportunity for organizational learning. *Human Resource Planning, 25*(3), 29-43.

Odenwald, S. (1996). Global work teams. *Training and Development, 50*(2), 54-57.

Pan Fan, K., & Zhang Zigang, K. (2004). Cross-cultural challenges when doing business in China. *Singapore Management Review, 26*(1), 81-91.

Ramler, S. (2002). Teaching and learning in a global society. *Independent School, 61*(3), 100-106.

Robbins, S. P. (1993). *Organizational behavior: Concepts, controversies, and applications* (6th ed.). Englewood Cliffs, NJ: Prentice Hall.

Salk, J. E., & Brannen, M. Y. (2000). National culture, networks, and individual influence in a multinational management team. *Academy of Management Journal, 43*(2), 191-203.

Schein, E. H. (1992). *Organizational culture and leadership* (2nd ed.). San Francisco: Jossey-Bass.

Scott, J. C., & Martinez, B. F. (2003). Developing global managerial skills: Business educators' roles and instructional ideas. *Business Education Forum, 58*(2), 39-41.

Trefry, M. G., & Vaillant, G. (2002). Harnessing cultural diversity to stimulate organizational learning. *Current Topics in Management, 7*, 47-60.

Triandis, H. C., & Gelfand, M. J. (1998). Converging measurement of horizontal and vertical individualism and collectivism. *Journal of Personality and Social Psychology, 74*, 118-128.

Tuan, V. V., & Napier, N. (2000). Paradoxes in Vietnam and America: Lessons learned. Part I. *Human Resource Planning, 23*(1), 7-8.

Young, C. B., & Henquinet, J. A. (2000). A conceptual framework for designing group projects. *Journal of Education for Business, 76*(1), 56-61.

Negotiating Concluding Agreements with Global Partners

Jensen J. Zhao
Ball State University
Muncie, Indiana

International cross-cultural negotiations play an increasingly important role in reaching international agreements, facilitating global economic and social developments, and maintaining world peace. Effective global negotiation skills are required for business professionals and government officials to be successful in handling global business and international affairs. This chapter discusses how to develop effective global negotiation skills and strategies. The discussion begins with fundamentals of global negotiation, followed by an exploration of the cultural impact on global negotiation. Then, the chapter discusses varied skills and strategies for effectively preparing and conducting global negotiations. Finally, the chapter provides information about teaching negotiating.

FUNDAMENTALS OF GLOBAL NEGOTIATION

Negotiation is an essential part of human life. People negotiate when doing business such as buying or selling cars and houses and making or receiving job offers. As many people have experienced, although negotiation takes place in daily life, to negotiate well is not easy. To negotiate successfully with global partners is even more difficult. For example, in September 2003, the Fifth World Trade Organization (WTO) Conference was held in Cancún, Mexico. The main task of the conference was to make progress in negotiations on international trade issues. However, the conference ended without consensus. The conference chairman concluded that the WTO members have to learn from the lack of consensus; doing international business in one nation's normal way would not lead to success (WTO, 2003). The global negotiation difficulty indicates the importance of understanding (a) What is global negotiation? (b) When do people need to negotiate globally? (c) What are common negotiation strategies? (d) What is the common negotiation process? and (e) What are misperceptions about negotiation?

What Is Global Negotiation?

Negotiation is a back-and-forth communication process used by people around the world to reach agreements when they and their partners share some common interests but also have conflicts. Negotiation occurs at four hierarchical levels: interpersonal, group or collective, international, and multinational or global (see Figure 1).

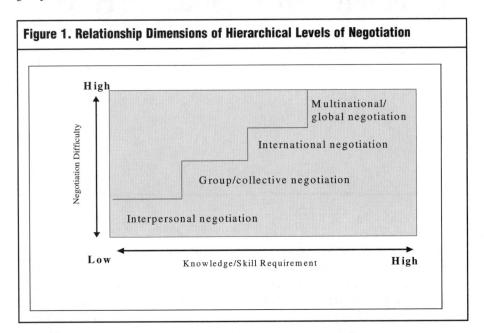

Figure 1. Relationship Dimensions of Hierarchical Levels of Negotiation

Global or multinational negotiation refers to negotiations among multilateral partners from different countries. Negotiators' various national interests, social values, cultures, religions, and languages do complicate negotiation processes. As Figure 1 illustrates, multinational or global negotiation is at the highest level of negotiation, which encompasses all the characteristics of the lower-level international, group or collective, and interpersonal negotiations. Therefore, negotiations at the multinational or global level are the most complicated and require the highest level of negotiation knowledge and skills.

When Do People Need to Negotiate Globally?

As Fisher and Ury stated (1981), "negotiation is a basic means of getting what you want from others" (p. xi). When people cannot get what they want domestically, they look to negotiate globally. For example, for getting cheaper labor, raw materials, or foreign market shares that they couldn't get domestically, many U.S., Japanese, and European companies have negotiated globally. Now Coca Cola gets 75% of its profits from overseas markets; Toyota sells more cars in the U.S. market than Chrysler does; and Intel, GM, and other foreign companies report strong sales in China (Chandler, 2003; Creswell & Schlosser, 2003; Newman, 2003).

Global negotiations are appropriate only if the following four conditions exist. First, there must be a lack of what a company wants to get in its own country. If a company can get what it wants locally, it needn't go beyond its national border to look for global partners. Second, there must be a conflict of interests. If there is no conflict, there is no need to negotiate. Third, there must be some ambiguity about the right solution to the conflict. If the solution is clear to each side, there is no reason to negotiate. Fourth, there must be an opportunity to reach an agreement that each side can accept, meaning that neither side may get exactly what it wants, but that each can live with the deal (Schoonmaker, 1989). These four conditions can serve as a checklist for negotiators to decide whether they need to negotiate globally.

What Are Common Negotiation Strategies?

Literature (e.g., Fisher & Brown, 1988; Schoonmaker, 1989; Zhao, 2000) indicates that common negotiation strategies include win-win, zero-sum, compromise, and cooperative egoism. The win-win strategy, also named joint-problem solving, relationship-oriented, or collaborative negotiation, is looking for synergy, meaning 1+1=>2. The strategy considers negotiation to be a way of working together creatively to explore opportunities that create value and minimize conflicts, allowing each side to win in the deal (Fisher & Brown, 1988; Zhao, 2000).

When the negotiation is for a short-term deal and the relationship is not as important to negotiators, however, some game theorists and bargainers believe that the zero-sum strategy works best. The zero-sum strategy considers negotiation as a game to maximize one's own gain from the sum of a deal without caring if the other side gets zero. Therefore, it is also called win-lose, pure bargaining, task-oriented, or competitive strategy. Zero-sum negotiators believe that it is suicidal to be open, honest, and trusting when the other side is deceiving and exploitative (Schoonmaker, 1989; Zhao, 2000).

Between the two distinct strategies of win-win and zero-sum stand the compromise and cooperative egoistic strategies. Negotiators who favor the compromise strategy believe in making fair deals; therefore, they like to negotiate deals by making mutual concessions as a compromise from each side. By contrast, negotiators for the cooperative egoistic strategy consider negotiation as a way to cooperate for getting what they cannot get elsewhere; at the same time, without damaging the cooperative relationship, they negotiate selfishly for maximizing their own benefits to the degree that the other side will allow (Zhao, 2000).

A study of 31 international and multinational business negotiation projects reveals that the win-win strategy helped generate the largest number of successful deals, 16, whereas the compromise strategy resulted in 3 deals; the cooperative egoistic strategy made 3 deals; and zero-sum generated 4 lose-win, 3 win-lose, and 3 lose-lose outcomes (Zhao, 2000).

What Is Common Negotiation Process?

No matter what strategies negotiators choose, effective global negotiators follow a negotiation process of three phases: preparing, negotiating, and closing deals (e.g., Fisher & Brown, 1988; Gliffin & Daggatt, 1990; Kublin, 1995; Zhang, 1995). The preparation phase includes forming a negotiation team, gathering and analyzing information, setting objectives and strategies, and preparing a negotiation agenda and rehearsing. In the negotiation phase, delegates implement their strategies and tactics for creating a deal-making atmosphere, negotiating offers and counteroffers, and breaking deadlocks. When negotiators reach agreements on the issues, they are ready for the final phase, closing deals, which includes finalizing contract terms, holding a signing ceremony, and implementing the contract.

What Are Misperceptions about Negotiation?

Misperceptions about negotiation hamper people's ability to learn effective negotiation skills. Thompson (2001) pointed out the four most prevalent myths about negotiation: (a) good negotiators are born, (b) experience is a great teacher, (c) good negotiators take risks, and (d) good negotiators rely on intuition. In reality, good negotiators are not born but trained and developed. Good negotiators learn and practice effective negotiation skills in a disciplined fashion, whereas most people do not have such opportunities. Second, it is only partially true that experience can improve negotiation skills. Without proper training and feedback, experience alone would cause biased self-confidence, which may lead negotiators to take unwise risks. Third, negotiators who take risks or gamble at the negotiating table are not good ones. Good negotiators know how to evaluate a situation, how to identify opportunities for each side, and how to propose solutions for maximizing the outcomes of each side. Finally, negotiators without training rely on intuition or gut feeling. Effective negotiators do not rely on intuition; rather, they are deliberate planners. They develop proactive strategies and tactics and know how to apply them to different situations.

In short, effective negotiators are not born but trained and cultivated. The following sections will explore the cultural impact on global negotiation and discuss how to develop skills and strategies for effectively preparing and conducting global negotiations.

CULTURAL IMPACT ON GLOBAL NEGOTIATION

Global negotiation is conducted among people from different nations and cultures. Each culture has its own traditions, values, and norms shared by its members. Knowing different cultures can help negotiators perform better in multinational cross-cultural negotiations. This section discusses, first, three major cultural dimensions and their impact on negotiators, then, the danger of cultural stereotypes, and, finally, the predictors of successful global negotiators.

Individualism vs. Collectivism

A key dimension in which many cultures differ is in terms of individualism and collectivism (e.g., Hofstede & Bond, 1988; Thompson, 2001). In individualistic cultures everyone is expected to look after oneself and the immediate family. When individuals' personal goals conflict with those of their family, work group, community, or country, their priority goes to their personal goals. Individual accomplishments are encouraged, rewarded, and protected by economic, social, and legal institutions. By contrast, in collectivistic cultures people from birth on are integrated into strong, cohesive in-groups that protect them in exchange for loyalty. Their social values and norms promote group and social harmony and interdependence. People in such cultures like working in teams, building relationships, and sharing resources; as a result, they need more time in making decisions and reaching agreements.

An obvious example of individualism vs. collectivism is people's name order. In individualistic cultures, such as those found in Canada, England, and the U.S.A., people put their own name first and the family name last. By contrast, in collectivistic cultures, like those found in China, Japan, and Korea, people put their family name first and their own name last. Another example involves different thinking processes. While people in individualistic cultures tend to think from specific to general, people in collectivistic cultures do so in a reverse order. This difference helps explain why Canadian, English, and U.S. mailing addresses start with an individual person's name, then his or her department or house number, street, city, state, postal code, and country; whereas Chinese, Japanese, and Korean mailing addresses are in an opposite way, starting with the country and ending with individual's name. The difference also helps explain why Americans prefer to negotiate specific issues first, while Chinese like to establish agreement on general principles before moving to specific issues (Zhao, 2000).

Cooperativeness vs. Competitiveness

Different cultures value cooperativeness and competitiveness differently. People from collectivist, feminine cultures tend to engage in more cooperative activities than do people from individualistic, masculine cultures (Hofstede & Bond, 1988). Cultures with cooperative orientation value more nurturing, supporting, and relating, whereas cultures of competitive orientation are more aggressive, assertive, and task-oriented. These cultural values affect negotiators' preference for either the win-win or the zero-sum strategy. However, with more and more global interactions, negotiators from both cooperative and competitive cultures realize the importance of balancing the use of cooperation and competition.

Direct vs. Indirect Communication

Communication is another dimension in which cultures differ from one another. Hall (1976) found that cultures range from high context to low context. In high-context cultures like those found in Asian countries, the social context (e.g., personal relations and nonverbal behavior) that surrounds a formal, written, legal document is far more important than the document. People tend to use implicit, indirect messages in communication because of such concerns as relationships, harmony, status, and respect. By contrast, in low-context cultures like those found in Anglo-American and Scandinavian countries, what counts is primarily what has been written in the legal documents and contracts. Therefore, people prefer using explicit, written messages for clear, direct communication.

Taking contract forms as an example, the Chinese Uniform Contract Law allows flexibility and states that contracts can be in written, oral, or other forms. In contrast, the U.S. Uniform Commercial Code states that a contract for the sale of goods for the price of $500 or more is not enforceable by way of action or defense unless a written contract is signed (Zhao, 2000). In negotiation, for instance, the Japanese are willing to meet face-to-face but feel uncomfortable with open conflict. They talk around it and give indirect hints that they disagree. The Arabs want direct, face-to-face discussions but tend not to bring open disagreements into a formal session (Hendon, Hendon, & Herbig, 1996).

Stereotypes Affecting Global Negotiations

Understanding cultural differences would help negotiators communicate appropriately with global partners. However, such understandings should not become stereotypes. Stereotyping national cultures, such as declaring the French to be arrogant and romantic and U.S. Americans to be impatient and aggressive, would affect negatively negotiators' ability to see people as individuals. Effective global negotiators are open-minded and flexible. As Griffin and Daggatt (1990) suggested, getting to know the negotiators from other cultures can be the best method of eliminating prejudices and stereotypes.

Predictors of Successful Global Negotiators

Research found that the following seven behavioral characteristics have value in predicting successful global negotiators (e.g., Kublin, 1995; Zhao & Parks, 1995).

Adaptation. Adaptation refers to the ability with which individuals act appropriately in new or ambiguous situations. Those who are willing to adapt to new situations always have high success rates in cross-cultural interaction (Zhao & Parks, 1995).

Respect. Respect is the ability to show admiration and positive regard for other people in interpersonal and cross-cultural relations. International business managers perceive showing respect as a very important skill for international business success (Zhao & Parks, 1995).

Empathy. Empathy is the ability to understand others' situations and feelings through giving and receiving feedback. Successful global negotiators show empathy by listening actively, maintaining appropriate eye contact, and mirroring others' facial expressions in a genuine manner (Zhao & Parks, 1995).

Interaction management. Interaction management is the ability to handle the process of human interaction. Those who are able to handle interactions such as negotiating issues, taking turns, entering and exiting negotiating sessions, and dealing with topical development smoothly have high success rates in cross-cultural interaction (Zhao & Parks, 1995).

Interaction posture. Interaction posture refers to the ability to respond to others in a descriptive and nonjudgmental way. International business managers consider the skill of withholding judgment as important in international business management (Zhao & Parks, 1995).

Flexibility. Flexibility is the ability to explain things to different people according to different situations in order to reach the same results. Flexibility predicts culture awareness and communication effectiveness in cross-cultural communication (Zhao & Parks, 1995).

Role behavior. Role behavior is the ability to perform both relationship and task roles and the ability to avoid self-centered roles. In cross-cultural interaction, developing a working relationship is the basis on which two parties can facilitate task roles (Zhao & Parks, 1995).

In short, cultural differences do affect global negotiation. Knowing different cultures can help negotiators develop effective behavioral and communication skills for successful global negotiation. The next section will discuss how to prepare successfully for global negotiation.

PREPARING FOR GLOBAL NEGOTIATION

A successful negotiation starts with good preparation. The better the negotiators prepare, the more successful their negotiations will be. This section illustrates how to prepare for a global negotiation: forming a negotiation team, gathering and analyzing information, setting objectives and strategies, and preparing the negotiation agenda and rehearsing.

Team Composition and Cross-Cultural Considerations

Negotiation teams for international cross-cultural business affairs usually consist of negotiators and foreign language interpreters. Using interpreters not only ensures accurate communication between the two sides, but also provides negotiators with more time to think before they speak. Negotiators need to be selected based on their negotiation experience, cross-cultural communication skills, and technical expertise. A team must have a leader who is able to think and act creatively and strategically, to lead consultatively, to be quiet and keen on observation, and not to involve directly in confrontations with the other side. Other members should have expertise in their respective areas and be able to play the assigned roles. For example, while an interpreter can be an information analyst and a liaison between the two sides, a technical specialist can play the role of a tough task-oriented negotiator, and the team leader can play a friendly, relation-oriented role (Schoonmaker, 1989; Zhang, 1995).

There is no magic number of members for a team; the decision is based on the size and complexity of a negotiation project. Traditionally, people from individualistic cultures tend to negotiate as a small team of two to three, whereas people in collectivistic cultures like to form larger negotiation teams of five to ten or even more. This explains why Chinese and Japanese negotiation teams are usually larger than the U.S. teams (Chaney & Martin, 2004; Pye, 1982).

Information Gathering and Analysis

Information gathering and analysis include two SWOT (strengths, weaknesses, opportunities, and threats) analyses. The first is the self-SWOT analysis. A negotiation team needs to gather needed information and to analyze its strengths and weaknesses in terms of its products, services, technologies, know-how, intellectual properties, production capacities, financial, human, and natural resources and then identify its market opportunities and threats. If there are good opportunities in the domestic market, there is no reason for negotiating with global partners. Otherwise, a SWOT analysis of prospective global partners is necessary. This analysis helps your team to know your counterparts' domestic and global competitions, negotiation urgency, and negotiators' authority and background (Zhao, 2002).

Based on the SWOT analyses, your team needs to (a) list all issues such as price, product/ service quality, technology, know-how, training, and warranty that either side may raise in negotiation; (b) separate your issues from theirs into two parallel groups; and (c) prioritize your issues and then theirs based on your information. This process identifies differences between the two sides. Every difference in priority can create a win-win opportunity. For example, U.S. companies move manufacturing facilities to Mexico for cheaper labor, while Mexico welcomes U.S. companies for better-paying jobs and more advanced technology (Zhao, 2002).

Team Objectives and Strategies

Knowing the prioritized issues of each side, your team needs to set objectives, which means setting a bottom line and a goal for each issue. The bottom line is the worst deal you will accept, and the goal is the best deal you want to get. A clear goal with a firm bottom line will help your team increase certainty and comfort and prevent it from conceding too much or not enough in negotiation. Next, through research and communication, not assumption, your team should try to figure out your counterpart's possible goals and bottom lines for its issues and their perceptions of your objectives. Knowing both teams' goals and bottom lines, your team can identify opportunities for persuading the other team to adjust its perceptions and expectations, creating win-win solutions or determining bargaining ranges to maximize your share if you do not care about the long-term relationship with your counterpart (Zhao, 2002).

To achieve your negotiation objectives, your team needs to plan your primary and alternative strategies and relevant tactics. Cooperative negotiators usually use the win-win strategy as the primary approach. A commonly used win-win strategy (Fisher & Brown, 1988) focuses on building a working relationship that can deal well with differences. The first step is to separate relationship issues, such as dealing with people honestly or deceptively, logically or emotionally, from substantive ones that are typically included in an agreement, such as money, terms, and conditions. It is easier to build a working relationship if negotiators deal with the relationship and substance independently and vigorously. Fisher and Brown's strategy is to be unconditionally constructive, which involves a process of pursuing six basic elements:

1. *Rationality.* Even if others are acting emotionally, balance emotions with reason.

2. *Understanding.* Even if they misunderstand us, try to understand them.

3. *Communication.* Even if they are not listening, consult them before deciding on matters that affect them.

4. *Reliability.* Even if they are trying to deceive us, neither trust them nor deceive them; be reliable.

5. *Non-coercive modes of influence.* Even if they are trying to coerce us, neither yield to that coercion nor try to coerce them; be open to persuasion and try to persuade them.

6. *Acceptance.* Even if they reject us and our concerns as unworthy of their consideration, accept them as worthy of our consideration, care about them, and be open to learning from them. (p. 38)

Competitive negotiators, however, like to use the zero-sum strategy as the primary approach, because they consider the win-win strategy as naïve and believe that pure bargaining is the way to help maximize their gains, especially when the other side wants to develop a long-term relationship. Zero-sum strategy includes (a) an overall bargaining range with well-defined starting points, goals, and walk-away points and (b) a best alternative to a negotiated agreement (BATNA), which is an alternative that can be pursued if the current negotiation fails. Six general guidelines for zero-sum strategy (Lewicki, Hiam, & Olander, 1996) are as follows:

1. Stick to your planned target and walk-away points.

2. Do not reveal your target point too early.

3. Never reveal your walk-away point.

4. Get the other party to make big concessions.

5. Keep your concessions few and small.

6. Know the other party's concern for the outcome and its cost of walking away (pp. 90-91).

Planning only one strategy is risky. While zero-sum negotiators have their BATNA as an alternative, negotiators with win-win as their primary strategy also have alternatives. For instance, Chinese negotiators are trained to probe the other side's strategies not only in words but also in deeds, meaning checking if the other side's verbal statements and negotiating behaviors are consistent, and then act accordingly. In doing so, they can prevent those who are driven by the zero-sum mindset from taking advantage to gain unreasonably huge profits (Zhao, 2000).

Negotiation Agenda Preparation and Rehearsal

A negotiation agenda serves as the guideline for a negotiation. Without preparing your agenda, your team will be led by the other side's agenda at the negotiation table. Effective negotiators usually draft their issues into contract terms before negotiating and then list them as agenda items for negotiation. General contract terms include (a) duties of each party, (b) rights of each party, (c) dates for ordering, shipping and delivering, (d) prices in U.S. dollar amounts, (e) quantities, (f) training, (g) payment terms, (h) insurance, warranty, and claim, (i) governing law, and (j) termination of the contract. In addition, the agenda should also include when and where the negotiation will be held. For example, if a U.S. company intends to export its products, it should invite prospective foreign buyers to come to the U.S. to negotiate the deals. Doing so enables the company to show not only its products but also its research and production facilities and capacities, thereby facilitating the negotiation (Zhao, 2002).

The final step of preparation is to rehearse or role-play the negotiation, especially when a deal is huge and the negotiating issues are complex and conflicting. Part of the team plays the role of the other side and simulates its possible positions, strategies, and styles. Effective negotiators even videotape the role-plays for adjustment and improvement (e.g., Schoonmaker, 1989; Zhang, 1995).

In short, negotiation preparation is a process of forming a team, gathering and analyzing information, setting objectives and strategies, and preparing the negotiation agenda and rehearsing. The next section will discuss how to conduct global negotiation with success.

CONDUCTING GLOBAL NEGOTIATION

After careful preparation, the team is ready for negotiation. This section discusses how to start negotiating with global partners, how to break deadlocks, how to close deals, and how to implement agreements.

Starting Negotiation with Global Partners

Starting the negotiation with global partners involves creating the right atmosphere, communicating positions, and making offers and counteroffers.

Create the right atmosphere. The negotiating atmosphere sets the tone for the negotiation. Negotiators need first to create an atmosphere that fits their strategies. Zhao

(2000) identified five negotiating atmospheres used in global negotiations, which could be arrayed along a continuum from friendly through formal to indifferent to adversarial to hostile. While win-win negotiators like to create and maintain a friendly atmosphere for building a long-term cooperative relationship, pure bargainers prefer the indifferent, adversarial, and hostile atmospheres to support their strategies. The methods for creating and maintaining a friendly atmosphere include (a) making small talks about personal interests, hobbies, education, or travel experience, (b) reserving a hotel for the counterparts, (c) meeting and greeting the counterparts at the airport, and (d) holding social meetings in restaurants. By contrast, the methods for creating an indifferent, adversarial, or hostile atmosphere include choosing a neutral third-party country as a place of negotiation and involving neutral third parties (e.g., the U.S.-North Korean nuclear-tensions negotiation in Beijing, China, in 2003), and using accusations, threats, or coercive power. Such methods are risky and often end up with lose-lose outcomes (Zhao, 2000).

Communicate positions. When communicating a negotiating position, research suggests (e.g., Schoonmaker, 1989; Zhao, 2000) using messages in a range from indirect to direct statements. Win-win negotiators prefer using indirect, polite requests such as "We suggest mutual benefit and long-term cooperation be our basic principles; what do you think about it?" (Zhao, 2000). By contrast, zero-sum negotiators like to withhold or distort some information while expressing their positions in direct, firm, declarative statements (Schoonmaker, 1989). For instance, a negotiator might ignore a question about why his or her company wants to sell a business because a frank answer would weaken his or her position; instead, he or she might state firmly, "This business is very profitable. The company would not even consider selling it if its other businesses were not growing that rapidly." Schoonmaker (1989) advises that negotiators should keep the position statement simple and put it in writing, use the counterpart's language, verify that the counterpart understands the position, and understand their counterpart's position.

Make offers and counteroffers. Who makes the first offer? In international trade usually sellers make the first offer. The first offer sets the ceiling of the price range; therefore, negotiators uncertain of the market and their counterpart should suggest that their counterparts make the first offer. Both sellers and buyers should make reasonable first offers; unreasonable offers will hurt the other side's feelings and damage the atmosphere. Offers can be Western-style package offers, which have room for negotiation and concession, or Japanese-style piecemeal offers, in which the basic price is quite low to attract the buyer but profitable extras are added on when the buyer asks for them (Zhao, 2000).

Tactics for making counteroffers range from accepting a reasonable offer, to requesting or giving justification, to making a counteroffer lower than the other side's bottom line, to rejecting their offer and asking them to reconsider it. Giving justification is most frequently used in global negotiations, followed by requesting justification. The least used tactic is accepting a reasonable offer without a counteroffer. While win-win advocates like to give justification with sufficient evidence and persuasion, cooperative egoists are just willing to answer questions but not to volunteer information. Compromisers prefer trading concessions as counteroffers, and pure bargainers like to make counteroffers lower than the other side's bottom line (Schoonmaker, 1989; Zhao, 2000, 2002).

Breaking Deadlocks

Conflict or deadlock resolution is a major part of negotiation. The win-win techniques for breaking deadlocks include (a) multiplying options rather than focusing on either/or, (b) being open-minded and creating more value for each side, (c) improving two-way communication and exploring more interests, and (d) leveraging price creatively with other issues of the deal, such as technology, delivery time, quantity, intangible value, service, training, referral, and market entry. In technology transfer, for example, when the negotiation of a price cut on the transferor's new technology is in a deadlock, the transferee should be willing to look at the transferor's mature technology. Very often the mature technology is more cost-effective for developing countries. If the transferee really needs the new technology, he or she could consider accepting the offered price if the transferor agrees to offer free training or consulting along with the technology. Or the transferor could consider making an exception and lowering the price to the level the transferee could afford in exchange for exclusive market entry or business referrals guaranteed by the transferee's government (Zhao, 2000).

Other techniques for breaking deadlocks include (a) making small concessions that appear painful to you and then demanding reciprocity, (b) leaving the deadlocks for a later time and negotiating other issues first, (c) suggesting a recess, and (d) walking out friendly. The last resort for conflict resolution in negotiations is to use a third-party mediation or arbitration (Schoonmaker, 1989; Zhao, 2000).

Closing Deals

When both sides have resolved the hurdles and are ready to close a deal, they may encounter disagreement about the official contract languages and governing laws. As an international general practice, English and the host nation's language both serve as the official contract languages. Concerning the governing laws, while the international trade and e-commerce agreements and contracts are under the governance of the United Nations' International Trade Law, the contracts of technology transfers and foreign joint ventures are usually governed by the host nation's laws. However, reasonable flexibility is possible for win-win negotiators. For instance, in a joint-venture negotiation, a U.S. company was not certain of China's intellectual property (IP) protection regime and insisted on using its home state law as the governing law. Knowing the cause of the deadlock, the Chinese explained about China's continuous improvement in IP protection and proposed that the contract governing law still be China's law, but the IP protection clause be governed by New York state law. The U.S. company accepted this creative proposal and signed the contract as a win-win outcome (Zhao, 2000).

Hold a signing ceremony is an important gesture for developing a relationship and implementing a contract cooperatively. The executives from each side should attend the ceremony. The host party usually also invites its local government officials to be present as a symbol of government support to the deal. Most signing ceremonies are accompanied by a band playing music and followed by a banquet or reception.

Implementing Agreements

In low-context cultures like in the U.S. and England, signing an agreement or contract means the end of the negotiation. Next, each side performs what it has promised in the contract; otherwise, it will be liable for the consequences of breaching the contract. By contrast, in high-context cultures such as in China and Korea, signing a contract just means the beginning of a formal business relationship. Therefore, at the contract-implementation stage, either side may propose to revise or renegotiate some contract terms because it believes that no one could predict future unexpected happenings during the early negotiation (Zhang, 1995; Zhao, 2000).

When low-context cultures collide with high-context cultures in this aspect, instead of warning the other side not to breach the contract, win-win negotiators prefer to listen to the other side's renegotiation proposal and to accept it if it is reliable, reasonable, and valid. Win-win negotiators consider the renegotiation and revision of contract terms as a way of continuous improvement of the cooperation and relationship between the parties (Zhao, 2000, 2002).

In short, conducting a global negotiaiton is a process of back-and-forth communication between or among parties from different countries and cultures. This process includes creating the right atmosphere, communicating positions, making offers and counteroffers, breaking deadlocks, closing deals, and implementing agreements. The next section provides some suggestions for teaching global negotiation.

INSTRUCTIONAL SUGGESTIONS

As the world has entered the global economy, teaching global negotiation skills and strategies becomes an important part of business education. The following list suggests some practical teaching approaches:

1. Global negotiation can be taught as an international cross-cultural component in courses such as business communicaiton, marketing, management, and foreign trade and investment. Instructors can choose from various teaching approaches according to the class time available for this subject.

2. For a 50-75 minute class session, the instructor can introduce the essentials of global negotiation to students through questions and discussions. For instance, questions such as, "What is global negotiation? When should people negotiate globally? and What are common negotiation strategies?" easily facilitate group discussions and individual learning. When teaching cultural differences and predictors of successful global negotiators, the instructor can ask students to identify their cultural behaviors and negotiation styles, to compare theirs with the predictors, and then to discuss their learning experience.

3. If more class time is available, the instructor can provide students with negotiation cases for hands-on simulation from which students can experience advanced learning, skill development, and fun. A proper simulation should follow the procedures discussed in the previous sections and start with team formation. For example, each team needs to decide who will be the team leader or coordinator, who will be negotiators and of what types, and who will be the secretary for taking minutes at the negotiating table. Then, each team will gather and analyze information and so on. After the simulation the instructor can hold class discussion for students to share learning experiences or ask them to write a short report about their learning experiences.

SUMMARY

Effective global negotiators are not born but trained and developed. Global negotiation is the most difficult of all the negotiations because of negotiators' different national interests, social values, cultures, religions, and languages. Therefore, if a company can get what it wants domestically, it needn't go to negotiate globally. When a global negotiation is needed, the company needs to select appropriate negotiators, strategies, and processes. Research found that effective global negotiators are able to adapt, to respect, and to manage interaction, as well as to be empathic, nonjudgmental, flexible, and balanced in the relationship and task roles.

A successful global negotiation starts with good preparation, which includes forming a team, gathering and analyzing information for each side, setting objectives and strategies, and preparing the negotiation agenda and rehearsing. When negotiating with global partners, effective negotiators first create a right atmosphere and then properly communicate their positions, make offers and counteroffers, break deadlocks, and close deals. Effective global negotiators are aware that while signing a contract means the end of the negotiation in low-context cultures, signing a contract is considered just the beginning of a formal business relationship in high-context cultures, and either side may propose to revise the contract at the implementation stage. As the world has entered the global economy, teaching global negotiation skills and strategies in business courses becomes more important than ever before.

REFERENCES

Chandler, C. (2003, November). China is too darn hot! *Fortune, 148*(10), 39-40.

Chaney, L. H., & Martin, J. (2004). *Intercultural business communication* (3rd ed). Upper Saddle River, NJ: Prentice Hall.

Creswell, J., & Schlosser, J. (2003). Has Coke lost its fizz? *Fortune, 148*(10), 125-127.

Fisher, R., & Brown, S. (1988). *Getting together: Building a relationship as we negotiate.* Boston: Houghton Mifflin.

Fisher, R., & Ury, W. (1981). *Getting to yes: Negotiating agreement without giving in.* New York: Penguin Group.

Griffin, T. J., & Daggatt, W. R. (1990). *The global negotiator: Building strong business relationshiops anywhere in the world.* New York: Harper Business.

Hall, E. T. (1976). *Beyond culture.* Garden City, NY: Anchor Books.

Hendon, D. W., Hendon, R. A., & Herbig, P. (1996). *Cross-cultural business negotiations.* Westport, CT: Quorum Books.

Hofstede, G., & Bond, M. H. (1988). The Confucius connection: From cultural roots to economic growth. *Organizational Dynamics, 16,* 4-21.

Kublin, M. (1995). *International negotiating: A primer for American business professionals.* New York: International Business Press.

Lewicki, R. J., Hiam, A., & Olander, K. W. (1996). *Think before you speak: The complete guide to strategic negotiation.* New York: John Wiley & Sons.

Newman, R. J. (2003). Chrysler in the crossfire. *U.S. News & World Report, 135*(16), D12.

Pye, L. W. (1982). *Chinese commercial negotiating style.* Cambridge, MA: Rand Corporation.

Schoonmaker, A. N. (1989). *Negotiate to win: Gaining the psychological edge.* Englewood Cliffs, NJ: Prentice Hall.

Thompson, L. (2001). *The mind and heart of the negotiator* (2nd ed). Upper Saddle River, NJ: Prentice Hall.

World Trade Organization. (2003). *The fifth WTO ministerial conference.* Retrieved December 15, 2003, from http://www.wto.org/english/thewto_e/minist_e/min03_e/min03_e.htm

Zhang, X. (1995). *International business negotiation: Principles, methods, and art.* Shanghai, The People's Republic of China: Shanghai Joint Publishing.

Zhao, J. J. (2000). The Chinese approach to international business negotiation. *Journal of Business Communication, 37*(3), 209-236.

Zhao, J. J. (2002). *Negotiation skills and strategies: Theories and applications.* Bloomington, IN: Tichenor Publishing.

Zhao, J. J., & Parks, C. (1995). Self-assessment of communication behavior: An experiential learning exercise for intercultural business success. *Business Communication Quarterly, 58*(1), 20-26.

Time: An Enigma of Intercultural Communication

Marcia L. Bush
Lincoln, California

Time is an enigma. If one thinks merely of being on time or scheduling time, it appears very simple. Yet, when one tries to comprehend time and space theories that have been the work of scientists throughout the ages, time can be extremely complex. Even in its simplest form, time dictates how individuals manage their lives, and the use or nonuse of time communicates a message about what is valued. The use of time also has a cultural identity; it is a puzzling factor that influences intercultural communication. This chapter raises questions about time, examines major events in the history of time, considers time as a medium of communication, presents cultural time orientations, ponders the impact of communication technologies on time use, suggests business strategies to improve intercultural communication, and offers instructional guidance for business educators.

QUESTIONS ABOUT TIME

Throughout the ages, people have been driven to try to understand time. Constant change was observed in the moon and the stars and the seasons. The continuing challenge was to devise some way to measure the change. The search for answers to questions as basic as "What is time?" and "What is timeless?" has been a common pursuit for each age and has marked the timekeeping progress of civilizations for thousands of years.

What Is Time?

Time can be defined as "the system of those sequential relations that any event has to any other as past, present, or future; indefinite and continuous duration regarded as that in which events succeed one another" (Flexner, 1987). Time is also an action in that one can time the speed of an object, time how long it takes to do something, or keep time in a musical sense.

Considering a definition of time, Boslough (1990) pointed out the possibility of asking six people to explain time and receiving six different answers and went on to give some examples of responses based on a person's perspective. A physicist would talk about time and space, a clockmaker would talk about his handiwork, a science-fiction fan would talk about the fourth dimension, and a banker would talk about money (Boslough, 1990).

Time in the modern business sense is a dominant factor in the United States. Consider timelines, just-in-time, work time, overtime, time-driven, and time-starved. Each of these descriptors has a definite daily meaning in the conduct of business.

What Is Timeless?

In contrast to a definite measurement, timeless is defined as "without beginning or end; eternal; everlasting" (Flexner, 1987). According to Boslough (1990), psychologists tell us that small children prior to the age of two are not aware of the passage of time, and scholars believe that people once lived in what could be called a "timeless present" (p. 111). In this type of existence, there would be no past and no future to consider or worry about. Instead, there would be a more definite awareness of and reliance on natural phenomenon. The sun, moon, stars, seasons, and personal senses and feelings are the driving forces instead of the clock, with definite measures to set sequences of events.

In business terms, timeless qualities are given a value, an infinite value placed on that which transcends time designations. Artistic creations are appreciated for their value irrespective of time, as are certain personal qualities. Classic styles continue to be accepted without a time deadline.

What Marked the Study of Time?

Time is one of the things that has piqued mankind's curiosity down through the ages. Nature's clock is ticking in everything, including people. The body clock runs by circadian rhythms that are explained by the natural body cycle of time for waking and sleeping. This natural body cycle is estimated to be 25 hours, close to the 24-hour clock measurement that defines the day. The circadian cycle, coupled with the observation of the rising and setting sun was what probably marked the first study of time, leading to the development of the sundial, the first instrument used by people to measure the flow of time (Boslough, 1990).

Other observations in nature also became studies of the passage of time. The rings of trees, rising and falling tides, and rock formations in canyons could all be observed to mark the passage of time (Boslough, 1990). Anyone who has seen the Grand Canyon is in awe of the passage of time, evident in the visual marking of the ages that have passed.

Thus, the quest to understand time continues to this day. Ultimately, each individual must answer his or her own questions about time. A review of major events in the history of time will provide a historical perspective on the efforts to understand time and to measure time.

MAJOR EVENTS IN THE HISTORY OF TIME

Concepts of time have changed with continuing exploration of theories and scientific verification. The range of understanding about time goes from the concept of a never-ending flow to proving that time is connected to motion and space, and the measurement of time intervals is affected by the motion of the observer.

Scientific Views of Time

Considerable debate has occurred about the ability to measure time as a physical reality. Victor (1992) pointed out that even the way scientists understand this physical reality has been revolutionized during the 20th century. Isaac Newton declared in 1687 (as cited in Boslough, 1990) that time is absolute, "flowing equably without relation to anything external" (p. 118). Albert Einstein shattered that notion in 1905 with his theory of special relativity. According to Victor (1992), others including British physicist Stephen Hawking worked to substantiate the relativity and uncertainty principles. The conclusion about time as one dimension of the time-space continuum is that there is a special relativity of time that is local and affected by the gravitational field that is unique to Earth. The theory predicts that a clock will slow as its speed of motion increases (Boslough, 1990). Even today the theory is still being tested. A Stanford experiment called Gravity Probe B will test Einstein's universe. Stanford researchers, one of whom has devoted 40 years to the project, developed highly sensitive gyroscopes to directly detect the curvature of space-time. Einstein's theory of relativity will be substantiated if the gyroscopes point in a slightly different direction at the end of the test (Chui, 2004).

The Measurement of Time

The idea that if time could be measured, it could be understood has continued to challenge people even to this day. Over the ages people have been driven to affix numbers to the passage of time. It was as if by creating smaller and smaller divisions, they would be able to control time. These attempts at control were also in the interest of understanding the phenomenon of time. Devising calendars and clocks has been one of people's most enduring intellectual pursuits, as evidenced by the progressive systems of time measurement that have been devised (Boslough, 1990). Landmarks in the organization and measurement of time are presented in Table 1.

The Organization of Time

Today a vast global timekeeping system keeps time for the military and for various civilizations. Atomic clocks at 50 timekeeping stations around the world from Washington and Paris to Moscow and Xian are amazingly accurate and help test Einstein's special relativity theory on a daily basis. Boslough (1990) pointed out that the clock lets individuals know what time belongs to their employers and what time is their own.

More attention has been given to measuring time than anything else in nature. The result of the work of scholars, scientists, and engineers is that today there are not only

Table 1. Landmarks in Time Measurement		
Time Period	**Location**	**Measurement**
2nd Millennium B.C.	Babylonia	360-day year; 12 months of 30 days
2686-2613 B.C.	Egypt	365-day year; 12 months of 30 days plus 5 feast days
1100s	China	First mechanical water clock
1300s	England	First mechanical clocks in monasteries
1582	Rome	Pope Gregory XIII endorses the Gregorian calendar
1600s	Italy	Galileo discovers the pendulum
1883	USA	Time zones established throughout the country
1884	USA	World time zones established based around Greenwich
1915	USA	Daylight Saving Time established
Note: Adapted from data from "The Enigma of Time," by John Boslough, 1990, *National Geographic, 177*, p. 108-132. Copyright 1990 by The National Geographic Society. Adapted with permission.		

more timepieces than all other machines, but also there is an intricate international timekeeping system (Boslough, 1990).

Thus, scientists are still testing theories of relativity, while people around the world accept the actual measurement of time by looking at a clock or a watch. The fact that the entire world is organized under one timekeeping system is amazing, considering the many different ways messages get communicated through the use of time.

TIME AS A MEDIUM OF COMMUNICATION
In one sense people may not understand time, but they are still able to convey a message or communicate with others about the way time is used, allocated, or saved. There may be a static measurement of time, but the perception about the length of time for any activity can vary. Time also takes on a social dimension with a perceived value when people set a priority for an event or booking an appointment. Even the length of the appointment can communicate the importance of the business to be conducted.

Temporal Orientation
An individual's orientation to time is multidimensional and includes how time is scheduled, how time is used or not used, and the judgment about the amount of time

spent on a particular activity. It might be communicated that time is of the essence, or that one has all the time in the world.

Matching the work of physicists on the measurement of time is the time-geographic model that looks at time as part of the social consciousness. This moves time out of the realm of scientific measurement and into a perspective of time as having an individual social identity: The sense of time and timing is unique to each person, just as each person has an individual personality style or personal likes and dislikes (Victor, 1992).

Another time dimension that is part of how a person communicates has to do with his or her past, present, and future orientation to life and living. Both individuals and collective societies have views about the relative importance of the past, versus the present, versus the future. One individual might indicate a particular focus for today's plans that lead to a future objective, whereas another individual could relate current happenings as leading from past practices (Block, Buggie, & Matsui, 1996).

Physical Measurement Versus Individual Perception

Time as measured physically is static, but different individuals' perceptions of the time spent in an activity can vary widely. According to Victor (1992), no two people view the passage of time in the same way. An hour may seem like a minute on one occasion and like an eternity on another. A person's perception is affected by how he or she feels, where he or she is, and what he or she is doing. Time may be relative, with time passing at different speeds, depending upon whether a person is busy or has little to do, whether a person is doing something pleasant or unpleasant, or whether a person is in a changing environment and waiting for something to happen (Block, Buggie, & Matsui, 1996).

In a business setting one can imagine the difference in the perception of time between the person preparing for a presentation and the person or persons who will be receiving the information presented. All parties will experience the same presentation, but how each one feels about the passing of time during the presentation will differ (Victor, 1992).

Time Use—the Social View of Time

The use of time from a social viewpoint involves individual planning processes and decision making. The approach that an individual favors for the use of time can be called a timestyle. Timestyle dimensions include the approach to planning that ranges from analytic or accounting for each minute of the day, to holistic, or being more spontaneous and thinking of time in larger chunks. People who exhibit a highly analytical planning orientation typically create small, mutually exclusive appointments. For example, they may plan their days in 15- or 30-minute intervals captured in a notebook or some other type of time management device. On the other hand, holistic planners think of time in terms of broad and potentially overlapping categories; they may plan for things to do this month (Cotte & Ratneshwar, 2001).

Other aspects of the social view of time include decisions about whether to spend time alone or with others. Individuals also differ in preferences to engage in one activity at a time or in many activities. For instance, the many activities could include education, full-time employment, and social club membership—all being undertaken simultaneously (Ezzell, 2002).

Thus, time takes on a social identity, individuals communicate through the use of time, and they perceive time in a very personal way. This individual time orientation and identity also extends across cultures.

CULTURAL ORIENTATION TO TIME

Culture has been defined as the "human-made part of the environment" by Triandis (as cited in Block, Buggie, & Matsui, 1996, p. 1) and accepted by others (Singh, Zhao, & Hu, 2003; Ulijn, O'Hair, Weggeman, & Ledlow, 2000). Communication styles and meaning, as well as realities, as perceived by individuals, are culturally induced. The concept of time and the use of time are compartmentalized according to cultural patterning. The perception of time varies among different cultures, and Hall's description of time (as cited in Victor, 1992, p. 232) as the silent language of intercultural communication is widely accepted.

Monochronic Time Versus Polychronic Time

Many who study cultural orientations (Adler, 2002; Beeth, 1997; Boslough, 1990; Cotte & Ratneshwar, 2001; Ezzell, 2002; Ihator, 2000; Varner, 2000; Victor, 1992; Wessel, 2003) identify Hall's silent language and two broad cultural approaches to time. Most individuals and national cultures follow one of these two general time orientations: monochronic or polychronic. Monochronic time is based on valuing time as a scarce commodity that can be scheduled, spent, and saved. The emphasis then is to focus on one thing at a time and to maintain a definite separation between work and family life. In monochronic societies such as the United States, business activities are timed at every stage of the implementation. Economically advanced nations adhere to monochronic conceptualizations of time in order to get all of the factors of production in the right places at the right times. Other monochronic countries include Switzerland, Germany, and Sweden (Ihator, 2000), to name but a few.

Polychronic time is characterized by involvement with many things at once. In a polychronic culture, time unfolds as circumstances warrant and is dealt with according to some prescribed pattern, such as the seasons for agrarian people, or highest priority, such as medical necessity for emergency-room services. In polychronic cultures people change plans frequently; consider schedules as goals, not imperatives; and focus on relationships with people. Many African, Latin American, and Arabic countries are polychronic (Ihator, 2000). Comparisons of the two time approaches to business and productivity tasks are illustrated in Table 2.

Clashes can occur because of different time orientations. Adler (2002) cites a monochronic manager or supervisor who perceives only a linear approach to work and cannot understand workers who have a polychronic orientation and perform more than one task at a time. In another instance, a businessperson with a monochronic orientation

Table 2. Monochronic and Polychronic Comparisons of Doing Business

Task	Monochronic	Polychronic
Schedule of activities	Appointment time is set	Appointment time is flexible
Tasks to be accomplished	Measured by output in time	Considered part of overall goal
Number of tasks	One at a time	Many handled simultaneously
Work time/Personal time	Separated from one another	Not clearly separated from one another

Note: Adapted from *International business communication,* by David A. Victor, 1992, p. 234. New York: HarperCollins Publishers, Inc. Copyright 1992 by HarperCollins Publishers, Inc., with permission from Pearson Education, Inc., Upper Saddle River, NJ.

arrives for an appointment exactly on time, only to find that he or she has to wait for other parties to arrive at the meeting. (Adler, 2002). According to Adler (2002), each style brings its advantages to a given work environment. Through situations encountered, Adler pointed out that there can be stressful situations when the two styles are in direct contact. The advice here is to recognize the advantages that each style brings to a given work environment. For example, a business associate with a monochronic time orientation will tend to have a linear focus and will be an asset on a planning team. Another associate with a polychronic time orientation can be more productive because of the ability to work on more than one task at a time.

Physical Time

In many western cultures time is carefully measured like a precious commodity that has to be conserved. Measurement takes the form of timetables, strict timelines, time in sequential order, and even payment based on time. In contrast, other cultures may not perceive time with the same focus. For these cultures human activities are not tied to the rigidities of time. The flow of social interactions determines timing, without serious regard to the ticking of the clock. Social and natural harmony takes precedence (Ihator, 2000) over scheduling.

In terms of physical time, there are some interesting examples of cultural clashes documented by Bluedorn (as cited by Wessel, 2003). A Russian team showed up 12 days late to the Olympics because it was using a different calendar, and an army with different understandings of time missed its rendezvous on the battlefield.

Life Pace and Punctuality

The pace at which life seemingly moves is also a variable across cultures. Levine and his colleagues have conducted pace-of-life studies in 31 countries (as cited in Ezzell, 2002).

Levine describes the ranking assigned to the countries by using three measures: walking speed on urban sidewalks, how quickly postal clerks fulfill a request for a common stamp, and the accuracy of public clocks. Based on these variables, Levine concluded that the five fastest-paced countries are Switzerland, Ireland, Germany, Japan, and Italy; the five slowest-paced countries are Syria, El Salvador, Brazil, Indonesia, and Mexico. The United States, at 16th place, ranks near the middle (Ezzell, 2002).

Punctuality is also a time factor with different cultural interpretations. There may be phrases to excuse lateness, but there is still a hierarchy regarding the usability of the phrases. Ezzell (2002) provided a Trinidadian example where it is permissible for the ranking official to arrive late and pass it off as "Any time is Trinidad time," while those in a lower echelon must be more punctual and abide by the "Time is time" adage (p. 75).

Personal Time

Personal time factors include views on the importance of past, present, or future; feelings about the timing of activities; and awareness of time during an activity. According to Wessel (2003), a culture's sense of time is ingrained, almost taken for granted until there is contact with people who operate at different speeds or under different time considerations. Some examples of personal time considerations include whether a person has a set time for daily events or prefers doing things unscheduled, whether a person is more comfortable knowing what time it is, or whether any attention is paid to the passing of time (Wessel, 2003).

Allen Bluedorn, author of *The Human Organization of Time* (as cited in Wessel, 2003), said that beliefs about time are some of the most basic ones people hold. A study done by Block, Buggie, and Matsui (1996) involved American, Malawian, and Japanese students at universities in their respective countries. The findings show a similar structure of beliefs about physical time and duration of time, with respondents differing most in beliefs concerning personal time. The researchers concluded that differences in beliefs about personal time seemed most likely to occur across cultural groups (Block, Buggie, & Matsui, 1996).

Thus, effective intercultural communication starts with self-awareness and understanding of others. One must interpret the silent language, appreciate the differences in how time is viewed and valued, and take all factors into consideration when communicating. Adding to this positive approach to improve communication across cultures are new opportunities with communication technologies that are now available.

THE IMPACT OF COMMUNICATION TECHNOLOGIES ON THE USE OF TIME

The continuing advancement of communication technologies is changing the way that business is conducted. There are new possibilities for intercultural communication where people from different countries have the ability to communicate on a daily basis, leading to a better understanding of the silent language of culture.

The Internet and the World Wide Web

The Internet and World Wide Web provide immediate access to people and information. Communication through the use of the Internet and World Wide Web makes it possible to alleviate many of the normal workday time constraints. Information can be exchanged to accommodate both monochronic and polychronic orientations. Some of the time pressures and other time considerations disappear with the use of e-mail or other online communication. Now the polychronic manager in South America can work on a project in the evening and still be able to meet an early morning deadline for the monochronic customer in the United States.

The growth of E-commerce and of worldwide acceptance of conducting business online is another way that technology is affecting intercultural communication. Web access crosses cultural boundaries, providing expanded opportunities to gain insight about how other cultures operate. The question has been raised about the content of Web sites and whether the Web is a culturally neutral medium. In a study of 80 U.S. domestic and Chinese Web sites conducted by Singh, Zhao, and Hu (2003), Web content analysis revealed cultural markers that give country-specific Web sites a look and feel unique to the local culture. The monochronic and polychronic characteristics are present. Ads in polychronic cultures try to be polite and make friends with the customer rather than directly selling him or her products. By contrast, Web sites in monochronic cultures use direct, confrontational appeals in the form of discounts, sales promotions, and aggressive selling. Singh, Zhao, and Hu (2003) concluded that Web designers still need to understand local cultures and local Web sites, including relevant temporal orientations.

Virtual Possibilities

Many companies use virtual teams of geographically dispersed people to work on short- and long-term projects. A virtual team conducts its work almost entirely through electronic technology. Technology and the expansion of global trade have changed the work environment for organizations of all sizes, allowing even small companies to compete in the international marketplace (Townsend, DeMarie, & Hendrickson, 1998). Virtual teams enable companies to accomplish things more quickly and efficiently. For example, Texas Instruments found that virtual meeting software such as WebEx reduced travel costs and saved time (Grosse, 2002).

A teaching project made possible with electronic media creates yet another possibility for using the Web to reveal the invisible aspects of a foreign culture and to give voice to the elusive silent language. An example of such a project is the Web-based cross-cultural curricular initiative entitled Cultura. Furstenberg, Levet, English, and Maillet (2001) reported from their experience with the Cultura project that it is clear that computer-mediated communication holds enormous promise in bringing to the forefront the hidden dimensions of culture, including different time orientations, and helps students develop an insider's understanding of another culture without having to travel to that country.

Thus, the use of technology provides time-neutral access and the possibilities of virtual teams and projects that cross cultural boundaries. The attention would then turn to the development of more global business strategies to improve communication across cultures.

BUSINESS STRATEGIES TO IMPROVE INTERCULTURAL COMMUNICATION

The globalization of business has created the need for companies to identify, study, and understand worldviews, mindsets, and habits of their global populace in order to effectively communicate. Those in business today must understand not only the words a person speaks, but also the differences in his or her cultural styles. According to Beeth (1997), if one learns a language and not the culture, one feels like a huge elephant in a dainty china shop—moving very carefully, but still sending china crashing to the floor. Lack of cultural awareness can lead to interactions that lack the essential emotional content that may be needed to effectively communicate in business and in personal situations (Beeth, 1997).

Multinational Companies and the Professional Culture

The emerging reality for business is that it is necessary to expand beyond normal limits and borders and to redefine how business is conducted. Cultural differences are no longer separate factors but must become an integral part of doing business in a global economy. Companies cannot strategize about innovation without considering global markets, foreign subsidiaries, or alliances. The understanding of different temporal orientations becomes just as important as recognizing different work styles or approaches to work. Temporal orientations no longer have country borders but become an integrated phenomenon of doing business. Think, for example, about the number of Chinese who do not live in China (Myers & Tan, 2002).

There is a new professional culture. Myers and Tan (2002) concluded from their cultural studies that it is now time to move beyond national culture. Educated individuals in polychronic societies are adopting the western time culture, and people across the globe have a raised awareness of the importance of understanding both monochronic and polychronic orientations.

Groeschl and Doherty (2000) pointed out that there are more opportunities today to live and work within cultures different from one's own. When a multinational firm such as Phillips operates in the United States, it becomes accepted as a U.S. firm. The operating style takes on the characteristics of western societies with explicit interaction, explicit time schedules, and a focus on the business at hand rather than on socializing to build working relationships. Varner (2000) substantiated that the corporate culture adapts to the national culture where business is being conducted with the example of a Mexican employee of Procter & Gamble who has completely accepted a corporate culture of timeliness and punctuality that, in the work setting, is replacing the traditional more relaxed time orientation of the Mexican culture.

Professional Culture Elements Important to Business Negotiations

The global village has been realized. In a sense doing business now requires one to think globally and act locally. If a person is doing business within a culture that is time-driven, where people are impatient, future-oriented, and have a bias in favor of quick fixes, that person should act accordingly. In another situation where the past is valued over the future, because the past is known and the future is hidden, the person's actions will be very different.

The impact of specific cultural practices is dwindling. The emphasis is on professional culture over national culture. Culture-specific practices create barriers to effective communication in intercultural negotiations (Sheer & Chen, 2003). There should now be an appreciation of communication practices that include both cultural values and strategic business practices. Assumptions in strategy research emphasize consideration of temporal perceptions that are quite useful to managers. There are four ways in which this might occur: (a) matching time views to firm choices, (b) matching time views to industry conditions, (c) anticipating competitors' strategic choices based on their different time views, and (d) using knowledge of current time views to change them (Mosakowski & Earley, 2000).

Thus, there is an emerging professional culture, and the strategy for businesses is to treat cultural differences as an integral part of doing business. What is needed next are business graduates who are ready to contribute to this new professional culture, and business educators who play an important role in preparing students for it.

INSTRUCTIONAL GUIDANCE FOR BUSINESS EDUCATORS

There is a definite need to educate business students for effective intercultural communication. Among other things, students must gain increased self-awareness about their own use of time, appreciate a variety of cultural values concerning time, examine pace and punctuality differences, and participate in practical applications to build their competencies with different approaches to the use of time. Business educators have responsibilities to provide related education at various instructional levels.

Gain Self-Awareness about the Use of Time

Business educators can facilitate students' discovery of their own time-related cultural programming with a class survey, analysis of data, and discussion of findings. Survey questions (adapted from Block, Buggie, & Matsui, 1996) could include the following:

1. My past will always be less important than my present or my future.

2. I usually pay attention to how slowly or quickly time seems to be passing.

3. When experiencing a period of time, I can estimate fairly accurately how long it is.

4. I like to know what time it is rather than not know what time it is.

5. I prefer to have a set time for daily events rather than doing things without a schedule.

6. When I am involved in a situation, I experience time differently than when I am not involved.

Once students in a class respond to statements about their use or perception of time, they can chart the data to show class patterns regarding the use of time. Analysis of the responses might show predictable patterns. For instance, male students might have a stronger preference for doing things without a schedule, compared to female students, who like to have daily events scheduled.

Students could be divided into groups based on shared time preferences. Once grouped, students would list what is important to them about their particular time-use preferences. After the shared preferences grouping, students could move to diverse groups, with the objective of hearing other viewpoints about time factors.

After the survey response analysis and group discussions, students could draw conclusions about their own self-awareness of time and their heightened understanding of time perception differences.

Appreciate Values Concerning Time

Business teachers can help their students gain insight into other cultural values concerning time by deciphering the meanings of sayings and proverbs. Consider these examples:

- *"Time is the master of him who has no master."* (Arabian proverb)

- *"Do everything at the right time, and one day will seem like three."* (Chinese proverb)

- *"Why kill time when you can employ it."* (French proverb)

- *"Time is the best adviser."* (Greek proverb)

- *"A day is long but lifetime is short."* (Russian proverb)

Business educators can direct students to a Web site with worldwide proverbs, such as *Creative Proverbs from Around the World,* http://www.creativeproverbs.com/, which gives proverbs from 300 countries and cultures. Teachers can then ask students to interpret the meanings of selected proverbs or explain what they tell someone about the time orientation of people from that country or culture. Students can work in groups on this activity, with each group sharing one interpretation or explanation with the class.

Consider Pace and Punctuality of Time

What are the priorities of different cultures in using time? Business educators can engage students in a simple investigation into the length of the workday and workweek, as well as the amount of annual vacation time that is usually granted or taken in various countries. Completing this investigation will help students to make comparisons and contrasts about time factors that affect the pace of life in various countries.

Business educators can also use a punctuality project. They can have each student choose a country and report in written or oral format what it means to be punctual in that country. For example, students will find that in Australia, Austria, Belgium, Chile, and China, prior appointments are necessary and that punctuality is highly regarded. In Brazil, by contrast, it is customary to arrive 10 to 15 minutes late. In England, Scotland, and Wales, it is acceptable to to arrive 10 minutes late, but never 10 minutes early. Students will find that in Hong Kong a 30-minute courtesy time allowance is extended because it is nearly impossible to predict how long it will take to get to appointments there. One useful source of information for this project is *Do's and Taboos Around the World* (Axtell, 1993).

In order to be successful in business activities such as sales, customer relations, joint venture planning, and the management and supervision of employees, business students should understand their own timestyles and appreciate that they have only one of many time orientations, as the instructional activities suggest.

SUMMARY

It is ironic that there are different orientations to the uses of time, yet across the globe people agree on one timekeeping system. With continuing advances in communication technology, a more universally accepted time orientation for doing business may evolve.

For the present, the choice of time orientations influences the ability of societies and their members to function effectively in a global business environment. Business people must be aware of contrasting cultural values, because the orientation to time is one of those values. One cannot assume that time just is and that all people experience time in the same way. Time is cultural, subjective, and variable. The lesson to ensure successful intercultural communication is for people to understand their own timestyles and to be open to adapting to different time orientations as business crosses international borders. Business educators must ensure that students graduate prepared to be leaders in a new professional culture that is attuned to time.

REFERENCES

Adler, I. (2002). One at a time? Whether you focus on one task or several at the same time, productivity is the goal. *Business Mexico, 12*(4), 18. Retrieved October 30, 2003, from the eLibrary database: http://ask.elibrary.com.

Axtell, R. (1993). *Do's and taboos around the world.* New York: The Benjamin Company, Inc.

Beeth, G. (1997). Multicultural managers wanted. *Management Review,* 86(5), 17-21.

Block, R. A., Buggie, S. E., & Matsui, F. (1996). Beliefs about time: Cross-cultural comparisons. *The Journal of Psychology, 130*(1), 5. Retrieved November 10, 2003, from the eLibrary database: http://ask.elibrary.com

Boslough, J. (1990). The enigma of time. *National Geographic, 177,* 108-132.

Chui, G. (2004, April 13). Einstein to be tested in Stanford experiment. *San Jose Mercury News,* pp. 1A, 13A.

Cotte, J., & Ratneshwar, S. (2001). Timestyle and leisure decisions. *Journal of Leisure Research, 33*(4), 396-409.

Ezzell, C. (2002). Clocking cultures. *Scientific American, 287*(3), 74-75.

Flexner, S. B. (Ed.). (1987). *Random house dictionary of the English language* (2nd ed. unabridged). New York: Random House, Inc.

Furstenberg, G., Levet, S., English, K., & Maillet, K. (2001). Giving a virtual voice to the silent language of culture: The Cultura Project. *Language, Learning & Technology, 5*(1), 55.

Groeschl, S., & Doherty, L. (2000). Conceptualizing culture. *Cross Cultural Management – An International Journal, 7*(4), 12-17.

Grosse, C. U. (2002). Managing communication within virtual intercultural teams. *Business Communication Quarterly, 65*(4), 22-38.

Ihator, A. (2000). Understanding the cultural patterns of the world: An imperative in implementing strategic international PR programs. *Public Relations Quarterly, 45*(4), 38-44. Retrieved October 30, 2003, from the eLibrary database: http://ask.elibrary.com

Mosakowski, E., & Earley, P. C. (2000). A selective review of time assumptions in strategy research. *Academy of Management Review, 25*(4), 796-812.

Myers, M. D., & Tan, F. B. (2002). Beyond models of national culture in information systems research. *Journal of Global Information Management, 10*(1), 24-32. Retrieved November 10, 2003, from the eLibrary database. http://ask.elibrary.com

Sheer, V. C., & Chen, L. (2003). Successful Sino-Western business negotiation: Participants' accounts of national and professional cultures. *The Journal of Business Communication, 40*(1), 50-85. Retrieved November 10, 2003, from the eLibrary database http://ask.elibrary.com

Singh, N., Zhao, H., & Hu, X. (2003). Cultural adaptation on the web: A study of American companies' domestic and Chinese web sites. *Journal of Global Information Management, 11*(3), 63-80.

Townsend, A. M., DeMarie, S. M., & Hendrickson, A. R. (1998). Virtual teams: Technology and the workplace of the future. *The Academy of Management Executive, 12*(3), 17-29.

Ulijn, J. M., O'Hair, D., Weggeman, M., Ledlow, G. H., & Hall, H. T. (2000). Innovation, corporate strategy, and cultural context: What is the mission for international business communication? *The Journal of Business Communication, 37*(3), 293-317. Retrieved October 30, 2003, from the eLibrary database:http://ask.elibrary.com

Varner, I. I. (2000). The theoretical foundation for intercultural business communication: A conceptual model. *The Journal of Business Communication, 37*(1), 39-57. Retrieved October 30, 2003, from the eLibrary database. http://ask.elibrary.com

Victor, D. A. (1992). International business communication. New York: HarperCollins Publishers, Incorporated.

Wessel, R. (2003, January 9). Is there time to slow down? *The Christian Science Monitor*, p. 13. Retrieved October 30, 2003, from the eLibrary database. http://ask.elibrary.com

Computer-Mediated Communication: Promises and Pitfalls

Elizabeth A. Regan
Morehead State University
Morehead, Kentucky

In today's global enterprises, computer-mediated communication (CMC) plays an important role in managing worldwide operations across national boundaries. It's unclear, however, just how and to what extent culture affects communication technologies, and, conversely, how communication technologies may be affecting cultures (Fornas, 1998; Tan, Wei, Watson, & Walczuch, 1998). Moreover, the growing body of research on computer-mediated communication, a topic also studied under the rubric of computer supported cooperative work (CSCW), virtual teams, groupware, and group support systems (GSS), has produced rather disparate results. Cultures where one might expect CMC to be problematic—such as Asian cultures that place significant value on strong personal relationships as a prerequisite to the development of productive business relationships—now seem to be embracing cellular telephones, mobile commerce, and other technologies at a faster pace than the U.S. As computing becomes more globally ubiquitous, intercultural issues of CMC take on growing importance. This chapter looks at worldwide growth of CMC technologies and their business application in different cultures. It then assesses current research on CMC technologies in intercultural settings with the objective of identifying common themes and sorting out the myths and realities. The chapter concludes with a discussion of the promises and pitfalls, the emerging concept of e-culture, and the implications for business educators.

GLOBAL GROWTH OF COMPUTER-MEDIATED COMMUNICATION

Computer-mediated communication technologies are evolving rapidly. Technologies generally included under the CMC umbrella include mobile commerce, cellular telephones, the Internet and World Wide Web, e-mail, e-commerce, enterprise resource planning (ERP), and collaborative and groupware technologies. Also included in the CMC research literature are MUDS, MOOS, listservs, Usenet, and the newer technologies of instant messaging, shared hypermedia, Web logs, and graphical chats.

Although the U.S. leads the world in the use of information and communication technologies (ICT), recent statistics indicate that use of these technologies in some parts of the world such as China, Hong Kong, Japan, and Eastern Europe is growing at a much faster pace than in the U.S. For instance, it appears that a number of nations now may be leading the U.S. in the use of wireless and mobile commerce. China is the world's fastest-growing ICT nation with a compound annual growth rate of 27%, according to the World Information Technology and Services Alliance (WITSA, 2002). Significant ICT spending increases were also noted in Eastern Europe. According to WITSA, these data suggest that countries in the developing world are committed to modernization through ICT investment (WITSA, 2002).

Technology research firm International Data Corp. (IDC) reported that the Asian ICT industry, excluding Japan, will grow by 11% to $88 billion in 2004. Growth, IDC added, would come from three emerging markets: China, South Korea, and India. These markets are growing because of an expected strong demand for consumer-related products and solutions that will be used both at home and at the office. The growing Internet population is also driving demand in these countries. At least 205 million people are expected to go online across Asia and the Pacific in 2004, up 22% from 2003 (Oliva, 2004).

Thus, globalization and diffusion of the Internet are fueling the growth of CMC technologies. This rapid proliferation, coupled with business trends such as distributed knowledge work and geographically dispersed work teams, requires a better understanding of the unique socio-economic and cultural considerations that may create barriers or incentives affecting adoption and use of CMC technologies.

BUSINESS APPLICATION OF CMC TECHNOLOGIES IN DIFFERENT CULTURES

This section looks at applications of CMC technologies in different cultural settings. A sampling of current research relating to four of these technologies was examined in an attempt to identify major themes or issues related to cultural differences.

Collaborative and Groupware Technologies

Use of teams and teamwork has increased significantly in the workplace, and a growing proportion of those teams is virtual (i.e., geographically dispersed). Many types of groupware and other CMC technologies are available to support geographically dispersed teams. The primary objective of virtual teaming is to capitalize on the expertise of available resources within or across organizations—and increasingly across international borders. Although a fairly large body of research has been compiled on group support systems (GSS) over the past twenty or more years, limited studies of GSS in cross-cultural environments are available.

Stough, Eom, and Buckenmyer (2000) studied the use of CMC technologies in global teaming with the objective of assessing the competitive advantages, examining managerial implications, and recommending ways to improve team performance. They concluded that use of CMC to support virtual teams can overcome many of the limitations of face-to-face teams. The success of these virtual teams appears to be invalidating the old organizational 50-foot rule: If people are more than 50 feet apart, they are not very likely to collaborate (Lipnack & Stamps, 1997). Stough et al. (2000) identified the following characteristics of virtual teams, which can reduce the barriers to collaboration often associated with geographical distance and time:

- **Transcendency.** Virtual teams can transcend time, distance, and place because CMC technology allows team members to communicate (synchronously or asynchronously) with one another 24 hours a day, seven days a week, from anywhere. Virtual teams provide an effective alternative to face-to-face meetings (same time, same place), which can be a shortcoming for traditional teams when members unable to meet at the scheduled time due to travel or other conflicts are excluded.

- **Infinity.** Virtual teams can have an infinite number of participants. With collaborative technology and groupware, participants from anywhere in the world can share information. For example, the NCR Corporation assembled a virtual task team of more than 1,000 people working at 17 locations to develop a next-generation computer system. With CMC technologies, the virtual task force team completed the projects on budget and ahead of schedule (Lipnack & Stamps, 1997).

- **Anonymity.** Virtual teams enable the members to keep their participation anonymous if desired and even to conceal the existence of the team itself. This characteristic can significantly reduce the limitations and problems associated with social, cultural, or political barriers to participation in traditional teams.

Anonymity provided by electronic GSS may be especially useful in situations involving Chinese, Japanese, and other Asian cultures based upon Confucianism where, for example, comments from women or younger people are given less importance (Aiken, 2000). The anonymity of group systems discussion has also been shown to help preserve face, another important value among many Asian cultures. Studies conducted on Chinese, Japanese, Korean, and Malaysian groups using their native languages in electronic meetings showed that participants generally enjoyed the same benefits of GSS use reported by English-speaking groups (Aiken, 2000; Aiken, Hwang, Paolillo, & Lu, 1994).

In a study comparing differences in decision making in Western (Australian) and Asian (Singaporean) cultures, Quaddus and Tung (2002) concluded that culture plays an important role in determining the effectiveness of decision making using GSS. However, while GSS offers benefits, such as increased levels of participation by group members and a systematic group process for managing conflict, a specific technique that has proven successful in one society may at times prove less effective in another society. Quaddus and Tung compared the societal norms of Australia and Singapore with respect to Hofstede's (1984) four cultural dimensions (see Table 2 and discussion later in the chapter). Major differences in results were noted in the Quaddus and Tung study between Singapore (high power distance and collectivist society) and Australia (low power distance and individualistic society), although they did not show any conclusive pattern. For example, the Singaporean group exhibited higher uncertainty avoidance than the Australian group. A higher level of interpersonal conflict was detected in the Australian group as compared to the Singaporean group. For Singaporeans, there was a greater acceptance of dissent and greater tolerance for defiance. The Australian group reported higher issue-based conflict in comparison to the Singaporean group. Overall, the lower levels of issue-based and interpersonal conflict reported in the Singaporean group were at least partially attributed to the fact that the Singaporean society values harmony (Quaddus & Tung, 2002).

A number of research studies suggest that trust is a fundamental issue in the success of virtual global teams. The influence of trust appears to be especially strong when only virtual interaction is possible. Some researchers suggested that the virtual context can constrain or even impede the development of trust (Jarvenpaa, Knoll, & Leidner, 1998). However, other research has shown that groupware, such as desktop or video/multimedia conferencing systems, can increase positive relationships among the members of virtual teams. A number of strategies have been used successfully to reinforce trust in virtual teams, in order to improve the team process outcomes. These strategies include proactive behavior, rotating team leadership, task goal clarity, role division, and frequent interaction with acknowledged and detailed responses to prior messages (Stough et al., 2000). Although CMC technology is not always a satisfactory substitute for face-to-face communication, it can facilitate the development of commitments among virtual team members and assist teams in becoming dynamic entities in geographically dispersed environments. In fact, Stough et al. (2000) concluded, "CMC may have a greater impact on the team dynamic than the traditional approaches of striving to improve face-to-face interpersonal communication" (p. 370). Major advantages and disadvantages to the use of electronically mediated virtual teaming in the global environment are summarized in Table 1.

Mobile Commerce
Mobile commerce may be defined as the use of handheld mobile wireless devices to conduct transactions through a wireless network. Leading locations in mobile wireless are Japan, South Korea, Hong Kong, Singapore, Sweden, Finland, and other European nations where government policy makers are moving rapidly and successfully in the development and establishment of m-commerce markets (InfoCom Research, 2002; Toda, 2001). The U.S. lags in establishing an interoperable infrastructure for m-commerce, and the U.S. m-commerce market is still considered to be in its infancy (Shim &

Table 1. Advantages and Disadvantages of Electronically-Mediated Virtual Teaming

Advantages or promises
- Enables organizations to streamline operations. An organization can be in every corner of the world without being hamstrung by a corporate headquarters and staff
- Relatively low start-up costs, assuming the computer infrastructure is in place
- Spatial independence, because the freedom of the system allows the participants to work in a high rise in New York City, or while ice-fishing on the Great Slave Lake in Canada

Potential disadvantages or pitfalls
- Loss of contact with management and workers
- Loss of culture where vision, mission, and core values play a significant role in success
- Resistance to the unstructured nature of the virtual organization
- Lower productivity due to people's inability to handle the freedom of virtual environments
- Lower level of idea transplant in communication because one is unable to observe body language, gestures, voice tone, inflection, pitch, and other nonverbal cues
- Miscommunication to be more prominent than ever as more importance is placed on written messages via e-mail and other forms of electronic communication
- Security problems resulting from data sharing, open lines of communication, and "hacker" intervention
- Less employee frankness and honesty in communication because of e-mail file retention and lack of privacy
- Dissatisfaction with the reward and recognition systems for outstanding performance

Adapted from ProQuest (http://www.il.proquest.com/proquest) document # 115926307, "Industrial Management & Data Systems," *100* (8), p.370.

Shim, 2003). Culture is a relevant and critical dimension of m-commerce. Consumers from different cultures may differ considerably in perceptions, beliefs, selection, and use of m-commerce (Colombo, 2001; Hofestede, 1984; Jarvenpaa, Lang, Takeda, & Tuunainen, 2003; Kim, 2000; Sarker & Wells, 2003; Shim & Shim, 2003).

An m-commerce survey by Shim and Shim (2003) reported that over 95% of respondents in Japan, Finland, Korea, and Hong Kong owned a cellular phone and over 90% had experience with m-commerce service/applications. In the U.S., only 88% of respondents owned a cellular phone, and only 65% had experience using m-commerce applications. Shim and Shim attributed this difference to the fact that most U.S. cellular phone owners use their phones only as a communications device and not for m-commerce services or applications, which are commonly available throughout Asia and Europe. Another distinction identified by Shim and Shim is the dependence on public transportation and the lengthy commute time typical in Asian countries, which is time Asians spend using mobile devices. Another important factor, however, was not culture related, and that was age. Shim and Shim found that the under-30 age group in all five countries had more exposure to recent developments in wireless and mobile technology. In all five countries the lowest percentages of mobile phone users were in the 40-50 age group and the over-50 age group. However, usage in these age groups was higher in both the Asian countries and Finland than in the U.S. The study also found that mobile phone users in Asian countries and Finland replace their mobile handsets more frequently than in the U.S. (Shim & Shim, 2003).

Another factor influencing use of m-commerce appears to be social status. In Asian, Greek, South American, and other cultures, higher status has been shown to be an important factor in adoption of cellular phones and m-commerce. In contrast, for U.S. users, functionality appears to be a far stronger influence than status on the adoption of cellular phones (Shim & Shim, 2003).

A cross-cultural research study involving 32 focus groups in Finland, Japan, Hong Kong, and the U.S in 2001 concluded that the success of m-commerce services is likely to depend on how flexible and malleable the technology is to allow users to shape it to their individual and group needs in various social and business contexts (Jarvenpaa et al., 2003). Mobility creates freedom of choice, which by itself, does not appear to be sufficient motivation for adoption. The prevalent opinion across all groups was that m-commerce is not offering any compelling new services for which they would be willing to pay substantial fees. "Only when mobility really made a difference did some participants indicate demand for genuine m-commerce services" (Jarvenpaa et al., 2003, p. 42).

Other factors affecting use of m-commerce were trust, age, services available, security, and willingness to pay for service (Shim & Shim, 2003). As of August 2003, there were 244.12 million Chinese mobile communication subscribers, making China the largest mobile communications market (Xu, 2003). However, as indicated in Table 2, less than 2% of those Chinese subscribers access the Internet using mobile wireless application protocol (WAP) and iMode mobile protocol phones, the lowest percentage of the eight Asian cultures studied by Xu (2003). China Internet (wireline) subscribers numbered 49.7 million as of the end of 2002 (Xu, 2003).

Despite efforts to increase services on the Chinese WAP network to include e-mail, stock information, news, games, shopping, banking, and other things, only e-mail services have proven popular with subscribers (Xu, 2003). This response contrasts sharply with the mushrooming growth of m-commerce in Japan, which uses iMode technology from NTT DoCoMo. As of March 2004, Japanese iMode subscribers totaled 40.1 million (NTT DoCoMo, 2004). (See Table 2.) Xu (2003) attributed the inconsistent response from the Chinese market at least in part to the inherent differences in the technologies underlying WAP and iMode. "The Chinese experience indicates that an advanced but less-than-user-friendly technology like WAP is not necessarily more commercially viable than basic but easy-to-use ones like short message services (SMS)" (Xu, 2003, p. 85). It also shows the value of an effective business model; mobile data communications must be an open system attractive to content providers, like the Internet itself, because the availability of content makes data communications attractive to subscribers (Xu, 2003).

Enterprise Resource Planning (ERP)

Implementation of enterprise resource planning systems presents a number of challenges in parts of the world with different cultural heritages (Corbitt, 2003; Davison, 2002). With their embedded Western business models, processes, and best practices, ERP systems generally require significant reengineering and organizational change. This requirement has presented a number of complications in non-Western cultures. Concepts such as open access to information and ad hoc reporting are not well accepted in Asian and other cultures, where information is often considered an individual rather than an organizational resource, and where bureaucracy demands extensive reporting. Reengineering and empowerment also run contrary to the cultural traditions of hierarchy and deference to authority. It became apparent by the turn of the 21st century that the one-business-model-fits-all approach is unlikely to be successful. There is a growing realization that the software written for e-business, whether ERP or other CMC solutions, needs to be adapted for different cultural markets (Corbitt, 2003; Davison, 2002).

Table 2. Mobile Users in Asian Cultures Accessing the Internet Using WAP and iMode Phones

Cultures	Percentage
Japan	36%
Hong Kong	15%
South Korea	10%
Philippines	8%
Taiwan	7%
Thailand	3%
China	1%
Other cultures	20%

Adapted from "Communications of the ACM" (http://www.acm.org/pubs/periodicals/cacm/), December 2003, 46(12), p.83.

E-Commerce

A recent case study of Greece, a nation that has been quick to embrace cellular phone technology but slow to adopt use of the Internet, shows that educational and cultural values may inhibit adoption of e-commerce (Georgiou & Stefaneas, 2002). According to the study, the growth rate of cellular phones in Greece, despite high subscription fees, ranks fourth in Europe behind France, Spain, and Italy. In contrast, the number of Internet users has been relatively small despite an infrastructure that provides good national and international connectivity and relatively low connectivity fees. The case study points to several cultural factors inhibiting Internet adoption. These include a dearth of Greek content, a user profile that is not characteristic of the population at large, and low use of credit cards (Georgiou & Stefaneas, 2002).

Thus, the provided sampling of research about the growing use of CMC technologies in intercultural environments highlights a variety of cultural and other factors that appear to be affecting the global adoption and use of CMC. The research literature sheds more light on the nature and extent of these cultural factors.

OVERVIEW OF COMPUTER-MEDIATED COMMUNICATION RESEARCH

Despite the globalization of CMC, much of the theory and practice is deeply rooted in North American culture and strongly reflects North American values (Boyacigiller & Adler, 1991; Tan, 1998). Moreover, some researchers (e.g., Cogburn, Zhang, & Khothule, 2002; Kanter, 2001; Katriel, 1999; Riva, 2002) question the applicability of face-to-face communication theory typically applied to CMC. They suggest that it may be necessary to "rethink some of the terms through which CMC is conceptualized" (Katriel, 1999, p. 95).

Relevant Theories of Sociology and Technology

A review of CMC research reveals a variety of relevant theories applied to identifying, assessing, and explaining cultural implications. Several are identified here. This multiplicity of theoretical approaches may account for some of the divergence in research findings.

- Linguistic approach – draws on work on the ethnography of communication and linguistics theory with a focus on language patterns and the conversational devices used in online forums (Churchill & Bly, 2000, citing others).

- Cues-Filtered-Out Theory – based on concepts of social presence; purports that online CMC essentially occurs in a social vacuum and is unacceptable in general terms because it reduces social reality to a form of physical connection between individuals (Sproull & Kiesler, 1991).

- Positioning Theory – replaces the well-defined concept of role with the concept of positioning, which is a dynamic process generated by communication (Harre as cited in Riva, 2002).

- Social Information Processing Perspective – posits that users adapt existing communicative cues, within constraints of language and textual display, to support processes of relational management, and thus online contexts allow the development of interpersonal relationships and even intimacy between the communicators (Walther, 1996).

- Social Identity Model of De-individuation Effects (SIDE model) – theorizes that in online environments, a social or group identity replaces individual identity. This phenomenon can lead some people to behave in more aggressive, uninhibited, and socially unacceptable ways than they might otherwise exhibit as an individual (Reicher, Levine, & Gordijn's study as cited in Riva, 2002).

- Miscommunication as a Chance Theory (MaCHT) – characterizes online communication as a pared-down or rarified form of conversation that lacks the rules on which effective interaction depends. If a user handles the CMC miscommunication processes well, he or she may even achieve results difficult to obtain in face-to-face meetings (Anolli's study as cited in Riva, 2002).

- Situated Action Theory – theorizes that action is not the execution of a ready-conceived plan but the subject's adaptation to context (Suchman as cited in Riva, 2002).

One interesting comparative analysis of social interaction theories in CMC suggests that some of these theoretical positions may be "limited by their assumption of technological determinism, a view that is reinforced by the general reliance on experimental methods" (Kim, 2000, p. 16). The researcher suggested that the limitations of many methodologies may overlook "the degree to which social and technical systems are mutually constructed—a primary tenet of social informatics—has been lost" (Kim, 2000, p. 16).

The literature suggests various dimensions of culture that may influence the adoption and use of CMC technologies. The most prevalent model appears to be Hofstede's model (1984), which identifies four dimensions of international culture: power distance, uncertainty avoidance, individualism, and masculinity. These factors continue to be used as a theoretical foundation for new research studies. Hofstede's "four dimensions of national culture are defined as follows:

1. Power Distance—the extent to which society accepts the fact that power in institutions and organizations is unevenly distributed

2. Uncertainty Avoidance—the degree to which a society feels threatened by uncertain and ambiguous situations, which leads it to support beliefs promising certainty and to maintain institutions protecting conformity

3. Individualism—a preference for a loosely knit social framework in society in which individuals are only supposed to take care of themselves and their immediate families, as opposed to collectivism, which implies a preference for a tightly-knit social framework in which individuals can expect their relatives and clan to protect them in exchange for loyalty

4. Masculinity—a preference for achievement, heroism, assertiveness, and material success, as opposed to femininity, which implies a preference for relationships, modesty, and caring for the weak and the quality of life.

Various research studies have shown a number of cultural differences in the use and adoption of CMC technologies along Hofstede's dimensions. For example, in high power distance cultures such as that of Korea, text messaging to individuals such as work supervisors was seen as a serious offense. In contrast, users from lower power distance cultures such as that of Norway did not see text messaging as being offensive, although some did indicate that text messaging could be potentially unsuitable for formal communication with someone unfamiliar, due to the frequent use of abbreviations and slang terms (Sarker & Wells, 2003).

Common Themes and Factors

It appears that culture is not the enormous barrier for virtual collaboration some have predicted (Davison & DeVreede, 2001; Qureshi & Zigurs, 2001). Rather, research indicates that people in different cultures adapt technologies in different ways (Massey, Montoya-Weiss, Hung, & Ramesh, 2001). A growing body of research points to the following factors that may have a stronger influence than culture per se to explain use patterns with CMC technologies:

- Age (Sarker & Wells, 2003; Shim & Shim, 2003)

- Business model (Davison, 2002; Xu, 2003)

- Compelling applications (Shim & Shim, 2003)

- Cost/price (Jarvenpaa et al., 2003)

- Ease of use (Xu, 2003)

- Emergent leadership (Cogburn et al., 2002)

- Government policies and infrastructure (Sheff, 2002)

- Media richness (Cogburn et al., 2002)

- Privacy (Katriel, 1999)

- Purpose (Riva, 2002)

- Security (Shim & Shim, 2003)

- Social status (Georgiou & Stefaneas, 2002; Tan et al., 1998)

- Task characteristics (Davison & deVreede, 2001; Evaristo, 2003; Massey et al., 2001; Qureshi & Zigurs, 2001; Tan et al., 1998)

- Technology self-efficacy (Sarker & Wells, 2003)

- Trust (Cogburn et al., 2002; Evaristo, 2003; Jarvenpaa et al., 1998; Shim & Shim, 2003; Stough et al., 2000)

Moreover, a growing body of evidence points to a number of ways in which CMC technologies are enhancing intercultural communication and understanding. For example, the increased mobility provided by CMC technologies appears to be bringing greater freedom of choice. Cultural differences placed on the value of this newfound freedom have been detected, however. In one study "participants from Western countries placed more significance on freedoms related to the individual sphere, while Asian participants especially valued new freedoms in interpersonal relationships and emotional expression" (Jarvenpaa et al., 2003, p. 42).

Cultural differences are also evident in the use of synchronous versus asynchronous communication (DeSanctis, Wright, & Jiang, 2001). For example, in their study of a multi-site global learning community, DeSanctis et al. noted "asynchronous communication is preferable in contexts where cultural differences are extensive, people are not geographically proximate, and team members are mobile" (p. 80).

Thus, evidence suggests that factors such as trust, task characteristics, cost, or purpose may have a greater impact on the effective use of CMC than culture. The influence of these factors, however, is moderated by culture, so that people in different cultures do not adapt technology in the same way.

PROMISES AND PITFALLS OF COMPUTER-MEDIATED COMMUNICATION
It is too early to conclude the extent to which cultural issues are barriers or incentives to use of CMC. However, some interesting themes and issues appear to be emerging.

1. Although culture influences the use of computer-mediated communication, one cannot assume that it decreases the interest or use. It may just be that the use differs—that the technology is applied differently.

2. Boundaries between online and offline have blurred (Churchill & Bly, 2000; Cummings, Butler, & Kraut, 2002; Fornas, 1998). It's not an either/or situation. The

material world and the virtual world are both part of an individual's total reality. So perhaps trying to study online cultures in isolation is misleading, as evidenced by studies that compare online and offline in ways that suggest that online is less rich (cues-filtered-out theory). Evidence suggests that the net benefit of online social relationships, for example, depends on whether they supplement or substitute for offline social relationships (Cummings et al., 2002). Perhaps it is more an issue of how one environment enhances or extends the other.

3. Cultural factors do not appear to be a determining factor in performance of virtual teams. Rather, performance is based on factors that build trust and support effective team performance, such as proactive behavior, empathetic task communication, positive tone, and rotation of team leadership. Successful global teams treat diversity as a source of strength rather than as a barrier to be overcome (DeSanctis et al., 2001; Evaristo, 2003; Jarvenpaa et al., 1998; Qureshi & Zigurs, 2001).

4. Multiple levels of analysis are needed to understand ubiquitous computing, which is simultaneously very personal and extremely global (Lyytinen & Koo, 2002). Understanding the benefits and avoiding the pitfalls requires transcending the traditional barriers between social and technical as well as levels of analysis—individual, team, and organizational.

5. Adoption and use of CMC technologies is driven more by compelling applications than by technology; i.e., killer applications drive use (Churchill & Bly, 2000; Georgiou & Stefaneas, 2002; Jarvenpaa et al., 2003; Shim & Shim, 2003; Xu, 2003). "It will be the innovativeness of users and uses, not the innovativeness of the technology, that will drive m-commerce growth to a new level" (Jarvenpaa et al., 2003, p. 44).

6. Increasingly, it appears that much of the leadership and innovation in the use of computer communications may be occurring outside the U.S. For example, this change is evident from the increased international participation at IT conferences and the growing prominence of international publications and research. As new Silicon Valleys emerge in previously thought unlikely places, such as India, Malaysia, and China (Sappenfield, 2003), it is difficult to anticipate what new and unforeseen directions CMC technologies may take. One example of this shift is India's growing level of technical competence and availability of high-tech workers and the current outsourcing of high-tech jobs that appears to have taken the U.S. political world as well as the high-tech community by surprise.

7. Risks of viewing and interpreting CMC research from the framework of old communication paradigms may be subject to misinterpretation or distortion, leading people astray in appropriate application.

8. The terminology computer-mediated communication (CMC) may itself be restrictive. The evolving focus already appears to be shifting from computer-

mediated communication to computer-mediated collaboration, which adds another dimension and significantly changes the dynamics. Perhaps the meaning of the CMC acronym should be redefined as computer-mediated collaboration.

9. The research literature exhibits a growing focus on the concept of online or virtual communities, with its implications of shared values, language, and identity (Fornas, 1998; Kelley & Jones, 2001; Raybourn, McGrath, Munro, & Stubblefield, 2000).

10. An evolving body of research suggests, preliminarily at least, the emergence of a new e-culture that transcends other cultural boundaries (Churchill & Bly, 2000; Fornas, 1998; Johnston & Johal, 2001; Kanter, 2001; Quaddus & Tung, 2002).

These themes may raise more questions than they answer about research involving CMC. Many questions such as the following remain to be answered: Are researchers taking a holistic view of communication and seeing online cultures as being made up of people who interact regularly with each other using multiple forms of communication technology, or are they tacitly or explicitly focusing on one genre of technology, as if communication in one environment could be isolated from the totality (Churchill & Bly, 2000)? How do software designers support multi-cultural collaborative virtual environments (Churchill & Bly, 2000) so that they minimize potential barriers and capitalize on new opportunities for enriched collaboration? What is the relationship between online and offline communication, and how can it be assessed? How does online inform offline and vice versa?

Thus, for CMC, although it is still important to be sensitive to cultural differences, it is equally important not to be misled by preconceived notions of cultural barriers. Although culture influences how and why technologies are adapted, it has not proven to be the barrier to virtual collaboration some predicted. Evidence indicates that people can deal with cultural difference to a much greater extent than expected and in ways that are different and sometimes more effective than in traditional venues.

THE EMERGING CONCEPT OF E-CULTURE

Some researchers (e.g., Johnston & Johal, 2001; Kanter, 2001) suggest that the Internet is an evolving virtual environment that has created its own culture with millions of users from all over the world. Rosabeth Moss Kanter's (2001) book *Evolve!* describes in some detail the characteristics of this evolving e-culture. Churchill and Bly (2000) contended "Online culture is not the sum total of all the offline cultures that the individuals bring in their norms of interaction, but is rather a separate entity in itself" (p. 9). Based on their research with Multi-User Domain (MUD) environments, they suggested the sense of shared cultures around work or other significant and meaningful experiences. This sense of shared culture spans organizational and country boundaries. In their observations of collaborations in MUD environments between people from different organizations or cultures, Churchill and Bly found that interactions among participants were seamlessly integrated with the communications of their local collaborators and transcended organizational and country boundaries. They concluded that this "occupational community—made up of people who are bound by a shared set of interests and overlapping working practices despite differing physical locations—is as real as the (organizationally and geographically) local community" (p. 7).

Noting the rapid emergence of global virtual teams, Davison and DeVreede (2001) observed that,

> ...some of the most interesting and valuable lessons can be learned from these cross-cultural experiences. The opportunities to learn from people in different cultures is inestimable, as all too often these people bring their own insights, perspectives, and values to bear upon the task context. Technology applications are adapted in local contexts to fit local norms and needs, with new technological and organizational forms emerging (p. 69).

The rapidly evolving development of digital cities is yet another phenomenon supporting the concept of e-culture. Digital cities are being developed all over the world (Ishida, 2002), using a wide combination of technologies including geographical information systems, two-dimensional and three-dimensional interfaces, Web-sensory information, databases, graphics, avatars, communications, and much more. Examples include Digital City Kyoto, Digital City Amsterdam, and Virtual Helsinki, to name just a few. Social interaction, including intercultural interaction, is an important goal in digital cities. In Europe more than 100 local authorities started different digital cities in the last eight years, and the European Digital Cities Conference started in 1994 (Ishida, 2002). "The concept of digital cities is to build an arena in which people in regional communities can interact and share knowledge, experiences, and mutual interests" (Ishida, 2002, p. 76). According to Ishida, digital cities serve a variety of purposes including tourism, commerce, transportation, urban planning, social welfare, health control, education, disaster protection, and politics. "Digital cities attract people because different experts contribute to building a new city and provide an opportunity to create for people a new information space for their everyday life" (Ishida, 2002, p. 81).

One researcher who strongly supports the concept of e-culture is Rosabeth Moss Kanter (2001). She talks about the notion of "a technology that makes place and face irrelevant" (p. 287). This culture, she concludes, "is best built and deployed in a context rich with human relationships" (p. 287). E-culture, she says, is a new way of working that "defines the human side of the global information era, the heart and soul of the New Economy" (p. 6). Effectiveness online is backed by strong relationships offline. Kanter sees a paradox in the seeming clash of individualism on one hand and greater interactivity and communication on the other. This hidden "I-Paradox," she says, is "that for all the personalization, customization, and empowerment of the Internet, rampant individualism (isolation and separatism) destroys the potential to develop economic and social benefits from the technology" (p. 17). She elaborates:

The best businesses involve this new individualism, operating more like communities—with fluid boundaries, voluntary action, stakeholders who feel like members, a shared identity and culture, collective strength, and community responsibility. . . . Operating as a community permits speed, releases human energy and brainpower, engenders loyalty, and reaches across walls and beyond borders to include volunteers, entice partners, and turn unknown audiences into fans. But if the Internet isolates people, it then undermines the very skills needed for the organizations that form around the Internet (p. 287).

Thus, e-culture appears to be emerging not as much as an isolated online phenomenon but as a new sense of community that transcends other cultural barriers. Or perhaps, more accurately, it's about communication freed from the boundaries of place and time that opens up new opportunities for relationship, understanding, and cooperation—a culture without artificial lines between online and offline—a culture that represents one reality with a greater, richer set of relationships and meaningful communication and collaboration in a more global context.

IMPLICATIONS FOR BUSINESS EDUCATORS

The bottom line for business educators is that virtual environments are the new reality. Driven largely by global networks, ever more powerful collaborative technologies, and the prevalence of geographically dispersed teams in the workplace, the ability to communicate and achieve results in computer-mediated environments has become an essential competence.

The implications for business educators are that the long-accepted concepts and principles taught in business communication courses cannot be assumed to extend to virtual environments. Moreover, just adding a unit on international communication or cross-cultural communication is no longer sufficient. Business communication has evolved to the point where anything short of integrating technology and global perspectives throughout the course is insufficient. A growing body of research suggests that CMC is not just another channel but is reshaping the dynamics of communication both online and offline.

Today's students need to learn to work in computer-mediated environments—to be able to function effectively as a group member online to successfully complete assignments and tasks. Fortunately, teachers have a rapidly expanding array of relatively low-cost collaborative technologies available, including online tools such as ICQ; NetMeeting; Lotus Organizer; instant messaging; e-mail; group systems software; course management systems that include group tools, file exchange, and chat rooms; and others. One suggestion is to have students team up with students in other schools, states, or countries to collaboratively complete projects. Students can also be engaged in a wide variety of Web-based projects, such as Web Quests, virtual tours, tutorials, and other online learning experiences. Helping students develop good teamwork skills is another essential requirement. Even though students socialize together, it cannot be assumed that they know how to work together. It is essential to provide guidelines for effective teamwork online and to assist students in building trust and rapport and in establishing clear expectations for group participation, including how they will evaluate both the group performance and their own contribution to that performance.

Another opportunity to provide students experience in virtual environments is to require that all students take at least one online course for credit during their high school years and again during their college years. A well-taught online course provides a rich learning environment and, in addition to content mastery, valuable insight into the power of virtual environments. Students can also be encouraged individually, as teams, or as a class to participate in online discussion forums, Webinars, and virtual communities. These are just a few of the expanding number of opportunities to engage students in CMC environments.

Thus, business educators should accept the new reality of virtual environments and embrace CMC, actively involving students in its many facets through related instruction and application.

SUMMARY

In summary, globalization and increased diffusion of the Internet are fueling the growth of CMC technologies. This rapid proliferation, coupled with such trends as distributed knowledge work and geographically dispersed work teams, has created a real need for a better understanding of how to support computer-mediated communication (CMC) in cross-cultural environments.

An analysis of CMC technologies used in intercultural environments highlighted a variety of cultural factors that appear to be affecting the global adoption and use of CMC. Currently, insufficient experience and research are available to draw scientifically based conclusions about the intercultural implications of CMC. A number of themes appear to be emerging, however, from the growing body of CMC research.

Although culture influences use of CMC, people cannot assume that it decreases the interest or use. Rather, evidence suggests that the technology is being applied differently in different cultural contexts. In fact, other barriers and incentives, such as ease of use, cost, age, purpose, and trust, appear to be stronger than culture in determining adoption and use of CMC. Thus, for CMC, although it is important to be sensitive to cultural differences, it is equally important not to be misled by preconceived notions of cultural barriers.

In reality, boundaries between online and offline are blurred. The material world and the virtual world are both part of an individual's total reality. In fact, the focus of virtual environments appears to be shifting beyond communication to collaboration, which adds another dimension and significantly changes the dynamics. The evolving body of research, preliminarily at least, suggests the emergence of a new e-culture that transcends other cultural boundaries. Business educators should embrace this virtual environment and integrate the use of CMC into instructional programs.

REFERENCES

Aiken, M. (2000). Multilingual communication in electronic meetings. *ACM SIGGROUP Bulletin, 21*(2), 3.

Aiken, M., Hwang, D., Paolillo, J., & Lu, L. (1994). A group decision support for the Asian Pacific Rim. *Journal of International Information Management, 3*(2), 1-13.

Boyacigiller, N., & Adler, N. J. (1991). The parochial dinosaur: Organizational science in a global context. *Academy of Management Review, 16*(2), 262-290.

Churchill, E. F., & Bly, S. (2000). Culture vultures: Considering culture and communication in virtual environments. *Bulletin, 21*(1), 6-11.

Cogburn, D. L., Zhang, L., & Khothule, M. (2002). Going global, locally: The socio-technical influences on performance in distributed collaborative learning teams. *Proceedings of SAICSIT 2002* (pp. 52-64). New York: ACM Press.

Colombo, F. (2001). Mobile telephone use in Italy in the 1990s: Interpretative models. *Modern Italy, 6*(2), 141.

Corbitt, B. J. (2003). Globalization, culture and e-business. In T. Thanasankit (Ed.), *E-commerce and cultural values* (pp. 1-16). Hershey, PA: Idea Group Publishing.

Cummings, N. N., Butler, B., & Kraut, R. (2002). The quality of online social relationships. *Communications of the ACM, 45*(7), 103-108.

Davison, R. (2002). Cultural complications of ERP: Valuable lessons learned from implementation experiences in parts of the world with different cultural heritages. *Communications of the ACM, 45*(7), 109-111.

Davison, R., & deVreede, G. (2001). The global application of collaborative technologies. *Communications of the ACM, 44*(12), 69-70.

DeSanctis, G., Wright, M., & Jiang, L. (2001). Building a global learning community. *Communications of the ACM, 44*(12), 80-82.

Evaristo, R. (2003). The management of distributed projects across cultures. *Journal of Global Information Management, 11*(4), 58-71.

Fornas, J. (1998). Digital borderlands: Identity and interactivity in culture, media, and communications. *Nordicom Review, 19*(1), 27-38.

Georgiou, D. J., & Stefaneas, P. S. (2002). Strategies for accelerating the worldwide adoption of e-commerce. *Communications of the ACM, 45*(4), 145-151.

Hofstede, G. (1984). *Cultures and consequences, international differences in work-related values.* London: McGraw-Hill/Sage Publications.

InfoCom Research (2002). *Comparison of Japan's telecommunications rates with France, Germany, UK and USA.* Retrieved May 19, 2004, from http://www.icr.co.jp/publications/book/pdf_hikaku_e.pdf

Ishida, T. (2002). Digital city Kyoto. *Communications of the ACM, 45*(7), 76-81.

Jarvenpaa, S., Lang, K., Takeda, Y., & Tuunainen, V. (2003). Mobile commerce at crossroads: Lessons learned from an international study of users of mobile handheld devices and services. *Communications of the ACM, 46*(12), 41-44.

Jarvenpaa, S. L., Knoll, K., & Leidner, D. E. (1998). Is anybody out there? Antecedents of trust in global virtual teams. *Journal of Management Information Systems, 14*(4), 29-64.

Johnston, K., & Johal, P. (2001). The Internet as a virtual cultural region: Are extant cultural classification schemes appropriate? *Internet Research: Electronic Networking Applications and Policy, 9*(3), 178-186.

Kanter, R. M. (2001). *Evolve! Succeeding in the digital culture of tomorrow.* Boston: Harvard Business School Press.

Katriel, T. (1999). Rethinking the terms of social interaction. *Research on Language & Social Interaction, 32*(1-2), 95-102.

Kelly, S., & Jones, M. (2001). Groupware and the social infrastructure of communication. *Communications of the ACM, 44*(12), 77-80.

Kim, J. (2000). Social interaction in computer-mediated communication. *American Society for Information Science, Bulletin of the American Society for Information Science, 26*(3), 15-18.

Lipnack, J., & Stamps, J. (1997). *Virtual teams: Reaching across space, time, and organization with technology.* New York: John Wiley and Sons.

Lyytinen, K., & Yoo, Y. (2002). Issues and challenges in ubiquitous computing. *Communications of the ACM, 45*(12), 63-65.

Massey, A. P., Montoya-Weiss, M., Hung, C., & Ramesh, V. (2001). Cultural perceptions of task technology fit: Acknowledging cultural differences helps companies build the strongest global virtual teams and determine the strongest tools they need. *Communications of the ACM, 44*(12), 83-84.

NTT DoCoMo. (2004, May 19). *Subscriber Growth.* Retrieved May 19, 2004, from www.nttdocomo.com

Oliva, E. L. (2004). *2004 Outlook: Despite Gloom, Growth Seen for RP ICT Industry.* Retrieved May 16, 2004, from www.INQ7.net

Quaddus, M. A., & Tung, L. L. (2002). Explaining cultural differences in decision conferencing. *Communications of the ACM, 45*(8), 93-98.

Qureshi, S., & Zigurs, I. (2001). Paradoxes and prerogatives in global virtual collaboration. *Communications of the ACM, 44*(12), 85-88.

Raybourn, E. M., McGrath, A., Munro, A., & Stubblefield, W. A. (2000). Research directions in designing intercultural interactions in collaborative virtual communities. *ACM SIGGROUP Bulletin, 21*(1), 3-5.

Riva, G. (2002). The socio-cognitive psychology of computer-mediated communication: The present and future of technology-based interactions. *CyberPsychology & Behavior, 5*(6), 581-597.

Sappenfield, M. (2003, December 29). Around the globe, new "Silicon Valleys" emerge. *The Christian Science Monitor.* Retrieved January 2, 2004, from http://www.csmonitor.com/2003/1229/p01s03-usec.htm

Sarker, D., & Wells, J. D. (2003). Understanding mobile handheld device use and adoption. *Communications of the ACM, 45*(12), 35-40.

Sheff, D. (2002). *China dawn: The story of a technology and business revolution.* New York: HarperBusiness, HarperCollins Publishers.

Shim, J. P., & Shim, J. M. (2003). M-commerce around the world: Mobile services and applications in Japan, Korea, Hong Kong, Finland, and the U.S. *Decision Line, 34*(5), 9.

Sproull, L., & Kiesler, S. (1991*). Connections: New ways of working in the networked organizations.* Cambridge, MA: MIT Press.

Stough, S., Eom, S., & Buckenmyer, J. (2000) Virtual teaming: A strategy for moving your organization into the new millennium. *Industrial Management + Data Systems, 100*(8), 370.

Tan, B. C. Y., Wei, K. K., Watson, R. T., & Walczuch, R. M. (1998). Reducing status effects with computer-mediated communication: Evidence from two distinct national cultures. *Journal of Management Information Systems, 15*(1) 119.

Toda, J. (2001). *Consumers and consumer industries in the ubiquitous network era.* Retrieved May 17, 2004 from http://www.nri.co.jp/english/opinion/papers

Walther, J. B. (1996). Computer-mediated communication: Impersonal, interpersonal, and hyperpersonal interaction. *Communication Research, 23*, 3-43.

WITSA. (2002). *Digital planet 2002: The global information economy.* Arlington, VA: World Information Technology and Services Alliance. Retrieved March 1, 2004, from www.witsa.org

Xu, Y. (2003). Mobile data communications in China. *Communications of the ACM, 46*(12), 81-85.